ARGUING WITH ANT

'It is something of a stroke of genius to make gift exchange the guiding thread of an introductory book . . . Sykes introduces many of the most important debates that dominate anthropology today. As that rare book that accessibly introduces students to the discipline without talking down to them, I think this book will be widely used.'

Joel Robbins, *University of California, San Diego*

Arguing with Anthropology is a fresh and original guide to key elements in anthropology, which teaches the ability to think, write and argue critically. Through an exploration of the classic 'question of the gift', which functions in anthropology as a definitive example of the entire human experience, it provides a fascinating study course in anthropological methods, aims, knowledge and understanding.

The book's unique approach takes gift-theory – the science of obligation and reciprocity – as the paradigm for a virtual enquiry which explores how the anthropological discipline has evolved historically, how it is applied in practice and how it can be argued with critically. By giving clear examples of real events and dilemmas in the history of the discipline, and asking students to participate in arguments about the form and nature of enquiry in recent years, it offers working practice of dealing with the obstacles and choices involved in anthropological study.

- From an expert teacher whose methods are tried and tested with students
- Clearly addresses the functions of anthropology, and its key theories and arguments
- Effectively teaches core study skills as the extension of a research and enquiry model of learning
- Draws on a rich variety of Pacific and global ethnography

Karen Sykes is a Senior Lecturer in Social Anthropology at the University of Manchester, where she teaches a popular introductory course in anthropology. She received her doctorate from Princeton University in 1995 and has conducted research in Melanesia since 1990.

ARGUING WITH ANTHROPOLOGY

An introduction to critical theories of the gift

Karen Sykes

LONDON AND NEW YORK

First published 2005
by Routledge
2 Park Square, Milton Park, Abingdon, Oxon OX14 4RN

Simultaneously published in the USA and Canada
by Routledge
270 Madison Avenue, New York NY 10016

Reprinted 2008, 2009

Routledge is an imprint of the Taylor & Francis Group

Typeset in Times by The Running Head Limited, Cambridge
Printed and bound in Great Britain by the MPG Books Group

British Library Cataloguing in Publication Data
A catalogue record for this book is available from the British Library

Library of Congress Cataloging in Publication Data
Sykes, Karen Margaret, 1960–
Arguing with anthropology : an introduction to critical theories of the gift / Karen Sykes
p. cm.
Includes bibliographical references and index.
1. Ceremonial exchange. 2. Gifts. 3. Anthropology–Philosophy. I. Title.
GN449.8.S95 2005394–dc22 2004021092

ISBN 0–415–25443–4 (hbk)
ISBN 0–415–25444–2 (pbk)
ISBN 13: 978–0–415–25443–4 (hbk)
ISBN 13: 978–0–415–25444–1 (pbk)

CONTENTS

List of illustrations vii
Acknowledgements ix

1 A sceptical introduction to theories of gift exchange 1

PART I
Modernist nostalgia **17**

2 The awkward legacy of the Noble Savage 19
3 Gathering thoughts in fieldwork 38
4 Keeping relationships, meeting obligations 59
5 Exchanging people, giving reasons 76

PART II
Postmodern reflections: historical criticism **95**

6 Debt in postcolonial society 97
7 Mistaking how and when to give 112

Postmodern reflections: critiques of subjectivity **131**

8 Envisioning bourgeois subjects 133
9 Giving beyond reason 151

PART III
A present without nostalgia **169**

10 Virtually real exchange 171

11 Interests in cultural property 187

12 Giving anthropology a/way 205

References and suggested readings 222
Index 237

ILLUSTRATIONS

2.1	Members of the Haddon expedition with assistants	26
2.2	'Hoisting the British flag in New Guinea'	29
3.1	The kula ring	42
3.2	'Scene in Yourawotu (Trobriands: preparing sagali)'	44
3.3	'Street of Kasana'I (Kiriwina, Trobriand islands)'	45
5.1	The ceremonial exchange of pigs	80
5.2	A gift of pigs as a form of bride wealth	83
7.1	The Kabyle house plan	116
7.2	Bourdieu's model of challenge and riposte	118
7.3	Cycles of reciprocity	120
7.4	Matrimonial exchange	122
8.1a	Miners' cottages at Coatbridge	143
8.1b	Accommodation for mine workers and families	144
8.2	*Coming from the Mill* (L.S. Lowry)	145
8.3	*Business as Usual*	147
8.4	'Manchester Free Trade Hall – For Sale'	149
9.1	'Yam house'	152
11.1	Malanggan carvings	201
12.1	Former Ladaven initiates	212–13

ACKNOWLEDGEMENTS

Although there may be other pathways of intellectual exchange the example of 'the gift' remains both eloquent and apposite to the present. This book emerges from a course of the same name, which I have taught since 1998 to undergraduate students. I owe a great deal to those people who have made my years teaching in the Department of Social Anthropology at the University of Manchester both intriguing and pleasurable. Over a decade ago, my doctoral supervisor, Rena Lederman, first suggested that it might be possible to teach undergraduate students about the history of the discipline through the lens of gift-exchange. Mauss had posed a good question; namely, why do people feel obligated to reciprocate what they have received? Anthropologists continue to respond to that question, and this book charts some of the replies. This is the 'how' of this book.

This book also benefits from conversations with colleagues in the Department of Social Anthropology at the University of Manchester and colleagues elsewhere. Debbora Battaglia's intellectual friendship gives greater value to this work. For chapter 8's insights I am deeply indebted to Anna Grimshaw and Keir Martin, who helped me to see the north west of England (and perhaps the Republic of Mancunia) in their different ways. Ann Kingsolver, Mark Whittacker and their son, David, helped me learn to see with the camera obscura on Eastbourne Pier. Joel Robbins read and commented on the entire book, but his comments are unparalleled. Joel, like Debbora and Keir, provided the kind of conversation about anthropological thought that keeps the discipline focused.

In the course of writing the final form of this manuscript over the past year, I have been fortunate to benefit from the friendship, wisdom and good judgement of a number of people. I hope they will recognize their thoughts in this book. They are Sandra Bamford, Debbora Battaglia, Stéphane Breton, Tony Crook, Melissa Damien, Mattia Fumanti, Ilana Gershon, Sarah Green, Anna Grimshaw, Eric Hirsch, Lawrence Kalinoe, Ann Kingsolver, Stuart Kirsch, James Leach, Rena Lederman, Keir Martin, Michele McComsey, Michael O'Hanlon, Victoria Price, Rosie Read, Joel Robbins, Will Rollason, Jacob Simet, Marilyn Strathern, Mark Whittacker.

ACKNOWLEDGEMENTS

I have enjoyed the benefits of fellowships and grants that have directly and indirectly made this book possible. These include: RAI/Leach post-doctoral fellow of the Royal Anthropological Institute; Life Member of Clare Hall, University of Cambridge; Visiting Senior Research Associate, Department of Archaeology and Anthropology, University of Cambridge and formal affiliations with Vassar College and the University of Birmingham; The British Academy, Small Grants Programme; Economic and Social Research Council of the United Kingdom; Manchester University Staff Research Grant; The Spencer Foundation, USA; The Woodrow Wilson National Dissertation Fellowship, USA; The National Science Foundation, USA; The Mellon Foundation at Princeton University. Parts of chapters 10 and 12 have been published earlier in 'My aim is true: postnostalgic reflections on the future of anthropological science' *American Ethnologist* 23(1): 156–74.

Several people gave invaluable help in completing the book. Anna Towlson of the London School of Economics, Anita Herle at Cambridge Anthropology and Archaeology Museum, Mark Woostonecroft and Peter Blore of the Media Centre of Manchester University and Catherine Trippet of Random House gave generously to the final steps of sorting out outstanding questions about the illustrations for the text. I also acknowledge the support of Lesley Riddle and Clare Johnson at Routledge, who are sterling editors, and must be thanked for their patience.

1

A SCEPTICAL INTRODUCTION TO THEORIES OF GIFT EXCHANGE

Anthropology is the study of social life as humans make it. In many ways it is an argument about how people do live and how to live. Exploring the history of the discipline itself is an excellent way of understanding this argument and that is one of the main aims of this book. Unlike other social sciences such as economics or politics, which aim to understand particular aspects of human life, anthropology approaches the study of social life as a totality. Anthropologists address the totality of social life because people live their lives out wholly and embrace the spiritual, political, economic and environmental as one. The earliest anthropologists took this total approach very seriously. For example, Boas founded a discipline that was a composite of studies into the material, intellectual and social life of men and women across the world. He argued that the totality could be encompassed in the idea of culture, which had different and particular emphasis around the globe. Similarly, Rivers, with Haddon's inspiration, examined the ways in which people claimed each other as kin, making this habit of social life the core of social anthropology for many decades. If the grasping of the totality of experience seemed and seems a somewhat daunting or fuzzy task, then it was probably right to proceed also with some inspiration from Durkheim and Mauss because they aimed to elaborate a social science that systematically theorized the totality of human experience. In this book about the many kinds of arguments that anthropologists make, I take up anthropology's claim to study the total picture of what it means to be human by examining a practice common to people around the world; that is the practice of giving and receiving gifts.

The gift can seem a small thing, but the habit of giving and receiving gifts resonates through human lives because the gift is more than the material object. It establishes or confirms a relationship between people and in this way has been described as a kind of cornerstone of society. The observation that some goods can be given to others as 'gifts' asks that anthropologists think more clearly about what kinds of relationships can be made in a material world and beyond it. For anthropologists, just as for many people, there is nothing self-evident about ownership or non-ownership of gifts. When I receive a gift, it opens more possibilities in my social life than it closes. I puzzle through what to do next. Why should I receive a gift with the understanding that it is the thought that counts, except to acknowledge that I do not necessarily like or need what I receive in order to be glad for it? The conventions of giving gifts remain both eminently reasonable and good mannered, and sometimes enigmatic because receiving a gift can acknowledge that more than one kind of relationship exists between giver and receiver.

Today many anthropologists undertake their work in capitalist societies (although not all do). It is something of an enigma that people give gifts, either small and intimate or grand and global, because the habit of giving and its associated ideas of generosity seem to run at odds with ideologies sustaining capital accumulation. At the very least, making a gift is an altruistic way of making a relationship when conventions and dominant modes of relating within capitalist societies suggest that calculated or rational self-interest should dominate decisions about human relationships. I am writing this in 2003 in Manchester, on the eve of the World Trade Organization meetings in Cancun, Mexico. I have been reading the *Guardian* newspaper supplement on 'Trade'. Many of the articles discuss the benefits and difficulties in *forgiving* the debt of the developing to the developed world, of *regulating obligations* rather than freeing international trade, of making (for example) pharmaceuticals and other medicines *freely* available at no cost in poorest nations, and of creating a *fair* trade organization. Some authors argued that free market capitalists could not lose sight of human *hopes for equality*, without risking the best aims of the work of trade. More so, the unnamed authors of the pamphlet argue for reforms to the practice of world trade that include a reconsideration of *alternative forms of distribution, using and sharing* of wealth. Rethinking fair or free trade in terms of obligatory relationships would entail hefty and complex arguments for any anthropologist to make, if not for journalists to advance. Fortunately, there is a tradition of thinking about gift exchange in anthropology.

When facing the analysis of a large problem, anthropologists take responsibility for their ignorance by raising difficult questions. In the early twentieth century, Marcel Mauss began to think about gift exchange as a totally human social act. Then, to put it in colloquial language, he began 'thinking through things' as if imitating the commonsense practice of making objects the focus of human thoughts, desires and memories. He framed a lasting question that grasps at the totality of social life: namely, why do people feel obligated to give back when they have received? There have been many answers to that question. By reviewing the kinds of arguments anthropologists make and have made about gifts, I aim to introduce some of the history of the discipline. I begin with those scholars who came before Mauss. In order to embrace examples from many societies, I will discuss most closely the kinds of relationships people make with the things they call gifts.

Mauss's insights help contemporary anthropologists to raise a warning against assuming that economic reason, especially utilitarian value, dominates human life. In line with his critiques of early twentieth-century economics, anthropologists can draw on the history of research on the gift in order to contribute to wider debates about the global economy. The reason they can do this recalls Mauss's basic insight, that any analysis of the obligation to give and receive things shows that human relationships cannot be contained wholly within usury forms of exchange. In particular, he argued that the gift contradicts the assumption that human relationships aim towards only utilitarian ends. Mauss's essay shows that Homo Economicus is a recent development, and perhaps we could add that it has been specific to the trans-Atlantic relationships between America and Western Europe that make many of us Euro-Americans. Its extensions to the Pacific in the period of exploration and settlement of that region presented extraordinary problems to traders and administrators alike. There is no reason to think that the idea of utilitarian humanity bears universal applications now, any more than it did in earlier years. Perhaps a time has come for reassessment of the legacy of anthropological theories of the gift if anthropology is to embrace the study of the totality of human experience. Talking, writing and thinking about gifts draw anthropologists into long conversations about how to examine what it means to be human.

Gift giving: a totally human act

It is possible to study some features, or phenomena, as a 'total social fact' in order to illuminate social life in its entirety. Anthropological arguments about exchanges, especially gift exchanges, shaped social theory since the Enlightenment and continue to do so today. I think that speaks to the future success of anthropology, more than its past. The scope of this book will appeal to the history of the discipline in order to generate the terms for future analysis. In this book, I return to the insight given to the discipline by Mauss, that giving gifts concentrates and constitutes a totality of human experience.

> In these 'total' social phenomena, as we propose calling them, all kinds of institutions are given expression at one and the same time – religious, juridical and moral, which relate to both politics and the family; likewise economic ones, which suppose special forms of production and consumption or rather, of performing total services and of distribution. This is not to take into account the aesthetic phenomena to which these facts lead, and the contours of the phenomena that these institutions manifest.
>
> (Mauss 1990 [1925]: 3)

Gofman underscores Mauss's words to mean that the totality of social life could be contemplated within a singularly human habit of association known as a total social fact. Total social facts are '[p]henomena that penetrate every aspect of the social system, they concentrate it and constitute its focus, they are the constitutive elements and the generators and motors of the system' (Gofman 1998: 67). Although Mauss did not fully theorize the concept of total social fact, the giving and receiving of gifts was his case in point. In this book I take the case of the gift as illustrative of the concept of the total social fact and explore its uses in anthropological argument.

Mauss's work is monumental in anthropology because he chose to describe gift exchange, as it constitutes social life or 'society' most generally and philosophically. Moreover, a less well-developed theoretical strand of his work remains important to the discipline. Mauss also poses a central question in what it means to be human by asking why a person should feel obligated to give back what he or she had received from another. The problem of 'the gift' comprises two kinds of questions: how people keep their social life at the centre of consciousness, and why it should seem meaningful for them to do so.

Mauss's theory of the exchange of gifts as the total social fact shows that the gift is a cornerstone of the whole of society because it encapsulates the concern with what it means to be human. He uses the example of the gift to make new advances over Durkheim's most philosophically inspired anthropology. Mauss finds in gift exchange an analytical idea that is uniquely ethnographic. Those people who were exchanging gifts also understood obligation to be an abstract idea; that is, an abstract idea that could be enacted in everyday life. This layering of significance, from the analyst's to the participant's work, makes the subject of giving and receiving gifts good to study.

In English, Mauss's *The Gift* is a short, four-part essay; but the unabridged edition in French is a longer book which was written at a time when he and his colleagues hoped to contribute to a growing debate over the nature of material life and government in their own country. By the 1920s, when *The Gift* was published, the intellectual community in France was discussing the importance of a social democracy to buffer the elaboration of capitalist investment in social institutions, and to counter the critique from the Bolshevik community that aimed to establish communal property. Recently, those researchers interested in the social history of Mauss's work (Gane 1992, Godelier 1999, Allen 2001) argued that Mauss carried forward the earlier Durkheimian project of pitching anthropological questions towards problems of the day. At the very least, this was a sceptical project in anthropology.

The essay on the gift: trials of reason

How do anthropologists approach the study of human experience as a totality? One answer might be to approach it sceptically. Mauss does not explicitly say that social anthropology requires a disciplined philosophical scepticism, but he assumes simply that he must work with that form of enquiry into the nature of social life and that the example of gift exchange presses ethnologists to think through things carefully, sceptically and philosophically. For the purposes of this book, it helps to recall that Mauss and other anthropologists inherit the disciplines of scepticism from the legacy of Enlightenment scholarship, and that this is deeply entangled in ideas about the 'Noble Savage' and the social grounds for a revolution of political and economic life – key issues in rethinking what it means to be human. Cartesian philosophy raised doubts in order to ascertain truth. Anthropologists argue from scepticism about how to make veritable claims, not from personal or societal beliefs.

Contemporary anthropologists hold an awkward position on the current view that capitalist political economy dominates the whole of human life when they acknowledge that people give and receive gifts. This is a common form of scepticism that challenges accepted conventions, in this case commodity-exchange habits, with alternative ones, such as gift exchange. Gregory (1997) discusses the different philosophical traditions of scepticism from South Asia and from the late medieval period in Europe. Holding a sceptical view means that anthropologists raise doubts about orthodoxy of belief by exposing contradictions in analysis, from which they elucidate arguments for more truthful claims about social life. A common example of scepticism arises in everyday acts of intellectual exchange, at a point when a person raises a question to shift the terms of discussion. This is true in fieldwork, as I learned when my acquaintances tested my reasons for living with them by asking for assistance. They changed their relationships to me in measure with my response to them. For example, when I was a student researcher in New Ireland, the elder man in the clan who took responsibility for looking out for me asked me for a plane ticket from Port Moresby to New York City, just to see what I might answer. I hesitated too long, and before I could answer he said that a radio would do just fine as a substitute for the trip, which would in any case tire him too much. From that time when he raised a first doubt about the terms of my residence in his hamlet, I learned to become responsible for his well-being too. Raising a question, a simple way of dissenting, can be a means to change implicit agreements and challenge conventional wisdom. Holding a sceptical point of view can be a matter of dissent, as when anthropologists present alternative interpretations or opposite points of view to more conventional claims.

Scepticism pervades the Enlightenment beginnings of the science of anthropology. Some Enlightenment scholars expressed doubts about how humans did live and could hope to live because they knew of a record of descriptions and stories of other lifestyles. During the 'age of trade', in the period preceding the Enlightenment, people began to wonder about the world. Seagoing vessels and overland caravans returned with objects for resale and with gifts from distant princes in Pacific islands or from civilizations to the east of Europe. Even in Shakespeare's day, the city of London was cosmopolitan, its streets busy with sailors and foreign traders, temporarily resident to sell their spices and goods. London Bridge housed small market stalls and temporary houses for the sellers, until it toppled under the weight of the improvised building and the residents were sent back to other lands. But years go by and the rebuilt bridge falls again. Problems of how to trade fairly and how to create social ties to distant peoples came into full discussion in public life well beyond the elite world of religious or secular scholarship.

The 'age of discovery' followed upon the age of trade. Explorers made maps of the known world of trade, and then laboured in order to fill in the gaps and discover the places they imagined they found. Explorers and scientists tried to determine what was known about distant places that they had only heard about or imagined from examining the new objects that came from distant islands and kingdoms. A journey up the St Lawrence river in North America took ships to impassable rapids. They were (and still are) named the Lachine rapids by explorers surmising ironically that China, the East, was only a little bit beyond the present horizon. Subsequent westward travel from Europe skirted around the continents and across the Pacific Ocean to circumnavigate the globe on the way to the Far East, to the same distant kingdom of China that earlier European traders had travelled eastward to find across the land-masses of Europe and Asia. *Bêche-de-mer*, sandalwood, spice, botanic specimens, tulips and orchids, new species of birds and animals – these were collected and catalogued. Stories circulated that needed confirmation. The Chinese told of the bird of paradise that descended from the heavens and never touched the earth, its legs non-existent because it kept its abode in paradise and had no need to rest on tree branches or the ground. Early storytellers of extraordinary things and places moved their listeners – and perhaps the tellers moved themselves in the telling – to rethink what they comfortably could claim to know about the world. Stories of distant places upset habits of thought and the grounds of belief came under scrutiny.

Earliest anthropological arguments recognized that different habits of organizing knowledge and thought, described on the one hand as custom and on the other as natural reason, each proposed different understandings of what it means to be human. Anthropologists recognized that the parameters of the epistemological crisis of the Enlightenment hung between custom and reason. That difference between natural reason and custom marks the terrain of scepticism in Enlightenment social science and its implications for social life in Europe, the 'New World' and the colonies. Some proclaimed that both the blur of customary thought and the damages of historical change obscured human natural reason and disabled the human capacity to interrogate and understand what others say. Others believed that only civilized humanity exercised natural reason most fully because civilized people interacted with each other in an intellectually generous manner, learning how to be consciously rational by communicating clearly with each other. Anthropologists posed a new question for themselves: how could they know to trust their sceptical reason if customary knowledge could so easily fog their vision?

Although the discipline of anthropology was yet to be refined, anthropologists used the Enlightenment genre of the essay to their best advantage in early arguments. In the eighteenth century, scholars following the earlier work of Montaigne used the essay as an argumentative form to show how the writer could compare cannibals and kings to criticize the present social conditions, which might be obscured by customary beliefs about the world order. If so-called 'natives' exercise reason without the same confusions of customary belief and superstition that peasants suffered, then how could Europeans free their thoughts from the burden of traditional belief? Whatever limits exist in these first assumptions about peasants, natives or custom, what should be remembered is that philosophers argued from idealized concepts of these life conditions and were not social scientists whose researches confirmed the extent of that belief. Thus, 'native reason' and 'custom' better describe the ways in which people see the world.

Ruth Benedict was inspired by the potential of these arguments for shaping the emergent discipline of anthropology into a critical exercise. She argued that for Montaigne natural reason (sceptical thought) and custom (knowledge embedded in practice) are each like spectacles; they are glasses that stand between people and the world they inhabit, whether that world is thought to be natural or the result of a history of mistakes (Benedict 1946, 1963). This creates a problem for anthropologists because natural reason can be as much the product of history as is custom. The point is that European reason, both now and then, is as much 'custom' as the thought of Hawaiians or Amerindians of the eighteenth century. Ruth Benedict, in a later period, defines anthropology as a way of seeing that anthropologists aim to make explicit through fieldwork and writing. She likens the craft of anthropological argument to the work of lens grinding, in so far as the lens grinder knows best just how to grind the spectacles that sit between a person and the world in which he or she lives. In the hands of the early Enlightenment philosophers and in the literary sensibility of Benedict and others of her era, the sceptical essay becomes the ultimate form of anthropology. In the contemporary period when scholars are encouraged to entrench educational orthodoxy in the name of democratization, perhaps it is good to remember scepticism's legacy.

Benedict, and others of her time, found an avenue forward for anthropological thought, leaving the Enlightenment dilemma behind. If natural reason could not be trusted as being a universal capacity shared around the globe, then surely a degree of scepticism was necessary to any claim by anthropologists that they might know something? Benedict's scepticism treads between different forms of customary belief expressed by people living in the 1920s with the state in Europe and America, and the belief of people living on the fringes of the state in the American south west, the Canadian north-west coast, or the Trobriand islands in the Australian Territory of Papua. These comparisons exude complexities and make things nearer to home seem a bit strange, as is often the case in ironic writing. This elucidation of the bizarre and the peculiar is an aspect of Benedict's style that might be misunderstood by those who fail to acknowledge her ironic sensibility. In the early 1930s Benedict published a book comparing Dobu sorcery with the Kwakiutl ritual of 'potlatch', and the Zuni rituals. It is a tidy triad of examples, but Benedict's ironic turn of argument disturbs the comparison and prevents the book failing on a false commensurability between the cases of what she describes as 'cultures as personalities written large'; Kwakiutl megalomania, Dobu paranoia and Zuni equanimity receive similar treatment in the assessment of the styles of life in each place.

Contemporary anthropological thought continues to find full expression in the essay because the form enables the author to utilize a sceptical stance to the best advantage of making a critical contribution to wider knowledge. An essay is a try at explanation – no more and no less – and that can be quite enough. Mastering its form remains difficult, largely because being a good essay writer in anthropology entails working with the sceptical argument, or even ironic style. This is not always straightforward because it can be easy to confuse scepticism and irony with emotional responses such as vitriolic sarcasm or dispassionate cynicism. In the early part of the twentieth century, anthropological argument received explicit attention from several different disciplinary 'fathers'. No doubt the effort undertaken to establish different schools of anthropology included attempts to clarify what counted as an anthropological argument in each of the respective schools. If anthropology could be a discipline of thought, if anthropology could be supported and taught in a university, and if colleagues could make assessments of each other's work, then anthropologists should standardize a particular form of essay writing. Anthropologists of the twentieth century worked within two shared assumptions. They shared one assumption with other scholars of the modern era: namely, they recognized for the first time that they conducted their scholarship within the traditions and terms of Enlightenment scientific legacy. Anthropologists shared the second assumptions among themselves. They acknowledged that they felt the first twinges of doubt about the value of the Enlightenment for the world beyond Europe.

Among the declarations for the creation of social science, some of the most compelling claims for anthropological argument arise from Durkheim's introductory pages of *The Elementary Forms of the Religious Life*. Durkheim aimed to surpass the philosophical impasse between Kant and Hume with the science of society. On the one hand, Kant insisted that shared forms of knowledge existed in the human mind prior to thought and these forms made it possible for humans to reason. On the other hand, Hume argued that human senses exposed patterns of the natural world which people learned to recognize and share as conventional knowledge. Durkheim, drawing on the different claims of Hume and Kant for the primacy of the role of sensual knowledge and the definitive role of apriori knowledge, argues that the problem of knowledge is posed in new terms. He argues that anthropology, as a modern science, should analyse the practices by which people make their experience coherent to themselves. In his example of totemic ritual in Australia he shows us that this exercise remains a project of something like 'critical reason'; that is, the Aborigine might well engage in totemic ritual as a rational exercise given to the end of self-knowledge. This act of explaining creates rational knowledge. In trying to explain themselves to themselves, people will find that they must reason through their experiences coherently, eloquently and clearly in order to agree an account of what they do.

In the midst of the act of explaining experience to themselves, people can also criticize their own actions. In this way, a critical form of reason (rather than dogma) emerges as one of the tutelary aspects of ritual. In religion as in science, truth will elude the practitioner of the faith or of the science, whether they are believer or agnostic in its devotions or methods. In anthropology the exercise of critical reason means that truth remains beyond the grasp, beyond the average ken. Its distance suggests that the spaces and gaps in the shortcomings of contemporary knowledge serve to darken rather than enlighten shared understandings of the modern world. If the anthropological aim is true, then knowledge cannot settle into received truths and new research should serve to illuminate an imperfectly understood modern life.

It helps to know something about these questions, because they point to the shift in Durkheim's thought, away from adherence to Comte's positivism, to outline the need to establish a critical programme for social science. It is part of his larger interest in moral reasoning and education. Durkheim spent the later years of his scholarly career discussing the role of education in modern society. He established a school of anthropological and sociological research, remembered to this day. *L'Année Sociologique* was nearly destroyed by the loss of so many of Durkheim's students in the devastations of the First World War, but its legacy of establishing social science research in a tradition of sceptical thought remains. He thought that education took the lead over other knowledge practices because it replaced religion and ritual for its role in the constitution of modern society. His research and writing on education comes at a time when the nation sought to formalize national education, in an effort to ameliorate with social planning the failings of the political visions for equality in modern democracy. Doubts about the success of democracy escalated throughout the late nineteenth and early twentieth century, and had an influence on the earliest attempts to formalize the discipline of anthropology in the university's roster of courses of study.

In what alternative ways have anthropologists tried to understand the nature of social connections between people? In the years leading to the turn of the century, the anthropologist and social psychologist, W.H.R. Rivers began his work in the Torres Straits, as a part of the Cambridge Expedition led by the university's new chair of anthropology, A.C. Haddon. Rivers tried to understand how people made claims on each other as kin. Most importantly, he made a lasting contribution to the discipline by creating the idea of genealogy, presented as a diagram or map of the ways in which people understood how they should keep their relationships to each other. Rivers worked with Torres Straits islanders to record the details of the chain or network of people they named as their kin. In this work, he invented what anthropologists later came to call 'the genealogical method' as a way of making diagrams and patterns to represent relationships made by childbearing and marriage. He argued that people also used goods to honour their relatives and remember that they had obligations to their kin. These illustrations can often be used to clarify how people think of each other as kin, and show how they disperse material goods among them.

In common with Mauss, Rivers's anthropological approach triumphed social interconnectedness as a fundamentally human condition. This made it possible for anthropologists to clarify the social matrix within which all humans claim to know each other. Rivers's personal influence in social anthropology finished with the end of the First World War and his early death, but the contribution to the epistemological matrix of the discipline persists. Most recently, Marilyn Strathern (1994) clarified that Rivers's early study of kinship and genealogy influenced British social anthropologists to pursue knowledge about social life as connected up relations, and to investigate the implications of living or participating in the shadow of each other's relationships. In her address to the Association of Social Anthropologists (ASA) decennial meeting in Manchester (2003), Strathern reminded her audience that practical knowledge of the world entails using knowledge that is socially mediated. She continued to argue that what a person *knows* is a matter of *how* they know it in relationship to another person.

Another way of expressing the concrete reality of relations must be to recall that anthropological science acknowledges that social scientific knowledge is conditional upon specific relationships. At the ASA Strathern argued that anthropologists' kinship theory remains a model of scientific thought in the discipline because it emphasizes that people are related by their knowledge of each other.

In summary, the work of early anthropologists explored many different paths of enquiry, only some of which I have mentioned here. But I do emphasize in the above examples that anthropology joins other disciplines in the legacy of Enlightenment science by trying to say something about social life. The contemporary form of Enlightenment science, social theory, makes the same claim to illuminate the character of social life. Social theorists cannot claim to argue about social life without first recognizing that knowledge is first and foremost social. An anthropologist can 'test', so to speak, a social theory by checking just how it is 'social'.

As I have outlined here, doubts about anthropological certainty can be raised in several ways. One way in which anthropologists can raise doubts about claims to the certainty of truth might be to show that what people say and do generates superficial knowledge. Durkheim contributed to general understanding of religious belief by taking seriously the contention that what people said and did could be very different from how the same people analysed their own actions. In *The Elemenatry Forms of Religious Life*, Durkheim suggested that scholarly human rationality excelled with a critical project. In a critical project, the researcher feels the tension generated between experiential knowledge and interrogative knowledge.

A second way in which anthropologists used sceptical enquiry in early ethnography acknowledged that knowledge grew or depended upon relations. The early research of Rivers shows how he astutely assessed that what any one person knew about the world could only be uttered or demonstrated in their actions, because they spoke or enacted those assumptions for another person. A person is a child only in relation to the parent. What people know can be made clear only in relation to another person; that is to say, *anthropologists recognize that knowledge is relative to social relationships that constitute and concentrate it as social facts.*

Third, anthropologists continue a sceptical project in ethnography through reflecting upon differences between the habits of themselves and others. This reflexivity exposes anthropologists' biases, or presumptions about what they can observe in their fieldwork. In reflexive anthropology, scepticism is simply a tentative stance in the field; it is a position articulated by expressing doubt. Some find this a double bind that immobilizes anthropologists from speaking their minds, and raises doubts about anthropologists' ability to share their insights as conclusions of research. In this approach, the anthropologist cannot settle into scepticism, as he or she might settle into another epistemology such as faith. Anthropology becomes a project of social criticism in the anthropologist's home society when it casts doubt about people's certainty that some truths are self-evident. *Reflexive anthropology works to unsettle 'received truths' or 'common wisdom'.*

Anthropological research has much to offer its students, not the least of which is the gift of disciplined enquiry and reflection on the total human condition. That kind of gift is hard to be rid of and difficult to carry. The anthropologist's obligations entail remaining open to the gifts received as wisdom, insight or argument. There is no surprise in finding that intellectual exchange traces the give and take of anthropological knowledge in argument. We could say that the logic of gift exchange lies at the centre of the discipline, and how ethnographic knowledge finds its way into the pathways of dialogue created by writing and talking leaves anthropologists to risk one last thing: What should anthropologists do with what they know, except give it away?

In the opening pages of this chapter, I suggested that current debates made the anthropologically informed discussion of gift exchange as important as it has ever been. Here, I modify that claim a little. Even without the increasing demand for clarification of concepts in the contemporary debates about trade, debt and reciprocal obligations, I do think that the history of arguments about gifts can be a rewarding study for anthropologists and their colleagues. Anthropologists who want to understand what kinds of relationships people make with gifts can find much in the history of the discipline: the nature of evidence, economic rationality, the comparative approach, grand theory, false consciousness, alienation, bourgeois values, sacrifices, property relations and ethics. Taking the question of what it means to be human in the round, I think this makes a few things clearer to any student of anthropology and the social sciences about what anthropologists do, have done and can do in each of their contemporary social milieus. By the end of the book I can return to the themes introduced here. First, anthropologists engage deeply in the concrete details of social life by examining human experience as a totality. Second, anthropologists argue in disciplined ways that criticize common wisdom that otherwise hides or overshadows broadly and deeply felt aspects of human experience. As this book unfolds, I will discuss how anthropologists practise this unique pairing in fieldwork and writing in a disciplined social science with doubts about how people live wholly, artfully and creatively.

Overview of the chapters

In this book I approach the history of anthropological theory through the lens of gift exchange. Like Mauss I privilege gift exchange as a focus of study, as a total social fact that concentrates and condenses social processes and thereby provides anthropologists with the descriptive and explanatory means to discuss how people live in the round. The analysis of gift exchange as a total social fact undermines the fallacious ground of utilitarian theories of value, as a partial view of society that finds pervasive expression today, just as it did in earlier eras. Anthropology as a discipline does not limit knowledge to matters of how people live politically, economically or spiritually because people live life wholly.

As this book was going to press Strathern, in her Huxley Lecture, proposed that anthropologists might become 'a community of critics', suggesting that over history anthropologists disciplined themselves to create a community of conversation and argument (Strathern 2004). Throughout the book, I address many anthropologists' sceptical approaches to the study of society. I aim to describe the different ways in which modernist anthropologists have used the gift exchange to understand the integrity and meaning of everyday life in small societies; in which postmodernist anthropologists have used gift exchange in assessing the extent to which the particulars of historical consciousness and the experience of subjectivity can be shared across a society, and in which anthropologists working in virtual society and across globalizing communities address gift exchange as a medium through which to describe social reality, the ontological challenges, and the ethics of exchange relations there.

Part I describes the work of gift exchanges as a constitutive and concentrating social process in small integrated societies, where everyday relationships are lived face-to-face. Four chapters comprise the discussion of modernist nostalgia in anthropology.

Chapter 2 describes how different anthropologists have used the rhetorical construction of the Noble Savage, and especially Rousseau's accompanying fable of the loss of the state of nature with the loss of common wealth and property, to launch critiques of state power. I examine ideas about the Noble Savage in evolutionary theories of the 'natural economy', in theories of political economy in the history of colonial relations, and in structural theories of natural reason as the grounds of communicative and social exchanges most broadly defined.

Chapter 3 describes the effort by Malinowski to recover through fieldwork the description of an apparently irrational economic practice of the exchange of 'kula' wealth as an institution significant to the internal coherence of a small society in the Trobriand islands. By comparing his method of fieldwork with the methods of others, such as Boas's historical particularism, I discuss Malinowski's goals in participant observation to provide an integrated holistic description. The numerous critiques of participant observation are reviewed and critiqued in turn for their ability to accomplish similar aims of providing a total description of social relations.

Chapter 4 describes Mauss's comparative approach to the study of gift exchange, such that it is possible to make a theory of society through comparative assessments of the practice in 'kula', 'hau' and 'potlatch'. I explore Godelier's thesis that the habit of keeping while giving enables participants in ceremonial gift exchange to contemplate the sacred as an expression of their common humanity in political economic processes. In concluding the review of the Godelier thesis, I pose some tentative claims for the further study of how power relations depart from Mauss's insight that gift exchange is a total social fact rather than a singularly economic institution.

Chapter 5 describes Lévi-Strauss's theorizing of gift exchange as an expression of rational principles of social organization and communication most broadly defined. I discuss the significance of the fact that the gift in matrimonial exchange is a woman, who is at once sister to some and wife-to-be to other clansmen. The feminist critiques of structuralism's project expose the ways in which women's outside labour, domestic work, reproductive capacity, sexuality and femininity cannot be contained by structuralist's theories of social variation. Strathern's alternatives to the structuralist theory of society are explored by referring to her critique of gender relations.

Part II distinguishes approaches to the problem of historical consciousness and the critique of subjectivity for the ability of postmodernists to enlighten understandings of the complexity, ambiguities and deceits of consciousness. Four chapters comprise the review of postmodern reflections on the discipline of anthropology.

Chapter 6 describes the limits of attempts by postcolonial anthropologists to resituate studies of exchange relations in colonial context. The transactions of gifts of beads, land, labour, money and identity are considered through three colonial encounters. These are: first, colonial Americans among the Iroquois; second, south Asian agricultural workers from the lowest rungs of the ladder of the Jati system of caste relations living with monetary policy enforced by well-meaning but confused colonial administrators; and third,

Fijian gift exchange misread as begging by early English traders seeking to make a little profit on the side of the larger trade of luxury wealth taken from the Pacific island's people. All three cases fail to provide a clear account of how to theorize context without reducing it to a background of the machinations of force.

Chapter 7 describes practice theory's efforts to address the extent to which historical consciousness is shared and reproduced in small everyday acts of gift exchange as well as in ceremonial ones, even where that knowledge entails non-conscious arrangements to reproduce social inequality. I compare the work of time in Bourdieu's practice theory of matrimonial exchange as it creates the ideology of prestigious honour and reproduces underlying kinship structures, with Lévi-Strauss's analysis of how the passing of time over generations in cross-cousin marriage is bound by principles of social structure. As afterthought, a question arises as to how anthropologists should address the uses of cultural stereotypes and conjecture in joking accounts of recent history, or farcical descriptions of ritual exchange, especially when the joke turns on misunderstandings or ambiguities of customary habits of exchange.

Chapter 8 describes the ways in which commodity exchange relations are hidden in order to make the bourgeois subject appear as if a singular individual, or a 'self-made man'. I draw loosely on the insights of Derrida, that a critique of the subject can be made aesthetically; that is, the art of exposing the self-deceptions necessary to commit an act of bourgeois generosity. This chapter examines visual arts and visuality to consider how people come to envision the bourgeois individual as separate from social relations. Through the case study of Manchester capitalism I explore processes of learning how to see the bourgeois individual and conversely how to see otherwise hidden exchange relations, whether gift or commodity relations. This analysis of nineteenth-century Manchester and the Free Trade Movement of Smith compares provocatively with contemporary efforts in the city and elsewhere to sell the symbols of free trade – for example, the sale of the Free Trade Hall building in Manchester or the sale of the photograph of the World Trade Center by street vendors in New York City.

Chapter 9 describes attempts by anthropologists following Bataille to provide a fuller picture of society by considering its excesses of production and its detritus, which are parts of social life that are often left out of analysis. By looking at potlatch on the north-west coast of North America, it is possible to describe how people give too much, how they live with the aftermath of their excessive giving and expenditure, and how the activity is variously judged to be reasonable. Is it a rational response to the social crisis initiated by the penetration of capitalist market exchanges into every social life or an irrational response to capital accumulation or an irrational form of exchange relations? The chapter examines the ways in which the aesthetics of exchange and its excesses are incorporated into the analysis of social life. Some of the implications include a fuller account of psychological dimensions of exchange relations to include the irrational aspects of human behaviour with rational understandings.

Part III describes the work of anthropologists of exchange relations who describe forms of human association at the close of postmodernity. Three chapters comprise this exploration of the anthropology of the present.

Chapter 10 examines the exchange of knowledge and of perspective by which technologically assisted life is made real in the virtual society that allegedly encompasses people in an almost intimate global village. How does a technology privilege a new mode of exchange such that a Cartesian space opens humans to disembodied transactions that dominate most of social life? Or does technology privilege new modes of exchange that evoke affective aspects of experience that are neither singularly bodily nor mentally/intellectually forged relations? Does this virtual reality require anthropologists to use new techniques of description?

Chapter 11 examines attempts to construct culture as the new commons in global debates about property, and thereby provoke a crisis of how to be in the world. In particular, cultural property debates challenge the people who participate in them to examine their assumptions about ontology as a matter of what interests them. I examine the different ontological assumptions of Mauss and Malinowski, and ask how people come to feel both interested in the ownership of the material forms of their culture and disinterested in possessing cultural artefacts as evidence of their own membership.

In chapter 12 I close the discussion of exchange relations in contemporary anthropology with a discussion of the ethics of representation in fieldwork. I focus on the transaction of vulnerability, and thereby depart from earlier documents that highlighted the protection of the informant and the responsibilities of the anthropologist. Using a case study in visual anthropology, which could be read in the context of the wider discussion of ethics in fieldwork more generally, I discuss how anthropologists can foreground ethical practice as transactions in vulnerability and thereby enable fieldwork in the present.

Part I

MODERNIST NOSTALGIA

2

THE AWKWARD LEGACY OF THE NOBLE SAVAGE

People do inherit ancestral wealth. As with a family member who inherits a legacy of personal effects, an anthropologist inherits numerous intellectual legacies: from her teachers, from the cultural areas in which he conducts his research, and from his or her reading in the discipline of anthropology. As with ancestors who leave a legacy of goods, heirlooms and even sentimental trinkets for people not yet born, anthropologists write with a sense of duty to leave ethnography for the readers of the future. In both cases, the problem remains what to do with it. It can be a blessing or a burden depending upon the ease with which a person can live with the restrictions peculiar to the use of any family wealth. Some people protect their legacy. The holder of a legacy cannot give it away, except to the holder in the next generation. They must care for it. Other holders lose or squander the wealth and thereby risk the network of connections between the family members who share in the legacy, and the family's connections to their own past. Some people want nothing of the legacy, and try to give it away by dispersing the goods judiciously according to the social values they hold to be important to the present times. The person's choice to use his or her legacy differently, to either destroy the possibility of passing it on (by dispersing the valuables), or to reject the privileges of the legacy (by not assuming them) bears most significance as it is known against the fact of their inheritance. A legacy remains inescapable. Similarly, intellectual legacies enable or hinder anthropologists *because* they cannot give them away. Coming to terms with the legacy remains the course of action. This chapter takes steps towards reconciliation.

The Noble Savage is an image, a term that denotes a particular constellation of ideas that hold importance from the earliest years of anthropological argument through to the present. As a term its first usage in English appears rather late in the eighteenth century and early in the nineteenth (Elligson 2001). It is clear that it is not a phrasing that Rousseau would have used in French. His essays are contemplations of the human condition in the state of nature; yet, he does not use anything remotely akin to this turn of speech. None the less, the discipline of anthropology bears this intellectual legacy from the Enlightenment, which distinguishes it as a unique intellectual undertaking. The balance of this chapter will describe how this legacy remains important. I will show that anthropologists cannot give away the image, or the idea of the Noble Savage, even when they try to rid themselves of it or insist they have left it behind. In reflecting upon the image, the ethnographer discovers that normative and descriptive social sciences have different ends. No ethnographer believes they describe 'Noble Savages' whether in ideal or real ways. What they describe makes anthropologists rethink the material and the immaterial conditions of their research; yet, few ethnographers believe that they provide only descriptions of places and people. These ethnographers think that the image helps to focus the account on the way of life that people might hope to have. In these ethnographies the image of the Noble Savage might appear as other things, such as ethnicity, poverty or violence. These accounts focus on sentimental or intellectual connections between what people know about the world and what they hope for themselves and for other people who live in it.

In *The Social Contract*, Rousseau tried to establish an image of how life might be lived outside the state. He discussed the natural state and the state as commensurate ideals of human existence, each one exposing the other's shortfalls and successes. He wanted to demonstrate the optimum claims that the individual person and the state could and should make on each other. Rousseau dignified the state of nature, envisioning human beings' natural condition as free. By contrast the state's restrictions on freedom emerged through histories of abuse and injustice, which remained sadly present in a world where history could not be wholly reversed. The aim of a new state would be to remove as far as possible the limits on human freedom that ignorant habits and custom secured. Then the state should make rational attempts to enable the kinds of human freedom known by the Noble Savage. Anthropological writing from the eighteenth century onwards remains deeply imbued with the vision of freedom in an image of the Noble Savage. Many anthropologists adjudicate the distance between how to live and how people do live by reappraising the ideals expressed in this image of the Noble Savage.

I take the Noble Savage to be a rhetorical image that gives shape and form to a capacity of all human relationships: that is the ability to reason about the world. Reason entails knowing how to conduct relationships and how to change them. Anthropologists find this in common wisdom, not only in elite intellectual traditions. More importantly, they conduct fieldwork because they believe that common people anywhere in the world can ably reflect upon who they are and the lives they hope to have, and discuss these subjects with an anthropologist. Why anyone should want to talk to anthropologists and how they do must be considered as part of the anthropological project. In what follows I will overview anthropological study under conditions of exploration, colonization and independence, by considering the different meanings of the Noble Savage as they unfold from one situation to the next.

Early anthropologists imagined that understanding the Noble Savage might enable them to better comprehend what it means to be human. Inspired by

Rousseau's essays, they sought to explain the social and political life of people in the natural 'state'. As the Enlightenment period unfolded from the seventeenth to the eighteenth century, scholars in Europe created a record of ethnography gathered from the history of exploration by drawing on records made by the naturalists and geographers who accompanied the voyages of discovery. Notable among these have been the voyages made by Captain James Cook, in the aptly named vessel *Discovery*. His encounters with early Hawaiian chiefs became the events of popular and even anthropological legend. Cook returned to Hawai'i after a storm at sea, but unfortunately did so at the time when the seasonally told mythic return of a Hawaiian deity would normally precipitate a fertility ritual to ensure harvest success. Confusion of characters, chiefs, deities and men led people to doubt what could be said or done with any certainty about the situation. Today, anthropologists still debate what happened in those days when Cook's crew got it all so badly wrong and, in the fight that broke out between the Hawaiians and the British seamen, Cook died at the hands of a Hawaiian chief. Sahlins (1985) argued that ancient Hawaiians struggled to understand the events and exposed in the most horribly public way the arbitrary grounds of belief, perhaps leading them to conclude that they could play with ritual, prohibitions and the signs by which they communicated with each other. In a somewhat different way, Obeyesekere argued that the various Hawaiian and English understandings of the event exposed the pragmatic conditions of each of their own systems of belief. The event destroyed English fantasies that they might be deities, and sustained Hawaiian belief that human actions folded different capacities of the social relationships into each other either as mythical reality or as historical myth (Obeyesekere 1992). The encounters between Europeans and others in the late eighteenth century can show how contemporary philosophers, scholars and anthropologists came to doubt the certainty of their belief.

Later anthropologists in the nineteenth century shared the legacy of this history of moral and political philosophy with sociologists, linguists and political theorists. Among the other disciplines, many anthropologists held an abiding concern in exploring the life ways of the Noble Savage in order first to describe the many aspects of inequality by exploring its contours in an allegedly egalitarian world of non-state society. Having done that they hoped, second, to expose how inequality came into the world with the advent of the political state. In fantasy anthropologists, in both the eighteenth and nineteenth centuries explored an image of what they did not have in their contemporary life, a free and egalitarian society. The Noble Savage was a fantasy used by anthropologists seeking illustrations of how to live in modern society.

This chapter describes the legacy of the fantasy of the Noble Savage in anthropological arguments that address inequality in non-state society. Not only do I expose the history of failure in the discipline; but also, I address the effects of holding on to this image. The 'savage slot' in research continues to fascinate anthropologists, especially when they make new things into the savage others. In the chapter's conclusions, I also seek to expose what might be called the 'real effects' of the fantasy of the Noble Savage for academic work and for political policy affecting others living in society beyond the state.

Rousseau's essays in the times of political change

Anthropologists bear a legacy from the philosophical work of Rousseau, largely for his insightful use of the ideal of the Noble Savage in constructing his political philosophy. This being the case, anthropologists have found that they struggle with dilemmas similar to those suffered by all heirs to such intellectual gifts. Bearing an intellectual legacy can spawn opportunities for the inheritor and at the same time keeping that legacy obligates the inheritor to the ancient benefactor in ways that confound contemporary social relations. Perhaps it is not surprising that in histories of intellectual legacy a student will read of the 'ghost' of an earlier writer exercising influences on the contemporary scholarship. Consider how the Noble Savage animates anthropologists' work.

It helps to know something about the historical period of Rousseau's basic intellectual project before I outline several enduring ideas in his early work that anthropologists continue to use in their own arguments about how to live. Rousseau's argument with anthropology begins in pre-revolutionary France and ends after the revolution, in the era of social reform. Typically, historians have seen the revolution as the beginning of the modern period, and point to the ways in which Rousseau and other philosophers of society and politics inspired a century or more of reason and enlightened social action that aimed to free people from oppressive regimes.

After his early essay, the discourse *On Aesthetics*, he developed three major works with care: *A Discourse on Inequality*, *The Social Contract* and *Émile.* Later scholars often understood these as steps in the development of his thought. As an essayist he influenced the time of enormous political transformation that followed their publication. *A Discourse on Inequality* coincides with the period before the French Revolution. It urged people to change the world they lived in by reasoning clearly, that is by using their natural intelligence to ascertain what in the world was wrong. *The Social Contract* coincides with the earliest years after the success of the revolution when the new republic tried to find its feet, and has been said to be a philosophical impetus to the political work of that era. In this period political futures were being re-written in dramatic ways for large numbers of people living across Europe. *Émile* coincides with the period following the establishment of the republic, when leaders sought the best ways to prepare the next generation to make wise political decisions and not deceive themselves with misunderstandings about history.

Rousseau's essay, *On Inequality*, which I shall discuss in this chapter, opens the questions for his longer-term series of political challenges to what has been called 'the ancient regime' of power that ensconced personal privilege and class differences through claims to aristocratic heritage. In *On Inequality*, Rousseau argues that inequality comes into the world by deceit, at a point when some people make private claims to have special access to what would otherwise be common wealth, and use that wealth for purposes beyond their physical and human needs and to further their own privileges. Many later scholars made Rousseau famous by quoting his paragraph describing the implications of the enclosure of common land as private wealth. Marx, of course, chose to write about this as history rather than philosophy. But Rousseau's concerns had been with establishing the rule of reason in political thought, and his goal had been to make better political philosophy for compelling events in his time, rather than to write a better history of events and things past.

I think that Rousseau expresses his views best over all three essays, each one developing the next stage of his thought, and mirroring his engagement with the questions posed by the changing political milieu in revolutionary France. Of course, his actual literary corpus is larger than these three texts suggest, and Rousseau is an avid thinker and writer of his day who was read and highly regarded by many people. Following the inspiration of Montaigne that writing should open the eyes of the reader to better and clearer reasoning about social life, Rousseau propelled the literary form to new importance for political results. Essay writing was a new activity in the eighteenth century, and Rousseau excelled at it. Early in his life, he won a competition for his essay *On Aesthetics*, and after this success felt inspired to turn his attention to the changing times. He entered another competition with the essay *On Inequality*, but won second prize. Yet, it is *On Inequality* that precipitates the work for which he is best known. The essay was a new literary form in Rousseau's day, and many believed that such a literary tool could be used to bring about political change. Rousseau argued for the advantages of reasoning clearly about the natural state, and the rights inherent to life as the Noble Savage. He assumed that the modern person could discover his contemporary link back to the capacities of that natural state by turning inward. A person should sharpen his intellectual skills to exercise the natural reason that was part of his internal human nature. For his time, Rousseau demonstrated some of the best executions of the essay as a form of writing and argument. He showed us the successful essay as the best product of natural reason, and he argued about the advantages of using natural reason in arguments about how to live, especially in the making of his contemporary political life.

In the essay *On Inequality* Rousseau provides an alternative picture of life as it might be lived without the state, and thereby critiques everyday life in his times because under the rule of the state some people prosper more than others do. He uses the concept of the Noble Savage to establish the dignity of human nature, as it is common to all people; and further, to elaborate the character of human relationships as they might be made within the 'state' of nature. He distinguished the human ability to reason clearly as a capacity of human nature that his political contemporaries had befuddled with corrupt, deceptive actions made against the best interests of all. This essay evokes the more hopeful spirit of the pre-revolutionary time, and inspired many to seek political change. In his second essay, *The Social Contract*, Rousseau elaborates how the best precepts of social life in the natural state can be brought to the effort to remake government and establish democratic rule in the new nation. In *The Social Contract* he argues that humans should enter freely into agreements to surrender natural rights to the government, keeping only the right to own the property that would be essential to their well-being. In the third political tract, *Émile*, Rousseau writes extensively about the education of a young man, as an example of an ideal education. Through a series of instructions about how to tutor a young boy, he provides a vision of education as a means to the rule of human reason in the democratic nation. He argues that a young man could take responsibility for making just decisions about how to live only if he understood how to distinguish between different moral choices. Some in Rousseau's day, and many more people later, used *Émile* as a manual for pedagogic practice. (It has been used as a set text in twentieth-century teacher training courses.) I think it fair to say that it would have horrified Rousseau to think that education could be reduced to following a rulebook. For him, human reason could not flourish in classrooms where students were inculcated with procedures and rules, but developed by doubting what seemed self-evident.

The fable of the tragedy of the commons

Consider Rousseau's essay *On Inequality*. In it he challenges his readers to consider how inequality came into the world. It is by a trick of argument that ensures that one man will succeed in the enclosure of common land as private property:

> The first man, having enclosed a piece of land thought of saying 'this is mine' and found people simple enough to believe him, was the true founder of civil society. How many crimes, wars, murders: how much misery and horror the human race would have been spared if someone had pulled up the stakes and filled in the ditch and cried out to his fellow men: 'Beware of listening to the impostor. You are lost if you forget that the limits of the fruits of the earth belong to everyone and the earth itself belongs to no one.'
>
> (Rousseau, *On Inequality*, Part 2)

Rousseau takes a lesson from this historic moment when the first man cheated the rest of his acquaintances out of their shared, common wealth. Knowing how to reason clearly protects the average person from lies of others and from being exploited by those lies into surrendering their rights to personal property.

Rousseau's essay describes the nature of human reason in the state of nature. It is clearly the corruptions of society that make men needy, greedy, prideful and selfish. Society blurs the best thought of even the best philosophers, such as Hobbes, and tricks them into imagining these corruptions as dishonesty of character. Rousseau argued, against Hobbes, that those human lives in civilized states, not in the state of nature, were nasty, brutish and short and that they experienced a 'war of all against all' not to be found in the state of nature.

Philosophers agree that Rousseau shifted his arguments, changing the definition of the state of nature, and especially the nature of human reason in that state. In Rousseau's argument human reason begins with effective communication, which itself is a social act. Human communication began with altruism and compassion. A person uttered the first words to another person in response to an alarm or cry for help. Natural reason begins with moral and ethical obligations to others. The most reasonable arguments are profoundly given to keeping obligations to others, but only obligations that reflect human beings' natural compassion for each other.

Field-testing the evolution of reason

The legacy of the Noble Savage in the nineteenth century presents a complex problem for understanding anthropological argument. As Stocking, the historian of anthropology, explains, Victorian anthropology was characterized by experiment and innovations. Mostly, the Victorian anthropologist worked to explain, even to account for and justify, the history of civilization as they knew it. Among anthropologists a strange idea emerged. Whereas Rousseau used the Noble Savage as a figure or an example to hold up as an example or image contrasting with life in his times, the later anthropologists came to believe it was an ancestor, living among them. Rather than understanding the capacities of the Noble Savage as the ability to reason shared by humans in any civilization, the Victorian anthropologists fantasized that the different people they encountered were manifestly Noble Savages in various stages of social evolution towards civilization. The anthropologists imagined the Noble Savage to be alive and well and dwelling among them. How did the idea of the Noble Savage emerge as a reality to be discovered, met and researched?

There are many answers to this question of how people came to assume that the Noble Savage was a real person, and not an ideal figure. One comes from Kuklick's (1991) account of the Cambridge expedition to the Torres Straits. The members of the group, which was headed by Haddon, are pictured in Figure 2.1. They contributed to the founding of the discipline across Britain and its individual anthropologists, Seligman and Rivers, initiated early methodological innovations in fieldwork and opened various pathways of investigation in the discipline (Herle and Rouse 1998). Kuklick traces the significance of evolutionary theory by showing that the arguments carried a purpose to change social life of the times and aid in the founding of British social anthropology in the late nineteenth century and after. Kuklick directs

Figure 2.1 Members of the Haddon expedition with assistants (l–r) seated: Jimmy Rice, Debe Wali; front row: Alfred Haddon, Charlie Ontong, Anthony Wilkin; second row: William Rivers, Sidney Ray; third row: William McDougall, Charles Myers, Charles Seligman (Museum of Archaeology and Anthropology, University of Cambridge).

attention to the intention of anthropologists to study selectively some forms of social life in order to advance the evolution of human civilization, adding to the best of Victorian knowledge about how to live. By paying attention to the way these scholars understood their own contribution to the evolution of human knowledge about how to live, she recovers for anthropology a vital part of the story of the beginning of the modern discipline that others missed, among them Asad (1973), Sahlins (1976), Stocking (1988) and Kuper (1992).

Kuklick and Kuper reminded their readers that the evolutionary anthropology aimed to describe a figure that had never existed, or at least had long since disappeared from the face of the earth. Sahlins wrote bemusedly about the attempt to revise Rousseau's ideas about human's 'native reason' by running a battery of tests to test empirically the capacity for logical reasoning of the residents in the Torres Straits Islands. Stocking (1988), and in different ways, Asad (1973), described anthropology as a kind of moral argument made for and against policies of the colonial period and the advance of the values of European civilization. By contrast, some members of the Cambridge expedition sought to test Spencer's evolutionist theory that historical events in medieval and modern Europe had twisted human reason and left Europeans less able than Torres Straits Islanders to think rationally about their existence.

Anthropologists' collective follies interest Kuklick, but she elaborates each anthropologist's intentions and purposes in her history of the evolution of the discipline of anthropology. In her book, *The Savage Within*, she recovers the ideas of evolutionary theory – selectivity, intentionality and progress – in order to explain the development of anthropology as a distinctly different discipline from biology, geography and psychology. That is, Kuklick recalls that the legacy of the eighteenth-century ideal of the Noble Savage presented anthropologists of the late nineteenth century with an opportunity to differentiate and distinguish their discipline in order to make better arguments about how to live.

Kuklick tells of the relationship between Darwin's and Haddon's theories of evolution, the latter being an innovative adaptation of the former. In *The Origin of Species*, Darwin did not argue that social evolution would proceed in the same manner as natural evolution. Haddon worked to extend the theory of natural selection to explain the evolution of some civilized societies. Kuklick reminds us that Haddon entwined his academic and intellectual efforts with his contemporary belief that people could rectify the injustices of social inequality by selectively choosing some social habits over others. He counted generosity and charity among the social dispositions that ensured the survival of a society and the evolution of more civilized forms of living among its members.

Some anthropologists revived the theory of cultural evolution in the period immediately following the Second World War, arguing that it was time to revive aspects of the theory that Boas's attack had ignored. Service, Wolfe and, in particular, Sahlins developed the theory of cultural adaptation to environmental conditions. Sahlins made a particular contribution with his review of social stratification in Polynesia (Sahlins 1958, 1963). He begins wittily that the series of small islands provided an unparalleled opportunity to explore theories of cultural change. He outlines the evolution of different forms of political life, from atomistic, leaderless, anarchistic association of individuals in Melanesia to chiefly noble 'states' of Polynesia focusing on the variations of their trade that can be deduced from the archaeological and ethnographic record. He ends desultorily, his project completed but his argument undermined by his failure to explain the course of evolutionary history with reference to the facts on the ground. Reflecting upon his efforts, he concludes that the theory of state formation and deepening of inequality did not cohere with the chronology of historical developments (Sahlins 1963). Sahlins showed that Pacific islanders over the centuries responded to the intensification of social relationships by leaving behind deepening inequalities and migrating further and further east in order to advance a frontier of most egalitarian social relations. This predicted that the western Pacific islands should appear to have the most complex and most 'civilized' forms of social and political structures while eastern Pacific islanders should appear to have the least complex forms of social structures. The opposite was true. Polynesia seemed more 'advanced' than Melanesia. Ultimately, this closed down future discussion of evolution within most anthropological debates outside biological anthropology.

Contemporary anthropologists certainly share Thomas's later cautions against colluding with the racist ideology that underpins much of evolutionary theory (Thomas 1984). Yet, to his credit, Sahlins (1963) had raised earlier serious doubts about the significance of the idea of cultural evolution by pointing out the recklessness of distinguishing the evolution of the eastern from that of the western Pacific islands. He broke the back of the body of his assumptions, even his ideal theory, on ethnographic reality elaborated in numerous fieldwork reports from the region. Cultural evolutionism had spent its legacy from the Enlightenment in two ways. It deployed sceptical ethnographic scientific description to critique the political ideology encompassed within the ideal science of the Noble Savage.

Ideological commitments to the Noble Savage's ideals

Anthropologists bear the legacy of the Noble Savage into the twentieth century even as the search for egalitarian society continued. Eric Wolf argued that the search for the Noble Savage blurred the anthropological vision of the other social relations that coexisted with village life. In effect, describing the Noble Savage as different and distinct from the modern human elided the long history of relationships between them. Rather than study humans in the state of nature, Wolf insists anthropologists must study the colonial territory, the administrators and missionaries who reorganized the everyday life of people into new colonies. One can imagine easily a picture of the social world of the Pacific that Wolf would have anthropologists investigate because newspapers carried

Figure 2.2 'Hoisting the British flag in New Guinea: Mr H.M. Chester, Queensland Magistrate calling for cheers' (lithograph from *The Illustrated London News* of 1885 from a photograph taken on the spot by Reverend W.G. Lawes). The illustrated newspapers in the nineteenth century, which often carried reports of overseas events, were extremely popular. This image records the British adoption of the territory of Papua on the island of New Guinea, with the families of the region looking on with apparent approval.

accounts of the colonial project in their reporting on events throughout the empire. Figure 2.2 is one of the many illustrations of the colonial world that were easily available to the middle-class readers of the late nineteenth-century paper *The Illustrated London News*.

In a definitive statement in his book, *Europe and the People without History* (1986), Wolf argued for a recasting of anthropological research. He showed that the history of colonial power changed the lives of the villager and the tribal people indelibly. He reminded readers that the anthropologist rarely described a society of people whose women and men had not already been trading for many years with Europeans, among whom missionaries had not been living for a generation, or whose leaders, chiefs or bigman had not been arguing with colonial administrators. He also argued that if anthropologists failed to include the ways in which colonial relationships, and even postcolonial relations, shaped what they knew about human experiences in any locale, then they would risk their own authority as truthful and reasonable scholars. In effect, Wolf argued that by not providing a critique of colonial power, that is, by forgetting the history that leads anthropologists to research the Noble Savage, anthropologists had forgotten the driving question about how to live that had inspired the Enlightenment project itself.

Wolf made his criticisms most pointedly against the structuralism elaborated in the anthropology of Lévi-Strauss, criticizing that school of thought for seeking to describe the deep structures of thought that shaped and organized social life without providing an account of the history of the power machinations that made those structures. Wolf may have been wrong to focus on Lévi-Strauss in his critique of ahistorical anthropology. Lévi-Strauss's work used Rousseau's critical insights in a different way, and will be considered in chapter 5. If anthropology was an argument about how to live, then it had to attend to the full range of human experience, including anthropological collusions with the administrative and state powers of the time.

Over the years, anthropologists made at least two sophisticated lines of argument that embraced Rousseau's critical efforts to use the example of non-state society in order to expose the creation of inequality by the state. Some researchers follow one line of argument to consider how they share a political problem with those who live elsewhere, perhaps beyond the reaches of the state. But, later day anthropologists admit that few people live without the effects of the state in their lives. In his brave reworking of Rousseau's insights for the late assessment of the emerging inequalities as they occurred with the rise of the African state, Diamond argues that modern anthropologists can find authority to speak about the experiences of the 'other' in the African or South American village because they share a common human problem: how to explain the suffering that the state brings to people everywhere, whether in the European metropolis or the African village. Diamond argued that anthropology best carries the legacy of Rousseau's intellectual gifts when it recovers the political philosopher's original impetus to criticize the explicit and implicit ways in which the state works against the well-being of common people. For Diamond this entailed examining colonial wars, the rise of inter-ethnic violence and the erosion of the capacity of the state to provide institutional services to its people. The anthropologist can analyse these experiences because they resound across political life in Europe, even when the reverberations might be felt differently there as the after-effects of decolonization, of immigration or surveillance, and of loss of social services.

Many anthropologists working since Diamond's time use similar terms to ground the claims of their work, although they do not cite his inspired revising of Rousseau. Among them, Scheper-Hughes (1995) called for a reclaiming of anthropology's legitimate role in describing existential crisis and suffering at the invisible or visible hands of the state. D'Andrade (1995) launched a criticism of the use of moral argument in these studies, raising doubts about the markers of good and evil for specific expressions of power that generated or sustained inequality. He asked anthropologists to understand inequality as a term relative to equality, and to withhold their judgements about the good or evil character of social relations until they held a fuller understanding of them.

Political power takes only one form under the state, and the state renders this a historical travesty by commanding all forms of power to its own purpose (cf. Clastres 1987). Gledhill (1994) examines the rise of the European capitalist state power against the fear of Byzantine power, whether evidence, allegation or fantasy sustained the supposed threat of the 'Oriental' state. In his history of the European capitalist state's efforts to overwhelm the dangers of the mysterious foreign Oriental state, he shows how agrarian reforms at home organized social life towards the goal of competing with and dominating the barbarian states of the east. In turn, the European states rushed to control and dominate the territories where many thought that numerous people lived in the state of nature. Driven by fear of the corruptions of Byzantine power, European capitalist states built colonies, incorporating and growing by drawing the livelihoods of people in distant territories into their larger project of civilizing the globe. The colonial and imperial policies of the European state that aimed to civilize the world, also disguised the machinations of coercive power. In Gledhill's analysis the disguises of the European state in the history of colonial and capitalist power hide but one coercive and racist form of power.

In a different way, Spencer (1997) asked for a better articulation of power in different societies after independence and after colonialism. Such scholarship would broaden anthropologists' knowledge of how power worked in postcolonial worlds, and enable their analysis of the beginnings of social movements there. He argued that political anthropologists should consider whether power or, by association, inequality could be differently understood in different colonial contexts. Spencer's radical argument asks that anthropologists consider different forms of inequality and power around the globe. Each different form of inequality predicts wide-ranging choices about how to live, yet distinct choices from other forms of inequality. This positions him differently from Gledhill. There are intriguing differences between these two positions: one that finds power to be differently disguised but similar in its coercive project of dominating others, and one that describes how power might be differently used by different people. Clearly, anthropologists deploy the concept of political power with difficulty.

Troubles in the Amazon before and after the Second World War

The personal journey of one intellectual leader of structuralist theory bridges the decades from modern times of the early twentieth century to the new modernity of the later twentieth century. Lévi-Strauss conducted his first research in the Amazon river basin in the 1930s, and published the book *Tristes Tropiques* (1955) as an account of a disappearing way of life among the Amazonian Indian villages there. This record remains with anthropologists as a primary example of the ethnography of that era, research conducted when even the anthropologist had become aware that nations in Europe had begun to prepare for war. Lévi-Strauss undertook great efforts to convey the elements of Amazonian social life, largely because he aimed to record the dynamics of a world on the wane. His account of the end of Amazonian warfare finds him asking in what ways did people in the Amazon basin make peace. They did not create treaties; there were no politicians to negotiate international agreements that would be written down for future reference. How could statecraft exist in this place without writing?

In the Amazon river basin of South America, deep in the interior of the continent and far away from the bustle and noise of cities in North America and Europe, distant from the parliaments, government departments, and officers that made the political world, the exchange of women secured the principal means to peace after warfare between language groups and tribes in the region. They negotiated an end to warfare by showing goodwill to the enemy, as emphasized and symbolized by the gift of a woman. Thus, the peace was kept through ongoing negotiation of relationships between her clan and the clan of her husband. As these connections thickened with histories of the give and take of small everyday gifts, then too did the reasons deepen for the end of conflict between the former enemies? Often they did. Lévi-Strauss explains how negotiations can achieve peace between warring enemies. He described all manifest and surface meanings of the exchange of wealth and the interchanges of communication as evidence of the successful accomplishment of peaceful social life (even at times when that would appear otherwise).

The analysis offered by Lévi-Strauss does not offer any explanation of why the warfare existed, or why people wanted peace. These were not his concerns because these lead to statements of belief about human nature, that the basic human condition was either warlike or peaceful.

Other anthropologists took up the question of what motivated people, and posed critiques of Lévi-Strauss by exploring examples of violence in human society. Chagnon (1977) offered a new evolutionary account of the successful accomplishment of peaceful social life out of the condition of war. In his effort to understand the human nature that informed Amazonian Indian behaviour he undertook to describe environmental and historical causes for the events unfolding in the time of Lévi-Strauss's visit. Chagnon described the lifeways of the Yanomami, whose identity now falls famously into the view of anthropologists of the region. The Yanomami people feature as the subject of a thirty-minute ethnographic film. Chagnon used the film to provide evidence of the nature of social life in the region in order to support his own larger theory about the evolution of political structures. Whereas Lévi-Strauss decried evolutionism as a theory of social variation, Chagnon championed it.

In particular, Chagnon aimed to show the facts of human social make-up, using film to record evidence of warring behaviour in everyday life and going beyond the claim that warfare could be best described as ritualized activity. He claimed that the film showed important descriptive material, and used it to support his claims about the evolution of political society following the old argument that states emerge with the aims of ending the warring condition and of containing the legitimate uses of violence towards winning peace.

Chagnon had worked hard with the film maker Tim Asch to create a compelling portrayal of events in the Amazon. Asch's own record of Yanomami life extends to well over thirty films, few of which portray the violence that Chagnon had tried to theorize. Ruby (1995) explains that Asch's corpus of films do not promote theoretical projects. Asch's principal concern was the development of collaborative methods in visual anthropology. Both Ruby and Grimshaw (2001) underline the ways in which Asch used collaborative work with anthropologists to answer questions posed by both anthropologists and a new generation of film makers inspired by Rouche's explorations of cinema. The more interesting film by Asch, *The Feast* was inspired by Mauss's essay *The Gift*. Asch made two innovations in film making in it: the uses of still frame highlights shown at the beginning of the film, and the minimal use of subtitles on the observational representations. He used the text to enhance the possibility for the viewer to understand the meaning of the actions, without relying upon words to interpret them. For the creation of *The Ax Fight*, which appeared to be a realistic shot of the events that developed naturally in front of them, the film makers worked to create the violent conflict on the screen. They focused on the build-up of antagonism more than on the restitution of peaceable relations. From this Chagnon aimed to show the emergence of structures of control in the village, which enforced the argument for the origins of political evolution in the management of conflicts.

One anthropologist pursued the question of violence in the Amazon somewhat differently, by focusing on historical events, rather than on the stages of political evolution. Maybury-Lewis asked why warfare existed with such intensity in the Amazon basin during the twentieth century. His answer finds somewhat different solutions assessing the context of broadly social and economic changes in the region. As a result of changing land policies for white settlers and businesses in the Amazon, many of the indigenous communities moved into territories previously used by other clans. Maybury-Lewis argued that the divisions between people emerged through political changes to the environs brought about by the colonization of the region and the advent of Amazonian states. Directly addressing Lévi-Strauss (rather than Chagnon), Maybury-Lewis argued that the 'dual organizations' of wife givers and wife receivers did not exist as social forms reflecting the mental constructs of the Amazonian Indian. These groups emerged because of recent history, and were not important to the development of a grand theory about the structure of society. Anthropologists must conduct good history before they theorize about the variety of societies around the globe. Maybury-Lewis insisted on good history first, whether the anthropologist pursued the evolutionist's question of why a politically negotiated peace exists or the structuralist's question about how that peace might be made in any society. In the final analysis Maybury-Lewis believed that the anthropologist could not know what human nature constituted, nor how human cognition shaped social life. Instead, the anthropologist could know what people did and describe simply that. As a rejoinder to larger theories of social and political evolution, Maybury-Lewis's argument offers an objection with a description of historical events, but neither a new theory nor a defence against the efforts of arguments elaborating theories of social evolution.

By offering a structuralist theory of how societies varied across the world, especially one that did not depend on evolutionary assumptions of the superiority and complexity of some societies over and above others, Lévi-Strauss offered a powerful intellectual alternative both to evolutionary theory and to historical accounts. It can judiciously be said that as an alternative theory structuralism provides a powerful counter to the theory of social evolution because it can explain how people develop political structures to address violence, but in entirely different ways. It is a particular advantage of the structuralist theory of social difference that it does not imply either racism or elitism, two of the ideological predispositions that some evolutionists relied upon more than others. It is also an advantage of structuralism that it did not rely upon a theory of human nature; so much as upon a theory of human society. Within structuralist theories of social variation, social relations never can be reduced to differences in human nature. Instead, structuralists argue that differences are always an effect of human social capacities, and a reflection of human abilities to make the world comprehensible in speech, act and artistic forms. Structuralists argue that potentials of human communication rather than nature ground human difference.

Conclusions: the legacy of the Noble Savage in anthropological argument

I began with a very brief introduction to Rousseau's idea of the Noble Savage, placing it in the context of his contemporary political milieu of revolutionary France and Europe, showing only how he reasoned through an argument about how to live. He wrote a series of essays about the life of humans in the state of nature and from this work emerged the concept of the Noble Savage as an ideal for human association. He writes first of the Noble Savage to describe the state of humans in nature, then of the Noble Savage within the social contract and as an accomplishment of that contract where a noble and natural lifestyle could be protected. Finally, he writes of how to educate youth so as to cultivate their natural reason, so that they might remain Noble Savages even as civilized humans. Although Rousseau and his contemporaries found the idea compelling, the Noble Savage remains today a perplexing and difficult concept. The legacy of the Noble Savage after the Enlightenment complicated and burdened anthropologists more than at first appears, largely because the idea of the Noble Savage benefits and constrains the intellectual orientations and ideological positions of the anthropologist, but a bit differently in each case. This chapter has discussed, in turn, the evolutionists' (both nineteenth- and twentieth-century versions), the Marxists' and the historicists' uses of the concept, and the structuralists' use of the legacy of the idea of the Noble Savage.

What are the lessons for anthropology that a student can learn from considering this legacy of the Noble Savage in social science research? In the first case, the theory of social evolution stumbled because the ideological claims for the advancement of human values could be sustained by ethnographic evidence. But that oversimplifies a complex problem. The ideal of the Noble Savage came to have material effects in the colonial history of social transformation. Early researchers mistook Pacific islanders for Noble Savages. They found Polynesian nobility in the fantasy of incipient Pacific 'states' built on charity, and Melanesian savagery in the fantasy of cannibalistic practices that fed the perseverance of an anarchic society. In the subsequent generations European admiration for the nobility of the eastern Pacific peoples proved to be insipidly destructive, changing Polynesian chiefdoms into state bureaucrats in two generations. By contrast, European angst about the alleged savagery of western Pacific peoples continued into the present as fear of the anarchism and threat to world order posed by allegedly weak western Pacific states.

The play or the difference between the ideal of the noble and the material effects of making colonial and state policy based on that imaginary person plagues anthropological work, at the same time as it enlivens it. Michel-Rolph Trouillot named the unstable image of the Noble Savage, 'the savage slot', but not because he hoped to dismantle the ideal in favour of the material evidence that humans are not 'savage'. Instead, he aims to show that anthropologists in the first place mistakenly divided the material form from the ideal. It would be a tragedy if anthropology gave up on the search for the better way to live, and it would be a tragedy if anthropologists continued to mistakenly turn their examination from enquiries into how humans tried to make good lives, with descriptions of the lives they did make. Simple material evidence of the failures or successes of the greatest human efforts simply do a disservice to the social sciences if they are not considered as a part of a wider anthropological discipline of arguments about how to live.

Some contemporary anthropologists have expressed concern about the awkward legacy of the deployments of the concept of the Noble Savage by anthropologists across the centuries, and have focused on the failure of scholars to match their work to the real lives of people in the places they described. Summing up this kind of search for the 'primitive' in anthropology, Adam Kuper rightly shows how it has been an extraordinary failure. He cynically exposes a history of failure in anthropology given to the exploration of a fantasy; the primitive did not 'really' exist. He discusses the history of kinship theory as a fantasy that illuminated an African past, but hid the social processes of resettlement and social-economic development in the Africa contemporary with anthropological research there. Kinship theories of Fortes and Evans Pritchard wobble under the weight of Kuper's inspections because allegedly they grasped for the fantasy of the African past. The extended case studies, or rational actor theory of the Manchester School, were a more viable model for research in the decolonizing world. However, if the members of the Manchester School had not measured simple economic rationality as a universal capacity, they could have mapped a better course of action for themselves. Kuper remains despondent about his anthropological bearings.

Trouillot challenges anthropologists to escape the narrow role they have made for themselves. Moreover he argues that anthropologists must find a way out of the mire of problems in the 'savage slot' if they only reason more clearly about how to live. He points out that whatever criticisms have been made of research with the elusive 'primitive', it is likely that anthropologists remake other equally abstract topics into the contemporary 'savage'. For example, research into such abstract concepts as poverty can denigrate the material aspects in the lifestyle of people in the condition of poverty in order to ennoble the ideal elimination of poverty. Perhaps it is better to ask the complex question of who is doing what with whose money? In seeking to describe the material forms of the abstract idea, anthropologists often shift their focus away from other arguments, such as those about the creation of inequality. I agree with Trouillot that contemporary anthropology must proceed fully aware that the Noble Savage was a fantasy that fuelled the imagination of the researchers, and with cynicism about the implications of that fantasy for contemporary anthropology. One way to take up Trouillot's challenge would be to examine how anthropologists used the concept of the Noble Savage to understand the problem of inequality.

Summary of chapter 2

The Noble Savage leaves an awkward legacy in anthropology because it cannot be given away or forgotten without making its role ever more potent and important to critical thought. The Noble Savage is best understood as a rhetorical construction, used by anthropologists working in the shadow of Rousseau to write critically about their contemporary political and social conditions. Often, as it did in Rousseau's day, the Noble Savage represented an alternative lifestyle from that lived by European people in his time. Social criticism using the image of the Noble Savage has been directed most often at the nature of state power, and has been used as an impetus to change and to create new ways of living. Over the decades the Noble Savage has been used to establish the capacity of humans to reason critically and reflect upon their lives by explaining how people in other societies live differently. Evolutionist accounts have used the label of the Noble Savage to describe other societies, as if they were contemporary ancestors of allegedly civilized people. Historical anthropologists charge social evolutionists with writing false history because they fail to account for social change as a product of purposeful human actions. While acknowledging this complex claim, historical anthropologists reassessed the colonial relationships in which most ethnographers worked and argued that ethnography should be examined in the context of that history. The reframing of studies about the Noble Savage as an artefact of colonial history did not produce a new anthropological theory about social change and cultural diversity. The more successful rejection of evolutionary accounts of social variations put a new theory in place in order to argue that the Noble Savage and the contemporary civilized human shared the ability to make rational insights into their respective conditions. In a case study from the Amazon the anthropologists posed the question: if rationality of thought underpins all social relations then how can anthropologists account for the power of violence in social life? We see that the answer to that question cannot assume that violence exists separate from social relationships and that it is wrong for anthropologists to 'slot' violence into the place of the 'savage' and study it as if separate from our humanity. Recently, anthropologists argue that the discipline needs to make self-consciously a rhetorical space for the Noble Savage so that researchers do not reinvent it in new forms and mistake it for objective reality.

3

GATHERING THOUGHTS IN FIELDWORK

Many anthropologists agreed it was time to return to fieldwork in order to gather their thoughts after the philosophical arguments by numerous scholars about how to live, especially the well-observed thoughts about how to live within the state. In fieldwork anthropologists cultivate anthropological knowledge, in a unique disciplined approach to the study of humanity. Early researchers likened contemplation and enquiry into the order of things to a kind of detective work, where they confirmed with ethnographic evidence simple modest proposals about human action, rather than grand theories about humanity. Collecting evidence is detective work; but collecting is an approach to knowledge that assumes that 'things add up' to make an alternative explanation from the conventional understanding of events. From the facts, using the evidence, an anthropologist builds up a case about how people act and even how they think. An account takes shape through an accumulation of evidence. They use the evidence to show how people do act and what they say about how they live to elaborate a fuller picture of a time and place. At the critical point when the collected evidence takes shape or presents some regularity to the sense of the anthropologist, an interpretation of details or a rule of behaviour can be stated. By accumulating a wealth of detail an anthropologist prepares to make an argument, especially an argument against the common wisdom of the day.

Although in the past decade some anthropologists accepted the assertion of the cultural critic James Clifford (1988) that participant observation was an accidental invention of Malinowski's, this seems unlikely if a contemporary anthropologist looks at the evidence. In the following I will collect some evidence to define the method of participant observation. I begin by discussing the way in which Malinowski, and his contemporary Boas, used ethnography against the speculative theory that Western civilization was more complexly evolved than were other societies. Second, I discuss the intellectual company that Malinowski kept during the years when he invented the method of participant observation and assess the relative importance that different thinkers might have had for his project. Finally, I review the arguments against the validity of results that can be had with Malinowksi's method, rejecting the claims that participant observation is purely subjective or deeply compromised by colonial power. The evidence is assembled to show that participant observation emerged as a method that functioned within a larger framework of the development of social science.

A story that often is told about the beginnings of participant observation takes listeners and readers to the time of the outbreak of the First World War, when the anthropologist Bronislaw Malinowski met difficulties with the Australian government. Legend has it that as a citizen of the Austro-Hungarian empire, with residence in the United Kingdom, his alliances seemed uncertain to the Australians, and so they detained him for a while. His choices were few. He could find accommodation in an Australian detainment settlement for those citizens of enemy nations who did not normally live in their home country. The better option must be to travel to the solitude of the Trobriand islands, of the territory of Papua in the south-west Pacific Ocean, where he might conduct an extended study of the livelihood of the people who lived there. Two years of residence passed before he returned to Australia, and ultimately London. This period of his residency in the Trobriands, from 1914 to 1916, largely came about because of the circumstances of the war. Here, the anthropological method of participant observation was born. Malinowski found in this time, the means to advance the cause of anthropology.

There is a myth that anthropologists discovered their fieldwork methods by accident or happenstance. It would be easy to assume this about Malinowski's experience because he came to the Trobriands under duress, rather than fully by will. None the less, it was his plan to do such research, and he had anticipated the duration of his stay with years of study before that day when he first found himself set down on the beach of a quiet lagoon. He did not discover fieldwork methods by accident; participant observation emerged as a method after years of cautious and careful deliberation about what a person could know from direct experience of living in a different place and from people who adhered to the cultural habits of another society. By the time Malinowski began his fieldwork, there already had been many examples of how to conduct research in the new discipline of anthropology. He learned a great deal about solo fieldwork from Seligman, who aside from working in Africa had been part of the group expedition to the Torres Straits. In the previous chapter, I referred to the nineteenth-century history of that expedition, led by Haddon to the Torres Straits, and recalled that the team of researchers from Cambridge wanted to adapt the field methods used by scholars of special or biological evolution to the analysis of social evolution. They used the best of observational techniques and methods to create a model of evolutionary social change. But, by the early twentieth century, Malinowski felt that fieldwork by naturalists and by anthropologists should differ dramatically. Before I discuss the aims and scope of Malinowski's method of participant observation as a solo or individual project, it helps to know that a number of others had established the value of solo research.

Recording the particulars of cultural life

One anthropologist in particular shared a similar intellectual history with Malinowski. Franz Boas was a European student of physics at the end of the nineteenth century. As a physicist, Boas pondered the limitations of human perception in discerning facts about the physical world. He lived on Baffin Island in the Canadian Arctic over a winter in order to assess how people understood the colour of snow. Snow as frozen water has no substantial colour except for the shades of the world it reflects; and so human perception of the environment becomes central to the 'naming' of the colour of snow. Another solo researcher in Africa, namely Seligman, recommended the value of working alone to the scholar of anthropology who needed to learn how the community worked. This could be accomplished by participating in it, and fieldwork became a kind of initiation into the social life of the village.

The tradition of fieldwork distinguishes anthropology both from the history of the civilization's evolution, and from the philosophy that sustained that history. Boas used anthropological evidence to critique evolutionism, particularly the evolution of culture and civilization. During Boas's early career at the turn of the twentieth century many European philosophers discussed phenomenology, which is the assessment of experience as it can be felt directly by consciousness as 'meaning'. The philosophers of phenomenology experimented with this approach of the human or historical sciences to advance a theory of cultural life, as a form of human experience that insisted itself in consciousness as 'meaning' and was shared by people in almost all societies in a variety of expressive artistic forms and habitual styles of living. But Boas criticized the general evolutionary model underlying phenomenological approaches because they triumphed only one vision of culture, rather than the multiple forms of expression that culture might take. Immediate experiences in the research location quickly led fieldworkers to doubt the apparent 'success' of the evolution of Western culture over and against the many cultures of the American Indian or the African village resident.

Like Malinowski, Boas remains most clear about the value of the descriptive efforts of fieldwork in creating arguments against the dominant evolutionary models of the day. Boas argued rigorously, and even more overtly than Malinowski, against the efforts to generate the evolutionary theory of social change. Boas argued that anthropologists should work first to describe the cultural life in the community in which they lived as researchers, rather than to fit it to a larger theory of culture as the artistic and literary expressions of the grand history of human civilization. Adamantly disputing the evolutionary models of his day, Boas proposed that ethnographers should be 'historical particularists' and reject the search for idealist or transcendent truth. That is, ethnographers as historical particularists should create as closely as possible a description of the particulars of everyday life during the period of their stay so as to keep the written account relatively truthful to the research interlude itself.

From the careful record of early ethnographic descriptions, Boas believed that later anthropologists could build up better explanations about what it means to be human. In Boas's day, the ethnographic record exposed as conjecture the claims that the history of civilization found its fullest expression in the urban and cosmopolitan centres of Europe and America.

Boas's criticisms of evolutionary anthropology won him a rebuttal from those contemporaries who were more committed to that theory, who dismissed Boas's historical particularsim as 'atheoretical'. Others named it a form of 'salvage anthropology', as if it were an effort to describe the maladaptive social developments in evolutionary history. It was not that. However, it is true that Boas sought to keep the record of cultural life for future use, and it was equally true that he saw that the lifestyles of the American Indian had quickly vanished from the world around him with the encroachments of the development of modern cities upon the American frontier. Others have recorded the complicity between evolutionary theory and the ideology of modernity that supported change in the name of the progress of a few centres of culture and social life that eventually should lead the rest on the same path. If Boas's historical particularism was a history of mistakes, the mistake was surely not to create a record of disappearing communities. Rather his ethnography is testament to the mistakes made against other cultures in the name of modern progress. A fairer assessment of historical particularism includes its record of criticisms of evolutionary theory, as a science colluding with the worst results of the ideology of modern progress.

Beyond Boas's adamant critique of evolutionism, Malinowski established a definitive fieldwork method for social anthropology that ultimately undermined the theory of social evolution for a long time to come. Participant observation described the aim and scope of an anthropological method that made the description of the lifestyles of other societies its ultimate result. Rather than add to the assumptions of evolutionary anthropology, Malinowski added to the growing body of knowledge about what it means to be human. In his introductory pages to *Argonauts of the Western Pacific*, Malinowski (1935 [1922]) is very clear that the idea that so-called primitive economy was a kind of foundational model of human economic behaviour must be put to rest once and for all. He reasoned that if by postulating that primitive economics exists scholars also came to understand European economics as civilized, then the discipline, to justify its own existence, had entered truly into the intellectual domain of generating myth and legend.

The kula trade in the Trobriand islands

The place and subject of Malinsowski's research is famous in anthropology, and even beyond. The Trobriand islands trail off in an archipelago to the south and east of the main island of New Guinea (Figure 3.1). Today Milne Bay province constitutes the political unit to which belong the Trobriands (or

Figure 3.1 The kula ring, from *The Encyclopaedia of Social and Cultural Anthropology*, edited by Alan Barnard and Jonathan Spencer (2002), London: Routledge: 18. Reprinted by permission of Routledge.

D'Entrecasteaux islands) as well as the Louisades lying further to the south and east and the shores of the mainland of New Guinea.

Some islands remain a vital part of the anthropological imagination, among them Woodlark, where Malinowski conducted research into the 'kula' and other institutions of Trobriand life, and Dobu where Reo Fortune studied sorcery. Kula itself is most important to the anthropological imagination because it did not conform in any way to notions of barter where basic goods were traded off against other goods which trading partners mutually deemed to be of use. Kula valuables are luxury items, necklaces ('soulava') and armshells ('mwali') that partners can admire aesthetically and for which they can recount the long list of previous traders who once held the item in their care. Kula must be conducted with definite and complex rules within firm and lifelong relationships of kula partners, such that an elderly chief will have a hundred partners to the south and an equal number to the north of his village. Malinowski described elegantly the trade of necklaces in a clockwise direction (always towards the south) and arm-bracelets in a counter-clockwise direction (towards the north). Men entered eagerly into trade, deploying magic and recounting myths, while seeking to meet up with established trading partners, especially those reputed to hold famously beautiful valuables.

Here is an account by Malinowski of how the exchanges progress through time and space, as taken from the words of a kula trader:

> Let us suppose that I, a Sinaketa man, am in possession of a pair of big armshells. An overseas expedition from the Dobu in the d'Entrecasteaux Archipelago, arrives at my village. Blowing a conch shell, I take my armshell pair and I offer it to my overseas partner, with some such words, 'This is a vaga [initial gift] – in due time thou returnist to me a big soulava [necklace] for it!' Next year when I visit my partner's village, he either is in possession of an equivalent necklace, and this he gives to me as yotile [restoration gift]. This means that the main gift has to be repaid on a future occasion and the abasi is given in tone of good faith – but it, in turn, must be repaid by me in the meantime by a gift of small armshells. The final gift, which will be given to me to clinch the whole transaction, would be then called kudu [equivalent gift] in contrast to basi.
>
> (Malinowski 1920: 102)

In this very helpful short, early essay on the kula, Malinowski continues to remind readers that partners hold close to their selves the virtues and spiritual aspects of the kula. The 'abasi', or 'basi', is given as an emblem of the good faith with which the kula traders operate. Upon the receipt of basi, a trader must trust that a more valuable gift will follow in the future. Kula involves elements of trust and a sort of honour. A kula partner shows his own trust of his trading partner when he demonstrates his deeply engrained ideas with liberality of giving. Generosity is the most important of virtues. Trobriand men can shame a man by saying he is mean and miserly in his kula dealings. Just as importantly, kula traders must conduct their work with magic at every step of the journey, from the earliest work of carving a canoe prow decoration so that it speeds the traders safely over the sea, through the magic to ward off witches who would endanger the lives of men should they fall into the waves, to the work of enticing the trading partners at their destination to be reckless in their generosity and lavish on the traders the best of gift necklaces or arm-bracelets. These virtues and the spiritual aspects of kula distinguish it from ideas of 'primitive barter', as advocated by anthropologists (such as Morgan) and historians (for example Engels) who sought to explain the evolution of civilization.

Collecting the facts against evolutionism

Malinowski's fieldwork description of life in the Trobriands played a large part in toppling the efforts to establish a general theory of the ascent of European civilization. In elaborating his approach, Malinowski made certain distinct

Figure 3.2 'Scene in Yourawotu (Trobriands: preparing sagali)' (Plate IV, *Argonauts of the Western Pacific* by Bronislaw Malinowski, first published in London in 1922, and under the same title in 1978, reprinted 1991 © London School of Economics and Political Science). Malinowski's photo of women's participation in sagali (ceremonial distribution of wealth) was taken at his doorstep shortly after his arrival (Malinowski 1922: 8). His caption reads 'A complex but well-defined act of sagali is going on. There is a definite system of sociological, economic and ceremonial principles at the bottom of apparently confused proceedings.'

efforts that his students and generations of anthropologists after him remember very well. First has been the one already alluded to in the above paragraphs, namely, Malinowski's language and word use. He insisted on the importance of relinquishing the use of the word 'primitive' as a label for any of the social institutions of the islanders he studied. In his introductory pages to *Argonauts of the Western Pacific*, Malinowski claims that his research, once and for all, jettisoned the abusive and obscurant label from scientific study.

Malinowski's students recalled his habit of establishing the 'facts' of Trobriand life. He urged that fieldworkers rigorously build up their descriptions of both everyday life and of ceremonial events so as not to impose their prejudices. Although the researcher must work slowly to put each fact in place, they can finally know the structure of the society. A viewer of the photograph of the 'sagali', a funeral feast in the Trobriand islands (Figure 3.2), might think that all social activity is anarchic and disorderly, but the anthropologist would put together a detailed account of the rules by which this society normally functions in ritual and everyday life. A student of anthropology might be tempted to see the street scene in the village in the Trobriand islands (Figure 3.3) as a precursor to the form of a modern village, or a simpler version of the British village (see Figure 8.1a). Sometimes the effort to create a perspective on social

Figure 3.3 'Street of Kasana'I (Kiriwina, Trobriand islands)' (Plate III, *Argonauts of the Western Pacific* by Bronislaw Malinowski, first published in London in 1922, and under the same title in 1978, reprinted 1991 © London School of Economics and Political Science). Malinowski's caption reads, 'An everyday scene showing groups of people at their occupations'.

life, in this case a common photographic perspective on street scenes half a world apart, can create meaningless or even false similarities between the places.

Famously, Malinowski returned to his field notes to establish the verity of his claims about Trobriand society, even as they met challenges in much later years of his tenure at the London School of Economics. Shelves lined with notes and journals from those years could be consulted for what details they yielded up about the livelihood of the residents of those islands. The value of such facts lay in disarming the speculations of armchair philosophers who waxed eloquent about human nature, while holding more parochial personal understandings of it based on the limited experiences of their own societies. Anthropology served to undermine such philosophy with evidence to the contrary of the most common wisdom with which they reasoned through their theories.

Third, Malinowski admired inductive reasoning as the means to establish certainty about what was true, and more so his students admired this habit in him. His seminars at the London School of Economics operated with the aim of establishing what could be known within reason, and many other universities came to imitate this style of anthropological discussion. Even today, his field notes are kept in the departmental library and students with specialist interest in the region can consult the voluminous record. A student of Malinowski brought the habitual investigation of the facts of ethnography to one American university, where it continued into the 1970s and finally emerged as a debate in virtual society, with a web-site address where the Malinowski Seminar can be joined on-line as an on-going discussion group.

Malinowski's efforts to establish ethnography as a descriptive science, in the broadest sense of the term, also can be understood as a part of the effort to institutionalize the discipline of anthropology. Malinowski, and those of his era, showed us that anthropologists do much more than 'hang around' in the process of participating in social life and observing it. Anthropologists create ethnographic reports from the careful record of planned research.

Participant observation: Malinowski's prescriptions for anthropology

Malinowski writes clearly about how anthropologists might conduct their work. They must begin with the facts, as these can be discerned through inductive reasoning. This is particularly the case if the researcher wishes to understand the nature of unusual or foreign knowledge and belief. Malinowski's concern to explain the principles of the kula trade begins with his fascination with the kula as a ritual institution. He chooses to study the kula trade because Trobrianders undertook it against the basic or subsistence interests of their community. The trader launched a canoe with a few luxury goods such as necklaces and arm-bracelets, hoping to exchange these for other similar valuables of renowned men living on more distant islands. In order to conduct this trade, in which he had invested enormous hopes that more prestigious men than himself might recognize him as their peer, he crossed hazardous seas in a small canoe with only magical protection from the elements and buoying up his preparations for successful trading. Such economic practices easily escaped modern understanding.

Malinowski addressed this social practice, hoping to isolate its peculiarities for closer understanding. He used the analogy between anthropological fieldwork and laboratory science, referring to the field as a natural laboratory. He showed the controlled experimental conditions with limited external factors on the focus on the research (which the lab scientists created with much difficulty) which the anthropological fieldworker found available to him in distant places, far away from the influences of modern life. In Malinowski's eyes the contrivance of research design in the physics laboratory threatened the validity of the results. The presence of colonial administration, missionaries, and other Europeans endangered the accuracy of the account of 'native' life. As in the natural science, the researcher must minimize these influences on the aims of the research.

Malinowski writes famously of the arrival of the fieldworker at the lagoon, and in describing the setting shows his reader how far separate he is from the white man, 'who is unwilling to waste any of his time on you'. He writes of a person immersed into the natural laboratory.

> Imagine yourself suddenly set down surrounded by all your gear, alone on a tropical beach close to a native village, while the launch or dinghy which has brought you sails away out of sight. Since you take up your abode in the compound of some neighbouring white man trader or missionary, you have nothing to do but to start at once on your ethnographic work.
>
> (Malinowski 1935 [1922]: 4)

In these pages we learn that Malinowski aims to develop an approach to the 'natives' that is different from that of his white hosts and thus begins his enquiry with the most banal and technological investigation possible. This first approach to the field should also influence his reception by the people living in the village. He does not come to take a census, nor does he come to enquire after infractions of the law. Rather, he comes to make an enquiry into the routines of village life that even the villagers understand to be mundane information, and of no importance to the Europeans present in the territory.

Malinowski establishes three recommendations for the student: to have scientific aims which include knowing the value of good ethnography, to put himself in a good condition for work, and finally to apply a number of methods of fixing his evidence. The first of these is best discussed by examples of Malinowski's own work. The value of a good ethnography lies in its aim of destabilizing received common wisdom about human nature, by showing that people residing elsewhere – with fewer contrivances of modern living, and with different assumptions about what in their social life should be valued from day to day – do things differently and hold different beliefs about their own human nature. Malinowski shows the value of ethnography of Trobriand economy by bringing it to scrutiny as an alternative vision of humanity to that fantasy of the Noble Savage, in Western imagination.

The second set of recommendations includes an elaborate discussion of the conditions for fieldwork, in which we learn that Malinowski encourages the future student of ethnography to approach his work holistically. Holism in research can be accomplished only if the fieldworker makes the fieldwork location his or her entire world, cutting him or herself off from home society and immersing himself or herself totally in village life. After the extended residence there, the fieldworker will begin to 'acquire the feeling for manners, for humour, and for recognizing matters of significance' (1927: 8).

In the third point of the set of recommendations, Malinoswki says that fieldworkers should rigorously test the facts of their knowledge in a systematic manner. On this point, he writes rather explicit and copious directions for the fieldworker to advance inductive truths throughout his research. He reminds his readers that neither people in England nor those in the Trobriands can utter general truths about their social life with ease, whereas a fieldworker can accept generalizations as scientific abstractions. When the Trobriander or the

English speak these truths, they hold the status of folk wisdom, not general knowledge of social life.

The fieldworker should ask about particular cases, and from these interpret the data without letting the fieldworker's own common sense overtake the data or cloud the information. In order to assess what he knows, a fieldworker might make a tabular chart of the details, distinguishing between information inferred from indirect experiences and that recorded as direct experience. This inductive reasoning about the social life allows for a record of the ambience and sensibility of life as it is lived. In this way, ethnography surpasses science.

Malinowski's pragmatism

Malinowski's ideas about empirical knowledge, about the ways in which a researcher can know something by his direct experience, reflect the concerns of his day. In his student days, a number of different European (and some American) philosophers experimented with challenges to rationalism. They argued that knowledge of the world could be won through direct experience of it, rather than through rational analysis. Direct experience could be understood as 'meaning', as felt insights into the workings and processes of life ways. Malinowksi does not leave a record of his thoughts about this movement, known as phenomenology, nor does he record his relationship to the work of the pragmatic philosopher of religion, William James. Yet, in the introductory chapters of *Argonauts of the Western Pacific*, he remains clear that he values inductive reasoning as it facilitates the aims and scope of his ethnographic method to record Trobriand lives. Perhaps the virtue of Malinowski's ethnographic work is that he eschews theories and the intellectual trends of his day in order to show readers the depths of Trobriand knowledge.

In Firth's (1957) collection honouring Malinowski, Edmund Leach argued that the work should be judged as an early contribution to pragmatism, especially as Malinowski had been deeply concerned with myth and magic and the nature of religious thought in Trobriand society. As Gell (1992) pointed out in later years, the magic that moves the canoes of the kula trader flying across the water causes kula traders to consider deeply the nature of their more mundane and fantastic work on the seas. On the one hand they use magic to protect themselves against harm in rough waters, and on the other they use magic to draw others to them through the seas. In many respects, the study of Trobriand religion, myth and magic is the way to the better understanding of Trobriand economics. Gell argued that the myth of the flying canoe shadows everything of Trobriand exchange, and the imagination of possibility presages ethnographic fact. Were one to follow the insights of the pragmatist philosopher William James, it might be possible to argue that Malinowski, like James, argued that belief is established in religious practice rather than in religious doctrine. But that would be to put the theory of pragmatism before the assessment of ethnographic evidence, a habit of thought that Malinowski rejected.

Malinowski's debts to James do not stand up well against any tests of direct influence, even though these are arguments that he could have formed with influence from the American philosopher's thought. Perhaps Stocking is correct to argue that there is a more compelling connection between Malinowski's thought and that of the German physicist, Mach. At least Malinowski lived in the same country as Mach did, during the time at which Mach taught in the German university where Malinowski studied for a while. But this too is an overly tenacious claim by Stocking, who had enthusiastically pursued the links between anthropological thought and nineteenth-century philosophy. Mach as purveyor of phenomenological insights in physics research drew large crowds of students into his classroom, making him one of the most influential lecturers of his time. The gist of Mach's argument was that direct knowledge of the natural world could be had through the sensory means. A human touching a tree could learn much about the qualities or essence of 'tree'. Mach's claim for the power of direct experience could have been a greater influence on Malinowksi's thought than we know. Unfortunately, we do not know that Malinowski ever studied with Mach or that the two of them came into direct contact.

While it is tempting to dismiss the power of Mach's ideas on Malinowski on the grounds that the two probably never met, Gellner (1988) recalls that Malinowski held some beliefs in common with this philosopher of science. First, it is clear that Malinowski remained certain of the common biological unity of humans, and understood this as the common grounds upon which humans could know anything. This remained an important feature of his commitment to the science of society. The power of the body on the mind remained a common feature of human experience, and one that predicted the possibility that anthropological science could be practised equally well by Trobriander traders as by Polish scholars. Neither should be bound to the transcendent power of categorical thought over and above sensual knowledge. It remained Malinowski's aim throughout his career to understand the way in which the human mind might comprehend the world without pre-supposing a number of categories to filter that experience. Gellner finds a historic influence for Malinowski, not Mach or James, but instead the classical philosopher of science, Zeno.

I think that Malinowski would resist all efforts to reduce his research in the Trobriands to a philosophical pursuit in any of these traditions. The more important influence on Malinowski's thought remains the thought of Trobriand islanders themselves.

Malinowski's functionalism

Throughout his career, Malinowski remained resolute. The study of history, especially evolutionary history, could not inform the anthropologist about the lives of the people of the present. He advocated that the meaning of contemporary social institutions was in their relations with each other, most narrowly the function that one institution played in the work of the others. Each of Malinowski's books or major essays, *Argonauts of the Western Pacific*, 'Baloma: spirits of the dead', *Crime and Custom in Savage Society* and *The Sexual Life of Savages*, discusses one institution of Trobriand life, in the round. Firth (1957) points out that Malinowski never produced the ethnography that knit together their relationship, although he often asked his students to do so. Firth judiciously points out that Malinowski does accomplish this, but as a matter of his life's work, not in a single book.

If anthropology could have a method without theory, functionalism would have been it. Its theoretical underpinnings generally emphasize more 'Western' or 'European' ideas about the self, the social contract, and some of the biological basis of human nature. This uncritical acceptance of many of these assumptions left Malinowski's work vulnerable to a number of charges. Most often he is accused of writing social change out of the lives of Trobrianders, as if Trobrianders could be people trapped by the force of their own belief within the bounds of history.

In many ways, Malinowski's student Raymond Firth correctly protests that later anthropologists unfairly judge the work, expecting a theory where Malinowski gave them none. (Later, Radcliffe-Brown would try to fill in the theoretical absence from Malinowski's work with his own theory of structural-functionalism.) Malinowski's functionalist method remains no more than a method. It is not a theory. It is especially not a theory about the nature of society, or what it means to be human. It is possible to argue that all methods imply theories, and that Malinowski can still be held accountable to his own. However, this would be to ignore that Malinowski did not aim to build a theory, largely because he wanted to undermine the most corrosive aspects of theories about human social evolution. In his hands, the functionalist method emerged as a tool to carve out the evolutionist fallacy of creating a historical account. The synchronic approach of Malinowski's functionalism presents the possibility that history of Trobriand society could be no better than 'false history', or even a dangerous and racist ideology. Confirming this general suspicion of historical argument, Gellner (1988) re-analyses Malinowski's experience in Krakow (Polish) politics in order to show what the anthropologist knew all too well. Those arguments about the past served the present far too well to be truthful about that past. Malinowski reasoned that it was better to avoid the clouds cast over research by such claims than to reduce the strength of the argument by sprinkling it in badly argued history.

Subjective bias? The diaries and the verity of participant observation

Did Malinowski find that his method of participant observation could be easily undermined by personal concerns? Was his attention unadulterated as it needed to be in order to record pure perceptions? These are concerns that preoccupied Malinowski well before the period of extended fieldwork. His record of contemplations about the influences of previous experiences, his personal emotions on his observations prove to be very interesting in later years.

Many anthropologists reassessed Malinowski's method of participant observation when new information about his years in the Trobriands appeared in print in 1967, nearly a generation after his death. A posthumous publication of Malinowski's diaries, released by his daughter, set the anthropological world astir. The diaries written by Malinowski during his fieldwork in the Trobriands revealed the doubts of a complex personality, conducting a difficult project, within a multifaceted social milieu. A contemporary anthropologist looking back on these events might ask if it should be any surprise that Malinowski's approach did not go as planned, and he often redirected his aims as he drifted off the course he chose to pursue.

Malinowski's own diaries posed a challenge to his ethnography because the writings betray a man ridden by angst throughout his time in the Trobriands. His fieldwork created long lonely periods, when he wrote about his frustrations with everyday life in the village. The diaries contain some honest confessions of dislike for individuals, and for village people more generally. More disturbing sections use racial epithets which, although common to his day, do not convey the impression of a professional fieldworker with sympathy for the daily routine of Trobriander life.

Do the diaries stand as the true, but unpublished, ethnographic record, revealing the backstage real fieldwork account? Do they overcome the value of the carefully written, published ethnography, as Clifford later argued? First, assuming the ethnography of Malinowski as a genre of writing, a kind of literary effort to describe the lifestyle of Trobriand islanders, Clifford then assesses Malinowski's work for its personal tones, insisting that the subjective account is all that Malinowski understands about the Trobriands. The ethnography that comes to the attention of so many later anthropologists appears to be grounded in misperceptions, and wrong assessments that were potentially drawn by a person who is harder to admire than the consummate fieldworker who won the respect of earlier students.

Here an enigma arises. Malinowski's apparently personal approach seems to be in direct opposition to the multifarious intellectual tradition that formed his earliest fieldwork style. Like Clifford, some of Malinowski's contemporaries, working in the traditions of continental philosophy, argued that all that could be known reduced to the insights of each single individual – yet, Malinowski's participant observation had aimed to overthrow such suggestions. Malinowski held that knowledge could not be objectively true, if its meaning lay only in its sense as the individual person sensed it. Different from Clifford, other contemporaries of Malinowski examined the terms by which experiential knowledge could be directly assessed as meaningful, but they did not all agree that this then implied that that knowledge gained from direct experience reduced to personal or subjective understandings. Many of these contemporaries of Malinowski elaborated their approach as a vigorous undertaking in establishing shared truths. Further, some of these scholars sought to explain how the meanings won from direct experience constituted a form of objective knowledge, free from the haze of prior personal opinion. They took issue with the claim that, at best, anthropology provides only a subjective account.

Geertz (1983) assessed the furore created by the publication of Malinowski's diaries in 1967. He recalled that Malinowski had aimed to create an objective ethnographic account with his fieldwork. Geertz's work contributed to a better understanding of the role of subjectivity in fieldwork, and he remarks on how Malinowski used himself as a research tool in order to better understand just what can be understood from experience. In elaborating this, Geertz drew on Kohut's psychological terms, 'experience-near' and 'experience-distant' knowledge. Geertz coined anthropological uses of the terms, pointing out that in the example of his own unconscious, he could say that it remained as distant from him as anything, forever impossible to capture in its entirety. 'Experience-near' anthropological knowledge described the puzzling array of understandings that make up the daily knowledge gathered from specific questions, mundane interactions and sentimental communications. 'Experience near' knowledge can be written down for future reference in field notes or in personal diaries. Fieldworkers then might use these more specifically close descriptions, allusively or for citation as they develop more sophisticated analysis of what they have understood from their experience. By comparison with 'experience near' knowledge, the ethnography analyses the fieldwork experience for the point of contributing to knowledge shared among anthropologists. The 'experience distant' knowledge, as Geertz calls this by comparison, might be the details and interpretations of the field notes. For example, the ethnography can report a description of the ways in which Trobrianders use shell valuables in a luxury trade, showing that they do not operate it as if a primitive economy. This brings Malinowski's ethnography away from the convolutions of personal experience, towards the wider aims of shifting epistemological understandings about the nature of exchange of goods.

Geertz did not argue that the record of the fieldwork was true, while the ethnography was false (as had James Clifford). Rather, the work of interpretive anthropology falls in between the fieldwork and the ethnography, in the space of interpretation. Geertz likens interpreting experience into field notes in the process of generating ethnography to 'getting a joke'. Field notes, or reports written close and near to the experience, become intelligible when the anthropologist draws insight from them in order to write about that experience differently. Getting the joke, finding the insight, is a matter of being able to find new terms of reference to describe that experience to the wider anthropological community. Meaning is made in the process of living, because understanding comes in the midst of translating between experiences near and distant to the fieldwork itself. Although some would oppose the claim, participant observation does generate objective knowledge by using the subjective knowledge as a tool to greater understanding.

Ideological preferences?

A different criticism of Malinowski's research emerged when his fieldwork methods came under direct evaluation, or restudy. An anthropologist revisited Malinowski's field site for the purpose of refiguring his fieldwork data. Although it was half a century later, her concern to get it right did not address the nature of social changes there. Rather, she was interested to see what difference being a female fieldworker made to the analysis of Trobriand social life.

In Malinowski's famous text, *Argonauts of the Western Pacific*, significant descriptions of the men's kula trade provide the reader with insights into Trobriand economics, but it is another form of trade that comes to the forefront in Weiner's book, *Women of Value, Men of Renown* (Weiner 1977). Weiner becomes interested in banana leaf bundles, collections that women amass on the occasions of funerals, in ceremonial trade with each other. Women make the banana leaves into skirts, which in turn are exchanged for yams, or sometimes for shell armbands used in the kula trade. By collecting skirts and redistributing them, a woman shapes the pathways of exchange between her husband and her brother. Her wealth of banana leaf skirts can influence the means by which men value their kula wealth of armbands and necklaces. In this way, women are 'of value', while men are renowned.

Weiner argues that Malinowski overlooked the importance of the exchanges made between women at the time of the mortuary feasts in the Trobriands. Banana leaf bundles could be traded at funerals and converted to other forms of wealth. They became a kind of measure of the value of women's personal labour. Did Malinowski dismiss as 'mere women's wealth' what Weiner exalts as *women's wealth*? If so, this perceptual shift in determining the significance of women's wealth provided a new departure for much of the literature on feasting, gardening and trading in Melanesia. It asked if the feminist point of view could be usefully brought to a re-analysis of social relations and the reproduction of power dynamics in the Trobriands.

In the Malinowski Memorial Lecture of 1981, Marilyn Strathern assessed the claim for feminist anthropology as it was posed by Weiner's work. According to Strathern, the problem lies in how the anthropologist first imagines the categories of analysis, then values those categories in research, and then centres or foregrounds them in the description, before going on to the work of interpreting such 'evidence' for general anthropological theory. These questions emulate the issues Malinowski so often addressed. Here, Strathern finds Weiner's imagined Malinowski to be no less than a 'straw man' to batter while feminizing anthropology. His fieldwork becomes emblematic of all of a patriarchal account, and Weiner attacks this emblem rather than the work itself. As a result, Weiner supplants the patriarch of Trobriand economy with a matriarch, while avoiding the work of reassessing the ethnography.

Malinowski might have approved Weiner's reassessment of his older ethnography had she simply carried out the full ethnography of Trobriand exchanges, including the account of women's exchange in the most rigorous methodological style. Unfortunately, this reassessment of ethnographic fact escaped Weiner's glass, as she set out to establish contrasts with selections of Malinowski's texts. Had Weiner reassessed Malinowski's ethnography on ceremonial exchanges at death in the light of the meanings of the yam gardens and exchanges, it could have been necessary for her to drop her charges against the male fieldworker. The problem arises around yam houses, yams, and the storage of yams in those houses. Yams, houses, and storage are concerns of direct importance to understanding the nature of women's work, which is given to gardening with her husband in order to fill her brother's yam house. Women's husbands stand in between them and their brothers, but conduct the important work of passing on the gifts of the yam. As well, experiences with yam gardens influenced the ways in which Trobrianders imagined the idioms to describe women's work and men's work. But the question arises as to how yam gardens came to the Trobriander consciousness as the place of fertility, and so how could they be likened to the work of production? Trobrianders, as much as Europeans, seemed to draw upon their experience in order to find the words, the images or the metaphoric language to communicate wisdom about how people kept social relationships alive to contemporary concerns.

Gardens give up, or bear, yams for exchange, as if giving up children to live within the village. The storage of yams in houses for future use accounts for the prestige of men and women who can disdainfully choose not to eat all that they have, even letting much of the crop rot so as to show that they have no need for it. The yam houses compare with the canoes, laden with kula valuables, taken by traders on long seafaring journeys. The full canoe, like the full yam house, indicates that the trader has no need for such wealth. He can risk it by leaving it in the hands of another person, or chance that it is lost to the rough seas. The presence of kula valuables, and the storage of yams, indicate that there are many more yams and kula valuables than the public display of these could ever reveal. Children give evidence of a married couple's fertility; yams give evidence that the garden is so full that the gardeners can relinquish great numbers of yams to storage towers until they rot; kula canoes laden with shell wealth give evidence that even more significant items of exchange exist beyond public sight. These terms engender social relations as male or female, and predict the way in which people choose to interact with each other as kin.

A feminist anthropology, drawing on Malinowski's fieldwork, would not only find the woman's point of view as distinct from the man's, but would go so far as to ask: what is a woman's point of view in Trobriand society? This suggests that the question of what is feminine can (and must) be posed before the question of what is a feminist analysis.

As with Geertz, who argued that ethnographers claimed authority to provide an objective account on the grounds that as anthropologists they knew by 'being there', Malinowski argued that ethnographers claimed authority over their objective accounts by thinking through their subjectivity as a kind of research tool. Strathern, rethinking Malinowski's ethnography in the wake of Weiner's critique, argues that getting the interpretation straight is a matter of reaching as far as possible towards the terms of analysis that Trobrianders would have used to assess relationships between men and women, in the world of work, procreation and ceremony. In sum, one could remain true to the facts, and still manage to complete analysis sympathetic to the questions of feminism, such as men's power, women's economic and social well-being, and the trade between the genders.

Did Malinowski erase the role of colonial power in his research?

Some contemporary scholars have charged Malinowski with the failure to account for colonial powers in the lives of Trobrianders. Indeed, the colonial concerns put Malinowski into the Trobriands in the first place. Even a cursory reading of the diaries and ethnography reveals that Malinowski did not fully remove himself from the company of Europeans and Australians living in the country. It is reported that he lived in a tent, rather than in a house with Trobriand villagers. The tent protected Malinowski's privacy, and provided him with the opportunity to write about his day's work. He also spent long periods away from the village, in the company of the Australians who were administering the territory, and seeing to the policing of the village. These aspects of Malinowski's fieldwork practice do not appear in his ethnography, and remain rather shadowy events and experiences in the background.

Some scholars raise a few questions about the importance of Malinowski's time with the colonial administration. To what extent could Malinowski truly participate in the lives of the people who lived in the Trobriand village if he kept company with such figures? It is possible that his village neighbours might dislike and distrust the colonial white people as law enforcers. It is possible that the Trobriand chiefs resented the power of the colonials. It is possible that by spending too much time in the company of Australians, by visiting their homes and sharing European and Australian food, Malinowski sent an implicit message to his Trobriand acquaintances. In so doing, he may have suggested with his actions that he also shared the values of the administrators.

Another question arises. If the administration kept such a presence in the Trobriand islands, then to what extent did Malinowski find himself to be participating in a Trobriand villager's life as that lifestyle was dying out? Did he describe only a corruption of that alternative, non-European lifestyle that he most wanted to describe?

Answers to these questions might first be found in Malinowski's published work that describes his fieldwork methods, and by analysing the significance of the diaries with reference to Malinowski's own understanding of the nature of human knowledge. In the next section, I return to the description of the fieldwork method.

Conclusions: participant observation in comparison with other methods of fieldwork

Malinowski forged a unique method for the discipline of anthropology with the definition of participant observation. Participant observation does require that the fieldworker lives in the village, and participates in life in ways to fit in as nearly as possible to locale conventions. It is a method defined by doing things with people, and thereby coming to know what they think about what they are doing and why it should matter. It is telling that Malinowski would suggest that the fieldworker initiate his or her work with the most routine or mundane work of the place. He suggests that it is wise to begin with learning small crafts and skills, telling his readers, 'I began by learning to cook and to mend roofs, the first activity primarily undertaken by women and the second largely by men.' But, by the learning of basic skills the anthropologist builds up trust with the community.

It remains the case that the fieldworker's time in the village is short, by comparison with the other residents who make their entire lives there. As researchers, anthropologists often have to remain focused on their work, and keep the single research question in view, rather than lapse into the work of the village itself. By staying focused on their intellectual enquiry, even while getting on with daily routines of living, they can solicit assistance from the members of the community in such a way as to be able to negotiate the provision of that help in an adult manner. Malinowski is consistent in this; he describes participatory observation as a kind of science.

Malinowski's experience refigured anthropological fieldwork for a generation of scientists working after the First World War. Participant observation is not the only transformation of fieldwork practice to have occurred after a war. I have not discussed how anthropologists dramatically changed the nature of their participation in fieldwork communities after the Second World War, and even more so after the Vietnam War. These transformations might compare intriguingly, even disturbingly, with Malinowski's own. For example, in the decades after the Vietnam War, some anthropologists sought to form intensely personal local relationships and insisted on becoming members of clans and using the appropriate kin terms as ways of addressing their informants. This was not an effort familiar to anthropologists of an early age, who did not seek to become kin with the villagers. There is nothing in Malinowski that suggests that the anthropologist should seek to be socialized into the community by becoming a relative with the inhabitants. He thinks that would be a false attempt to seek inculcation into village life, in the way that a child might be nurtured into social relationships.

In other cases of later years, fieldwork became an exercise of finding gatekeepers, key informants, and expert witnesses, as ways of figuring out who can comment helpfully on the anthropologist's own project being carried out. This search for a few key informants whose words could substitute for the anthropologist's own analysis came sometimes to typify the interpretive approach to fieldwork. The interpretive approach assumed that everyone analysed and made meaningful accounts of their experience. The anthropologist should simply work hard to find the few people able to give voice to the issues. Again, Malinowski's participant observation was not like interpretive ethnography. Rather than give them voice, he emphasized the unlikely possibility that the people of the community of research could reflect upon or analyse their own behaviours because this is the nature of human actions. For example, consider an analogy to the study of linguistics. If the speaker thinks about how language works while he or she speaks the language, then it ties the tongue of the speaker into knots, even in the act of speaking. It is difficult for humans to be vocal about the underlying rules, or the principles of association by which humans live. Malinowski argues that it takes another person who is different from the community in which the research is done, to create a reasonable explanation for the events.

The researcher planning his or her study to be an undertaking in participant observation will succeed in collecting insightful and sensitive evidence about the locale, the community and the individuals that comprise it. If an anthropologist of Malinowski's tradition (and today, many do exist because functionalist thought seems close to everyday common sense) dedicated him or herself to the job of exposing through systematic study the social institutions that teach the rules of life in that culture, the logic of people's association, or the unvoiced rules of behaviour that people observe in the course of their day's work, then they might be considering different options available to them as anthropological fieldworkers, and hence, as Malinowski had hoped, as research scientists.

Summary of chapter 3

Fieldwork in early anthropology aimed to create a descriptive account of the total social life of a society, often a small society. It was not an accidentally discovered activity, but a purposefully planned science of humanity drawing on insights into the methods of the natural sciences in which early ethnographers were trained. Malinowski worked to build a case from evidence so as to avoid subordinating the knowledge of other societies to a broader theory of evolution or world history. His functionalist approach argued that other societies were not fragments or artefacts of the past. Rather, other societies were 'integrated wholes' in which each part or institution was defined by its usefulness to the rest in terms of natural and psychological needs. By contrast Boas argued that the integration of the different parts of a society depended upon how people found them to be meaningfully shared, rather than useful to them, and hence societies were known as cultures (sometimes defined as linguistic groups). Critics of Malinowski's work – of its subjectivism by looking at his diaries without considering Malinowski's own ideas of the psychology of the fieldworker in research, of its debts to pragmatic philosophy by mistakenly associating it with other theorists, of its gender biases by criticizing its presumptions without creating the alternative account, of its ignorance of colonial power and history without considering the battle fought by Malinowski to defeat false history – often do not consider Malinowski's research within the social and intellectual context of his academic life. One danger of criticizing his fieldwork injudiciously is that contemporary anthropologists will fail to exercise an adequate level of reflexive scrutiny of their own work such that they can make it possible for the fieldwork community to respond helpfully to them.

4

KEEPING RELATIONSHIPS, MEETING OBLIGATIONS

People keep relationships by remembering their obligations to give to another; in giving gifts I remember that I have a relationship with you. Any attempt to understand the habit of giving and receiving focuses on the complementary processes involved in that work. On the one hand a person gives away wealth, and on the other hand, obligations are kept to others. When the renowned kula trader honours another kula partner who has given him armshells over the years, by returning a beautiful necklace to him, he keeps his relationship with that person by so honouring him and by enhancing the renown of both kula partners for their largesse. By habit, Kiriwinians of Malinowski's day gave away shell valuables in order to meet their obligations and keep their relationships secure.

Much of this seems straightforward, yet not. The exchange of gifts poses problems for anthropologists to understand. People use, feel and see some objects as if things were entities separate from human relationships. At the same time, to give is to do more than transact an object. How people give and receive is a matter of what kind of relationships they imagine they make and keep with each other; immediately immaterial or ideal concerns become a part of the issue. The habit of giving gifts complicates anthropological understandings of the material world, by introducing the idea of the relationship as essential to material life. Once a person understands how to receive and how to give a gift, then the material world can never be simply distinct from his or her ideas about the relationships he or she keeps in that world.

In this chapter, I discuss how people keep obligations by giving and receiving gifts. I discuss keeping obligations to reciprocate wealth as a distinct departure from those theories of political economy that emphasized the utility of wealth. The mistake of focusing on utility led social theorists to emphasize the centrality of the individual person in measuring the value of wealth for his or her singular interests, rather than the relationship of exchange. I follow Mauss, who wrote most thoughtfully about the obligation to give, receive, and to reciprocate. He discussed gifts as gift exchange. But Mauss is interested in the gift, as an exchange between people. The gift makes the ideal relationship a material fact because giving and receiving gifts creates and changes human relationships. The gift also makes the relations of exchange substantial. Yet, with all of these insights, Mauss knew that the gift is more than just words, intentions and perspectives. By giving gifts people create concrete or substantial forms of their relationships. I describe the advantages of comparison across cultures, and discuss Godelier's thesis that Mauss's comparative approach 'almost' succeeds. Throughout, I emphasize the complementarities between ideas about relationships and material forms of those relationships.

Mauss's gift

It is hard to write of Mauss without writing of the spirits and ghosts that seem to inhabit his oeuvre of publications. The anthropologist Maurice Godelier, himself working in the shadow of Mauss, tells about the complex intellectual legacy of the gift. Fournier remains a great intellectual biographer. It is from him that we learn how Marcel Mauss worked in France in the late nineteenth century, but comes to greatest prominence in the 1920s, just after the First World War. Much of this lies in his efforts to publish the works of his colleagues. In the earliest years, the research group used *L'Année Sociologique*, which they founded in 1898, to expose new ideas to a wider intellectual community, to advocate the widest implications of the work of the school. Mauss and Durkheim aimed to set more radical directions for socialism of the time (for a discussion of Durkheim's thoughts on socialism and an English language translation of Mauss's on Bolshevism, see Gane 1992). The contemporary appraisal of this period shows that the essay *The Gift* aimed to undermine the economic philosophy of Bourgeois, a contemporary of the two, but who had a popular following. Narotzky (personal communication) has argued that even in these years, Durkheim and Mauss held contemporary debates about socialist economics, and had developed a germ of an argument that the analysis of gift exchange could be used against the claim that utilitarian economic reasoning was natural to humans. The obligation to keep social relations was not so new, but the idea that objects had value locatable only in their utility was quite a recent notion.

The First World War takes many of the members of the school away from research because so many of them enlisted in the military. It cost lives and research careers, first in the work left undone by those who died too young, and later in the work of those whose own studies were usurped by the effort to publish the unfinished writing. Perhaps it is because of this history that Mauss begins a statement of his intellectual life, meant for a review of his invitation to the Collège de France (James and Allen (1998)). In his intellectual self-portrait of 1930, which Bailey and Llobera translated into English in 1983, Mauss tells his readers that

> It is impossible to detach me from the work of a school. If there is any individuality here, it is immersed within voluntary anonymity.

> Perhaps what characterizes my scientific career, perhaps even more today than formerly, is the sense of working as a member of a team, and the conviction that collaboration with others is a force that stands opposed both to isolation and to the pretentious quest for originality.
>
> (Mauss in James and Allen 1998: 29)

A decade earlier, after the end of the war, Mauss received a gift, both auspicious and burdensome. He 'inherits' from Durkheim the responsibility of guarding the future of *L'Année Sociologique*, the research group established to interrogate the nature of social life in the years of the turn of the century. Mauss's good luck to assume the directorship of the famous research group hides the burden of that gift of social power. He faces the problem of recovering the lost work of the members of the group who died in the war. The succeeding years of Mauss's work are given to establishing his dead colleagues' research. Some have wondered whether Mauss would have written more of his own thoughts down if he had not devoted his life to publishing the work to his dead colleagues. But I think it correct to say that Mauss's career grows by meeting his obligations to his peers.

The circumstances in which Mauss worked help to sharpen an insight into the theory of exchange which he offered in his comparative study of *The Gift* (Mauss 1990 [1925]). Mauss worked tirelessly to keep the relations that supported the works of the early *Année Sociologique* alive and to further the work begun by Durkheim in establishing a science of society. Mauss resolutely aimed to publish the works of his former colleagues. This immediate context, more than the ideological concerns of his time, gives greatest shape to contemporary understandings of how to approach the study of the exchange of goods.

In recent years, some anthropologists have addressed the ideological concerns of Mauss's day, in order to put his major research question into perspective. Western Europe reorganized its borders after the First World War, and it also entertained a new set of ideas about how to organize social life in a time when none of the old orders remained quite the same. The resettlement of people from the Russian Revolution ended the feudal rule of the Czars, and the subsequent movements of numerous people across Europe created the reasons for an intense debate, in both public and academic places. Most famously, the Bolsheviks presented the argument for an international revolution that would unite workers to share in the commonwealth of property. These intellectuals held high the ideals of communism as they fled during the rise of Stalin to leadership. They presented a threat to the new communist state in Russia because they believed that it did not realize their revolutionary ambition. Some believed the forcible union of all soviets compromised socialism's better ideal of achieving an egalitarian community. The same intellectuals advocated that the success of such a revolution could better come about elsewhere, in democratic states. Bolshevism, which had not yet proven itself successful in material or social fact, presented a challenge to the success of the democratic state in the early twentieth century. Ideas about economy had almost tangible force, and to talk about exchange led people into all-consuming debates about the relative virtues of capitalist forms of property, such as the commodity, and forms of communal ownership. How people understood their uses of wealth remained a significant matter. Did they muddle along with a false knowledge about the social relationships they made and kept through exchanging and transacting goods? Were people confused in their everyday life? Anthropologists and sociologists were committed to face-to-face research and to unearthing common assumptions about how social relations worked and should work. Better than ideologues, or philosophers who did not concern themselves with 'knowledge on the ground', anthropologists could contribute to this problem of understanding human knowledge by examining the concepts that people used as they went about their daily work.

It is interesting to ask what everyday social life might have been like for Mauss's peers in the 1920s and 1930s. From a different perspective, it is possible to capture the flavour of the life of the dishwasher in Paris of the years between the wars from the descriptive personal essays of the English Socialist, George Orwell. In *Down and Out in Paris and London* (1933), the reader learns that in times of economic duress a camaraderie still existed, or at least emerged, among the men who found temporary jobs in the restaurant and hospitality business of the city of Paris. Although the situation of the dishwasher in the Parisian world of hospitality that traded in services for financial gain raises disturbing questions about the foundations (and cellar kitchen lifestyles) that support a pleasant world of style and taste, Orwell judged that condition better than that of the homeless, unemployed individuals in the city of London. Londoners who were without work also were without home and often without bed, constantly moved on from one place to the next in the course of a night. Orwell's experience raises the important question of why the London unemployed poor had few, if any, ways of making social connections. Orwell's experiment in research and reporting won him accolades from his London publishers, The Red Press, because he had exposed that the poor of London needed even a tissue of society, especially as there were no social institutions that existed to help people to find ways of helping each other. Claiming an insight into the corrosion of society by capitalist business, the London radical left of Orwell's days, in the early 1930s, tried to facilitate and make the missing links of social life among London's non-working poor.

I think *The Gift* is a brave text in the best possible ways because it offers a third way of considering the nature of social life through people's use of material goods. This observation is shared by many anthropologists who seek the means of establishing arguments against the dominance of the concept of 'economic man' in the West. The basic observation about the nature of gifts is simple. Because they are received from others, gifts cannot be claimed as private property, nor can they be claimed as communal wealth. In the opening pages of *The Gift*, Mauss asks, 'Why do people feel obligated to reciprocate what they have been given?', recalling that having once received the gift, the claim on it is not absolute nor is it ended. His answer to that question comes over the remaining four short chapters by setting out a series of comparisons across both 'ancient' and 'primitive' society. To put it simply, people feel that the gift is a magical or spiritual aspect of human relations, an aspect that stands apart from other ways of keeping social associations. Looking back, Godelier sums up the problem: acknowledging this as a significant departure from longstanding debates suggests that an alternative to capitalist exchange exists. This alternative form of exchange does not immediately imply communal claims on property, as proponents of contemporary theories of exchange suggested.

Anthropologists can understand the obligation to reciprocate, which Mauss notes around the world, by analysing gift relations as more than economic transactions. It is on this point that Mauss differs from both Malinowski and Boas: the gift is not simply an economic relationship as they had assumed in the collecting of their evidence about exchange. How to assess why people feel obligated to each other becomes an enormous question. This is the puzzle with which he begins. I will discuss next the way in which Mauss lays out his puzzle, and then I will look at how his work can be assessed for its ability to substantiate an argument about society.

The Gift remains a definition by example of Mauss's concept of the total social fact. In other assessments of his work, he has been criticized for the vague notion of the totality of society, and the total social fact (James and Allen 1998). Even Godelier (1999) does not pick out the significance of this idea to Mauss's theory as much as he could. The gift is a total social fact because it is pervasive across societies, but also because it concentrates attention on social relationships and because it constitutes those relations. It is better that the concept of the total social fact does not have a narrow definition. As a definition made by case or by example, the total social fact remains useful because it heuristically describes social life in ethnographic manner. The total social fact is profoundly a sociological, not a philosophical concept, and as a sociological concept it is best discussed in ethnographic examples. I will look at the debate over the significance of the 'mapula'.

Mapula: a total social fact

The case of mapula, a father's harvest gifts to his wife's brother made in the name of his children, remains something of a puzzle in all theories of gift exchange. Annette Weiner used this puzzle as the centrepiece of her argument in *Inalienable Possessions*. Her discussion draws heavily on Malinowski's ethnography and on what Mauss made of that ethnography in his essay, and clarifies the distinctions between them. She recalls Malinowski's presentation of the mapula gift as having two distinct usages; one is that it applies to the gift reciprocated for the previous gift, what Malinowski called the repayment equivalent; a second is that mapula applies to the many smaller gifts made by a man to his wife and to his children for which there is no reciprocation, and so they are 'free gifts'. Mapula could be a Kiriwinian term by which Kiriwinans extend their understanding of what it means to keep social relations, but how to represent it as such remains something of a debate.

Malinowski was of two minds about this. In *Argonauts of the Western Pacific* (1922), his earliest discussions called the numerous small gifts of mapula a 'free gift' from fathers to their children. He pointed out that the mapula functioned as if it were a free gift that required no retribution, as when mapula completed a kula transaction, with the smaller countergift from the recipient of the major kula valuable returned to the first giver. Weiner recalls that the term 'free gift' could not be easily matched in the vocabulary of the region. Later, in *Crime and Custom in Savage Society* (1926), Malinowski withdraws his first claim and acknowledges his error in calling the gift free. He argues that the mapula gift reciprocates the generosity of the first giver of kula wealth, by acknowledging the custom of giving, but not the explicit value of the wealth. In this explanation, Malinowski aims to show that the concept of mapula upholds customary law, as a reciprocal gift that honours and confirms the legal or normative force of the custom.

Mauss uses the concept of mapula as evidence of something more than the institutions of either kula economy or Kirwinian law. Instead, he uses it as an example of the concept of the total social fact. Neither the first nor the second of Malinowski's explanations for 'mapula' answers the question that Mauss posed: just why do people feel obligated to give back what they receive? In considering mapula, Mauss acknowledges that Malinowski's research makes a major contribution to anthropological knowledge by exposing a transaction between people to be laden with the totality of what it means to be human. The mapula as both economic and political and even spiritual, combines most domains of human relationships into one. The gift of mapula can be taken as an instance of what Mauss saw to be foundational to society: that is, the gift exchange that created the social and is wholly imbued with it.

The comparative approach: the Godelier thesis

In his text, *The Gift*, Mauss describes the form and explains the meanings of exchange. He claims that the gift is a total social prestation, which means that giving a gift in ceremonial contexts is not just a part of society as Malinowski claimed, but comprises or embraces the whole of social life. Gift exchange does not present a theory of society that can be abstracted from the analysis of the social relationships in which gifts are transacted. There is some debate about whether Mauss intended the gift exchange as a total prestation to be the back bone of a theory of society, or whether he aimed to develop a comparative method without elaborating philosophically on the nature of social life.

If Mauss did intend to develop a theory of society, then others have been left to carry out that work, principally Lévi-Strauss and, somewhat differently, Godelier. Each provides a theory of society built on the gift, yet neither of their respective theories incorporates an argument about how to keep social relations that does not reach beyond the social to find an explanation, nor do they provide answers to the enigma of how to keep the obligation to give back what has been given. How people keep their obligations remained Mauss's guiding question throughout his work; and his phrasing of the question may have set later students down a difficult course. In the next chapter, I will discuss Lévi-Strauss's theory of society as the alliances made by the exchange of sisters. In the remainder of this chapter, I will discuss how Godelier develops Mauss's question about why people feel obligated to give. Godelier leaves unanswered an outstanding question about how people manage relationships, but fascinates readers with an adroit discussion of the spirit of the gift. Such an analysis of the keeping and releasing of relations can provide a theory of how a person can be social, and of sociality, without assuming that society can exist before individuals make it.

Godelier develops three main case studies as he contemplates the question posed by Mauss about the dynamic of the exchange of gifts: how do people come to feel obligated to give back what they receive? His insights into each case are compared against the insights of the previous cases. He aims to answer a series of questions in order to show that Mauss's essay provides a chance to build a theory of how people live humanely within society.

Godelier compares Mauss's treatment of the Maori 'hau', the Trobriand kula, and the Kwakiutl 'potlatch'. Certainly, there are uses of the ideas about gifts and votive offerings from the ancient period, of the Greek and Roman classics as well as from the Icelandic sagas, but Godelier claims that these do not truly advance Mauss's theory, so much as stand to show that Western civilizations hold the texts, practices and beliefs about the gift as significant in their own history. However, this aspect of Mauss's work might be usefully developed towards understanding the legal aspects of gift exchange, as I will discuss in chapter 11. Godelier argues that Mauss begins to answer his problem by comparing the socially and culturally specific ways of exchange. Each case explains a different aspect of the problem: why do people give, why do they feel obligated, and why do they reciprocate?

In the first case, Mauss shows that humans participate in a general practice of keeping obligations by giving each other gifts. He draws extensively on the ethnography of the Maori, the indigenous people of the south Pacific islands now known as New Zealand (or Aotearoa). Anthropologists often wrote about the Maori as an example of the Polynesian lifestyle, a way of organizing social and political life that spread in a wide region from New Zealand east and north across the Pacific defining what is known as the Polynesian cultural area. Mauss's choice of the example of the Maori hau compels us to think about the rest of the region.

The Maori conducted warfare in large seafaring canoes that made the distances between south Pacific islands disappear rapidly, as they seemingly raced through these waters. The Maori powerfully showed that they could command a region through a system of exchange practices, in which the deployments of power neither created states nor sustained political rivalries between disparate nations. The power of exchange, as practices in the spirit of the hau, was that it kept trade relations open to negotiation and renegotiation. Much of the work of the hau itself depended on persuasion and maintenance of good trading relationships with other Maori.

The Maori did launch large seafaring expeditions, and often entered wars as a part of their trade routes. Trade was principled, depending upon the participants to respect and honour the values of the exchange.

Maori traders helped to ensconce this way of trading, hau, in negotiations carried out in Maori debating houses. Maori chiefs might invite the members of other villages to discussions in their own Maori debating house, for the point of overwhelming them with its glory as well as to overwhelm them in debate. Among other things, they would consider the manifestations of hau in their lives. Of the Maori hau, Mauss wrote, in particular, material and immaterial aspects of human relationships entwine in the gift. Exchange partners of the hau took the spirit of the gift very seriously, just as they approached the exchange of goods. Mauss elaborates the mingling of material and spiritual dimensions of the hau in careful description. Following the Maori teaching on the hau, Mauss comes to better understand the exchange of gifts than by following his assumptions about European gift giving alone.

In Mauss's hands, the comparative approach provides a long answer to a short and profound question. He begins with a puzzle, a meditation on the meaning of the Maori commentary on the hau. Put down in words, incorporated into Mauss's writing, the ideas of the Maori become legendary. In describing a social and cultural habit known as the hau, Mauss drafts a short commentary about how to give to each other and what it means to give to others.

> The 'hau' is not the wind that blows, not at all. Let us suppose that you possess a certain article [taonga] and that you give me this article. You give it me without setting a price on it. We strike no bargain about it. Now, I give this article to a third person who, after a certain lapse of time, decides to give me something as payment in return [utu]. He makes a present to me of something [taonga]. Now, this taonga that he give me is the spirit [hau] of the taonga that I had received from you and that I had given to him. The 'taonga' that I received from these 'taonga' (which came from you) must be returned to you. It would not be fair [tika] on my part to keep these 'taonga' for myself, whether they were desirable [rawe] or undesirable [kino]. I must give them to you because they are a 'hau' of the taonga that you gave me.

> If I kept this other taonga for myself, serious harm might befall me, even death. This is the nature of the 'hau' of the taonga, the 'hau' of the forest. Kati ena.
>
> (Mauss 1990 [1925]: 27)

Mauss uses the hau as a clear example of the ways in which the 'spirit' of the gift can move a person to use wealth to create a circle of exchange. The Maori informant explains to the ethnographer Elsdon Best how the ceremonial exchange of goods works. After several transactions, people give back the gift; the last person in the chain remembers the first person in the circle of exchange. This description leaves the ethnographer with enormous puzzles about what to make of the felt need to reciprocate wealth. The spirit of the gift, the hau, does not translate easily into European terms. The script used by Mauss comes from the Maori, as translated by Elsdon Best (1909) into English. This becomes something of a problem for anthropologists as the translation can easily obscure allusions that shift the meaning of the text. Sahlins and Godelier each tell us that this requires great care. Their respective assessments of the hau differently position the implications of Mauss's essay.

Sahlins provides the enduring account of the hau as the basic concept operating within non-capitalist exchange. Notably, the hau is an example of how that person uses wealth without being committed to communal ownership, or without observing conventions of private ownership. In commenting on the Maori hau, many later scholars consider an exciting departure for scholarship, a third way forward that honours an alternative way of focusing on the uses of material wealth in social life. This has always been the compelling aspect of its contribution to wider political and economic theory. Curiously, Sahlins discusses hau as if the spirit could bear the meanings of motivations and interests in exchange. If the spirit of the hau moves the person to give, Sahlins reasons that the person's motives and interests can be activated by the hau.

Many have chosen to focus on the economic aspects of the gift, especially once Sahlins chose to locate the hau at the centre of the arguments about the nature of inequality in non-state society. For Sahlins, the possibility of describing inequality could emerge only if others took very seriously the claim that alternative forms of inequality exist. Did inequality lie in the substance of the person, or did it emerge in the forms that the relationships took over time? This effort to return argument first raised by Mauss to the concerns of political economy can be praised; economic anthropologists moved to address political concepts. However, Sahlins presses too far the argument for revising economic anthropology into political and economic anthropology. He misses important aspects of the gift that Mauss's work addressed more clearly than Sahlins gives credit.

Sahlins's greatest oversight in the retelling of the spirit of the gift must be the nuances of the legal aspects that Mauss so carefully reveals with his comparative study. Mauss's essay tells us that the hau remains significant to

Maori legal ideas, that is the ways in which legal ties extend beyond the person, obligating them to deal with the theft of an object beyond their own holdings. People can be moved to recover stolen wealth because they recognize it as a theft of an extension of their own possessions. The Maori point out that the thing received is not inactive because the hau follows after the thing, precipitating a response from the contemporary holder of the object. This feature of the hau compels more attention than Sahlins has given it. It makes a very different contribution to the concept of law and custom than had been comprehended by Malinowski who understood the custom of giving and receiving kula objects to be deeply tied to the elaboration of Trobriander legal codes. Customary law for the Trobrianders contained the motives and inspirations of the person, holding them accountable to the greater good of the society so that it functioned smoothly and justly. Although many (especially Parry 1986) would describe a marriage of Malinowski's ideas with Mauss's as an unholy alliance, Sahlins creates a common ground in his insistence that the spirit of the gift could be one and the same with the interest or the investment that the exchange partners held in it.

The meaning of mapula

In the second case, that of the ceremonial kula trade, Mauss, like Malinowski, argues that Trobrianders feel obligated because they compete for prestige over and against other kula traders. But, unlike Malinowski, who had described the competitive exchanges of the kula as economic strategies for the elaboration of Trobrianders' prestige, Mauss sought a more general explanation. Mauss uses the Trobriand explanation for their behaviour specifically in the dynamics of the kula ring to address generally the problem of motive. He justifies his generalizations because he believes kula cannot be a singularly economic practice. Instead, kula is meant to sustain ongoing relationships within the kula ring. Godelier argues that kula shows that exchange partners make peaceful society in the Trobriands first, by controlling social relations through the prestigious trade of goods. Later, the partners become prestigious through trading with others. It is an example of the general human concern with the continuity of social relations.

The ethnographic observation by Annette Weiner is relevant here. She notes that some kula goods can be kept back, as if they were sacred and not meant to be displayed or traded with others, thereby risking the goods passing into the hands of other clans. She describes this practice as keeping while giving, in so far as the trader gives away wealth to traders from other clans, but keeps the most valuable for his own clan. In everyday exchange, rather than only in the kula ring, fathers habitually hold back wealth from others so that they can give to their children. Weiner (1992) focused on this habit of giving while keeping as the principal definitive activity of social life because it bridged both the kula exchange and the cross-clan funerary exchanges. The question arises: how do some forms of wealth come to be known as more sacred or of greater spiritual value than others?

The idea of 'keeping while giving' is more complicated that it initially appears. First, keeping while giving persists as a dilemma of the person who gives because it is a contradictory act in so far as it assumes that the giver must be duplicitous. Second, keeping while giving creates a problem for the recipient because he or she discovers that their relationship to the giver is not what they thought. The conditions of 'giving while keeping' assume two things of primary importance: first, the authenticity of the sacred object, and second, the motives of the parties to the exchange. These assumptions can mislead anthropologists so I will describe them as Annette Weiner presents them in her ethnography of the Trobriands.

I think the suggestion made by Annette Weiner drew attention to the ways in which a Trobriand individual thought about the gift and giving. Her assessment that Trobrianders give, while keeping, became controversial throughout anthropological circles during the 1990s (see Mosko 2000). There is good reason for this. It is dangerously subversive of the common image of the gift as noble and generous, recalling the more pejorative slur that giving in order to 'take back' can be dishonest. But, that criticism easily disappears with any attempt to fully understand the work of giving in Trobriand society when one considers the wider context of mapula exchanges.

The whole picture of Trobriander life provides nuances of meaning to Mauss's understanding of the competitive kula ethos. Men perform kula because they have obligations to exchange partners, but also because they hope to find fame for their names with their wife's brothers and their wife's children. How children perceive their father's work matters a great deal to men. It influences a man's own renown in the village, but also has an effect on his afterlife. The gifts of fathers to children operate as a core ethos of exchange relations, an approach and ethics dedicated to the continuity of society in so far as a father's gifts express concern for the child, rather than self-interest in search of prestige as a powerful trading figure. Malinowski shows the reader that mapula, the gifts made by fathers to their children, can be given without obligating the child and his clan to give back the gifts of the father. By giving to the child, by using mapula, the Trobriander father expressed openly the cultural ethos of charity, of the 'free gift' as both Mauss and Malinowski called it, and recalled the value of supporting social life. The mapula gift demonstrated the rule that it is fundamentally correct to give to others. Mauss sees the mapula as an aspect or instance of the spirit of the gift, an opportunity for a nurturing relationship between father and child. In kula, necklaces (soulava) and armshells (mwali) circulate in alternate directions, and even in this ceremonial exchange partners compete for the prestige of giving away a special necklace or armshell. It expresses the spirit of the gift; but it is also about power.

If Weiner correctly assessed the nature of Trobriand exchange, then gifts from father to children emerged as rather significant to the social fabric. The mapula gifts keep fast the relationships between the clans, during the lifetime of the father. By making a mapula gift, the men of one clan honour the children and women of the other clan that holds the children as its members. Men honour the clan of their own wives and children with mapula, making them matter. Weiner analyses the mapula gifts of a father to his child as a total social fact, which must continue as a key mechanism of social solidarity in the region.

Weiner explains that the mapula, the small gifts given by fathers, do not seem to reciprocate any larger work. Instead, the mapula of father to child precedes the work of the children. The children will contribute to a ceremonial gift at the time of his funeral. Here, the mortuary feast recalls the reciprocation of the mapula gifts from the participants. Mapula can be made during the lifetime of one man with no recognition or reciprocation. At the death of the father, the child recognizes with a ceremonial presentation, an entire lifetime of nurture which the father bestowed upon him. Weiner understands this as a return of the gift, which belonged to the clan of the father in the first place.

In some cases, the father gives small gifts to his son, in lieu of the specialist magic his child might actually want from him. On many occasions, the father substitutes small gifts for the more significant and powerful gift of magic and ritual knowledge. The elder man may choose to withhold the magic and ritual knowledge from the child because he is saving it to give to another son. This would be the case when the magic can be given to only one child, not all children. An example of this comes to mind from my own field site where weather magic could not be shared among children, but could only be entrusted to the hands of one son. Elder men reasoned that only one son could use the knowledge sensibly in each generation, and that not all children could be trusted to make wise and just decisions about its use.

The ambiguity of the situation created a dilemma for the children who received the gifts of fathers. Each child accepted yet another small gift, and as he did, he assessed the situation in one of two ways. Either the gift pacified his desire for the more important bestowal of weather magic, which was yet to come, or the gift substituted for the grander bestowment of magic, which would be given to another child and never come to the hands of the youth who waited for it now. One might hypothesize a kind of double-bind scenario, whereby the father asserts his interests in his young within a matrilineal society with an innuendo of promise, but no actual promise is made to give a child the specialist knowledge that the son seeks and wants.

Giving to keep, in this scenario, might look strange and unpleasant to an anthropological observer, but it is not if the researcher focuses on the relationships made with the gift. Gifts can be understood as aspects of the relationships, rather than material objects that are possessed, or are not possessed. As such, they make relationships and inflect them with evidence of sentimental attachment or even foster sentimental relationships when the recipient enthuses about the gift that his father has given. Instead of focusing on the ambiguities of possession, the anthropologist who focuses on the kinds, even qualities, of the relationships made with mapula between fathers and children can find the connection itself significant. A father gives gifts to substantiate their relations, and by doing so demonstrates the social connections to his children. He holds these commitments over his and his children's lifetimes. He thereby makes the relationships, a fact which is of greater importance than the possibility of securing a recompense for the gifts at the time of his death.

Power and potlatch competitions

Godelier makes a further comparison between kula and hau that Mauss does not. He seeks to understand the power that resides in social relationships of exchange partners. He does this first with reference to the kula. The kula trade, as an elite trade, also aims to establish the renown of men. Most importantly, Mauss understands the kula trade as a smaller form of potlatch because participants compete with each other. Men reciprocate because they advance their fame, and in competitive gift giving show they have the power to pull kula goods into their sphere of influence long enough for them to pass them on in magnanimous gifts.

In order to explain the significance of the spirit of the gift, Godelier takes issue with Sahlins's misrepresentation of the hau. The hau can be better understood with reference to the bush spirits that men honoured with sacrifices at the time of the hunt. He shows that Sahlins correctly reinterpreted the Maori text to expose the ritual's wider context in the spiritual life of the Maori. But Godelier takes issue with Sahlins's final analysis of the hau as an exchange for profit in multiple social relationships. At the core of Sahlins's ideas about the hau, it is possible to find that he conceptualizes kula traders as if they were profit-maximizing individuals. Godelier then proceeds to show the end results of that process. Here Godelier spells out the fascination with power that resides in the work of the hau, but that Mauss elided from his account.

After pointing out the slippage of Mauss's attention away from the gift and on to matters of the power of the spirit of reciprocity, Godelier addresses the potlatch in detail. I will describe the potlatch ceremonies first. The occasion for a potlatch might be a commemorative funeral of a senior clansman of a major chief. The senior clansman might be commemorated for his name and spirit, having died years earlier; the potlatch is not simply the funeral of his death. Taking into deep consideration the wishes and urging of the spirits of the dead ancestors (who speak to him collectively in his dreams), a chief of a large matrilineal clan will host a potlatch ceremony with the help of his entire clan. The clan organizes enough food for all guests, and comes with additional gifts to give to those who visit. If they have them, then members of the clan will bring forward their best pieces of sculpture and carvings, so that these artworks may be displayed with those of the chief. Often these are made of copper, beaten into images of the different animal totems that the clans recognize to influence them, perhaps the eagle or the bear. This display is followed by an extraordinary ritual act, in which the sculpture is destroyed. Typically, the sculptures are thrown into the waves of the Pacific Ocean, waves that lap the shores of the north-west coast of North America where high mountains reach down to the sea.

The potlatch ceremonies hold peculiar importance in the history of anthropological theory. These ceremonial feasts on the north-west coast of North America commemorated the dead and established the power of the host, usually the senior chief of a matrilineal clan. At them, enormous amounts of the host's wealth were displayed for redistribution, but most of the wealth was destroyed. The early ethnographer of these events, Franz Boas, believed that the making of the feasts epitomized the activity of the human competitive spirit. His landmark ethnography discussion of the feast of the Kwakiutl, a language group of the region, describes the competition between chiefs to overwhelm each other with displays of generosity (Boas 1897, 1966).

At a potlatch the chief gave away ceremonial blankets, money, furs, food and copper sculptures. As legend had it (no doubt some of this was interlaced with the fears of the time) the event included the disposal of slaves to the control of others, and sometimes human sacrifice. Although the verity of the legendary suggestions of sacrifice does not hold up to scrutiny by historical evidence, at the least, the folklore contributed to a general sense of terror about the event. Is the contemplation of death the end result of the day in which a chief staged a display of his power by conspicuously giving away wealth? The events stirred the imagination of many people; even D.C. Scott, the head of the Department of Indian Affairs in Canada, wrote poetry about the disturbing events. Boas's student Ruth Benedict wrote more ironically of the comparison of the power displayed in cannibal feasting and in nationalist propaganda in Germany.

Later, Eric Wolf (1999) returns to Ruth Benedict's interests in power, but he does so differently. Instead of exploring its psychodynamics, he pursues the relations of power under the colonial circumstances created by the Canadian government, whose officers in British Columbia worked to contain and restrict the excesses of the potlatch ceremonies. The earliest descriptions of potlatch recorded by Boas and his assistant George Hunt were made at the time of the colonial administration of the territory (then province) of British Columbia (1895). The Kwakiutl presentation of potlatch ceremonies terrified early settlers and administrators of the region. They could not comprehend the displays of power in the feasts, and some complained about the ceremonies as pathologies. Boas considered the possibility that potlatch emerged as a failure of society, as evidence of a Kwakiutl world out of control. The feasts disturbed local white residents so much that they banned the potlatch in 1908.

In the potlatch, Godelier finds the fuller discussion of power that Mauss's account lacks. Most often, competitions between Kwakiutl chiefs made reciprocity almost impossible. Chiefs often kept back the most sacred copper relics and circulated false ones in their place. A sacred one is given to the gods.

Godelier argues that a comparison between Kwakiutl potlatch, Maori hau and Trobriand kula can significantly advance Mauss's theory of society. Godelier hopes to contribute a discussion of power to Mauss's work. He accomplishes this fascinating but difficult argument by thinking much more carefully about the wealth of potlatch. He argues that these gifts to the gods, which is what Kwakiutl chiefs claimed they were making, were more than sacrifices that established the community's common humanity, and their dependence upon and close connection to the ideal spirit world. Going beyond the analysis that Mauss's colleague Hertz might have given, Godelier argues that the key to the potlatch lies in the fact that the copper sculptures destroyed were copies of sacred objects that remained with the chief's clan. In the potlatch there always remained a degree of uncertainty about whether the wealth lost was sacred wealth or copies of sacred wealth. At the heart of the potlatch persisted the possibility of keeping while giving.

Godelier argues that Mauss never solved his problem, largely because he lacked an important insight into the nature of exchanges. That insight could be better drawn from Weiner's assessment that some things could be kept at the same time as they were given. She calls this keeping while giving. Godelier abstracts an insight from Weiner's work. He takes this to mean that humans held the coppers to be sacred, which for him is a communal or social trust in things which expands the self beyond the economic, as Mauss once insisted.

> It is our western societies who have recently made man an 'economic animal'. But we are not yet all creatures of this genus. Among the masses and the elites in our society purely irrational expenditure is commonly practised. It is still characteristic of a few of the fossilized remnants of our aristocracy. *Homo oeconomicus* is not behind us, but lies ahead, as does the man of morality and duty, the man of science and reason. For a very long time man was something different, and he has not been a machine for very long, made complicated by a calculating machine.
>
> (Mauss 1990 [1925] 76)

Conclusions: gifts to gods and gifts to humans

As I have outlined in this chapter, the account of social life given from the perspective of human motivations quickly degenerates into fantasy about the contents of the mind. This kind of analysis is to be avoided. In parallel, another failure would be to begin with the analysis of the individual person. This assumes the separation of the person from the world of material objects and from other people. This approach also falters on a number of difficulties in ascertaining the possibility of understanding that world wholly.

Does the gift to humans differ from the gifts to gods? If I ask that with the ghost of Mauss looking over my shoulder, then is the gift to gods the same as the gifts to humans? What is the spirit of the gift, this immaterial aspect of human social relationships, which Mauss grasped so willingly from the Maori explanation of the Taonga? The problem so far has different answers: Sahlins thinks it is 'Bush spirits', Weiner names it the father's generosity, and Godelier finds it to be 'the greatness of the human spirit'. These are replies to the question: what inspirits the gift as an object?

What if the question of the spirit of the gift lies in the human relationships rather than in the object? How would the question of the spirit of the gift then appear? The comparison of different forms of gift giving across cultures shows that the gift can be differently inspirited in each cultural context. This is neither straightforward as an anthropological analysis nor is it a worthy account of the workings of culture. It is better to distinguish between cultural processes of inspiriting of the gift as a sacred object in a specific cultural context, and enlivening human relationships to their ethical concerns within a given situation. The first is a religious act, the second the act of secular humanists. These are different aspects of the gift's animation, and creating categories of objects that are more or less spiritual does not illuminate the puzzle of different forms of power. It helps to separate spiritual and secular humanist answers to how the gift is enacted in social relationships, in order to think about the different implications of giving and receiving across cultures.

Strathern (1994) offers a secularist approach, somewhat different from Godelier's re-orienting towards the sacred in Mauss's comparative study. Strathern focuses on 'the relation', rather than the object, as the central unit of analysis in the exchange of gift. I think that Strathern's suggestion that anthropology should proceed with keener attention to the relation, rather than the person or the thing, keeps clearly in view Mauss's question of why people feel the obligation to reciprocate the gift. She insists that people, being fundamentally social (rather than primarily psychological) individuals, are moved to keep relations (rather than things). I take Strathern to be advancing Mauss's basic anthropological project of ascertaining the total social fact and analysing it across societies.

Strathern (1988) can show that it is possible to work closely to the comparative project Mauss first set out, but only if the academic researcher abandons the idea that the analysis of society must begin with any separation between person and things. Strathern grasped Mauss's key observation about gift exchange as a total social fact. People cannot be understood as isolates; they live entangled in each other's lives. Their work cannot be separated from that of others, in the same way as an analysis of individual things or persons cannot grasp the totality of social experience. Anthropologists cannot focus on the person alone in the effort to understand the totality of the person's experience. Similarly, they cannot understand mapula from the perspective of the individual and their motives. Instead, a full account of social life should focus on 'the relations' in which persons make their lives.

Summary of chapter 4

The question moving the essay *The Gift* is: why should people feel obligated to reciprocate what they have received? Mauss was enmeshed in the obligations of career as an academic and kept his duty to give his energy to the publication of others' work. Although he does not explain motives to reciprocate, people keep their obligations by giving things away. The gift cannot be understood as a utilitarian exchange of goods, rather it encompasses the total human experience. A case in point is dispute over the meaning of mapula, which Mauss reinterprets from Malinowksi's ethnography to be an example of reciprocal exchange between social groups, rather than a free gift from father to child. If mapula is not taken to be simply the transaction of an object, a thing, it can be understood better as the establishment and confirmation of a relationship through exchange of wealth. This compares similarly with the Maori hau, which is gift giving motivated by spiritual interests animating the gift (distinct from other forms of wealth); and it contrasts with competitive potlatch ceremonies in which giving away wealth makes the hosts of the ceremony prestigious. Godelier's thoughtful reworking of Mauss's thesis finds that some objects (withheld from circulation and destruction) hold a spiritual value and come to stand for the greater communal humanity. One might ask to what extent the spiritual is a version of the economic. Instead, when understood as a total social fact, gift giving concentrates many aspects of human relationships, but does not underwrite all of them as the economic.

5

EXCHANGING PEOPLE, GIVING REASONS

After the Second World War, new maps and alliances were drawn across Europe and around the world. The period of war had ended, but a period of reconfiguration of new trade and political associations continued. The era heralded a new time of respect for social and cultural differences, but new problems too. In anthropology a new theory emerged that supported the commitment to the commensurability of differences that would be necessary to modern times. The new theory, the structuralist theory of human variation, aimed to explain social variation without falling into habits of relying on evolutionary differences and drawing on old paradigms of race.

Structuralist theories of social difference make a major contribution to understanding the world in the era of a new modernity. Structuralism can account for both traditional and modern life, by explaining that these apparently different ways of living in the world are deeply connected. The period after the First World War and after the revolution in Russia, the decades of the 1920s and 1930s, ushered in a social revolution in which many people chose to depart from the old conventions of everyday life. At this time, many observers of social change remarked on the loss of traditional lifestyles. In Europe the industrial revolution had modernized agriculture as it had also in North and South America. In the new Soviet Union, and also in China, the creation of communal farming cooperatives ended the lifestyle of the peasant. Natural and social sciences aided the modernization of the village lifestyle. Following upon the popular inclination to think of the world as a transformed place, scholars began to mark the passing of traditional lifestyles of tribes, clans and villagers. A new doubt grew among anthropologists. Along with the sense that although a modern world emerged through the applications of scientific knowledge about its operations, some people felt that another was on the wane.

The years immediately after the Second World War may sound too much like today, when we have the restructuring of social life after the end of the Cold War and demands on people to adopt new ways of exposing information about their social relationships in the wake of a new war on political terrorism. Some of the older lessons might be carried forward to the contemporary situation, at least so that they can be examined for their value in answering to the current dilemmas about how to deal with social differences across the globe. Structuralist theories of difference assumed that behind the social forms of modern life – the institutions, organizations, arts and family associations – most societies operated similarly to the societies of the rest of the world. Structuralist analysis reached behind the mask of modern times, and behind the masks, rituals and myths of non-modern societies, to describe a common knowledge of how to live. Structuralists took surface meanings to be manifest evidence of deeper significance.

The contemporary anthropologist asks somewhat different questions because the world no longer divides so neatly into modern and non-modern, but he or she holds many of the same assumptions inherent to structuralism of the era immediately after the Second World War. It is commonly thought that the possibility of symbolic thought as written expression of literacy in Papua New Guinea, in Africa, or elsewhere does not change the basic concern with human communication across difference. Despite the best arguments by structuralists that the capacity to think about the world symbolically might be shared universally, some anthropologists such as Augé (1995) and cultural theorists such as Clifford (1988) argue that the new contemporary world differs significantly from the older contemporary world. Now the anthropologists meet with the informants who might dissent in print or agree in collegial academic seminars. Is that a difference that matters? What is yet to be seen is just what will come of the network of collaboration between people who might not have shared professional insights two generations ago. People meet and work together who are as disparate in their interests and persons as Melanesian anti-colonialists, Fijian anthropologists, the university professor and her students. Their means for that conversation requires a new understanding of what remains reasonable about people's interchanges and exchanges. At the very least, what contemporary anthropologists share with the questions of the structuralist anthropologists in the past is an attempt to understand what can be a reasonable way to live.

The subject of gift exchange in the structuralist theory of social difference assumes that it is one form of human communication, albeit non-verbal. It concurs with some of the fullest elaborations of structuralist theory which ascertain that communication is basic to social relationships. This would seem a reasonable claim, for is it not really the case that there can be no relationship between people who have said and can say nothing to each other? This might not obviously extend to people who are unknown to each other, but it does. Structuralist anthropologists argue that communication is the grounds of all social life, even if people imagine the possibility of communicating with an unknown person or group of people to be a problem rather than a pleasure.

The possibility of communicating with strangers – with people whom you never imagined existed – arises because human beings have the capacity to think symbolically, that is to represent their experience to each other. In the 1930s groups of adventurers went to the steep hills of the Highlands of New

Guinea with hopes of finding gold. Even in the early twentieth century, it was uncharted land on the maps of Australian, European or North American atlases. The explorers found people, numbered in thousands, in valleys they thought were empty of human life. Some of these encounters were recorded on film. A particularly fortuitous decision of the Leahy brothers to carry film to the central Highlands on their first expedition into the mountains produced the footage that made up the film *First Contact* which the Australian film makers Connelly and Anderson compiled with more commentary from the late twentieth century. The Leahy brothers surmised that the responses from the Melpa people they filmed showed that they were confounded as to whether white Australian men were ghosts or living humans. Is this fantasy of communion with non-humans possible? Later in the 1960s the anthropologist Roy Wagner made a record of his conversations with Highland New Guineans thirty years after another early encounter in the mountains at the northern boundaries of what would become Gulf province (then district), a different part of the Highlands of Papua New Guinea. Wagner met one of the Daribi, a group of New Guineans who remembered the shock on the faces of the Australians when they first came over the high mountains and realized that the unknown valley was filled with people making a livelihood in its fields and trading luxury goods in its villages. It is hard not to smile as Wagner reports the story of his Daribi friend – who concluded its telling by saying that he should have seen the look on those Australians' faces when they realized the valley was full of human beings! But the force of the explorer's, and the anthropologist's, assumptions that it must be possible to communicate with these men and women soon made them forget the shock. It is recorded best in the memory of the New Guineans who witnessed it in the faces of their 'discoverers', and not in the anthropological record describing the lives of the valley residents. The ability to think symbolically is taken to be a primary feature of social life because symbolic thought makes social life possible by making communication possible. Symbolic thought depends upon the ability of the human mind to make distinctions, to separate light from dark, male from female, wet from dry, or nature from culture. The point being that knowledge of one entity is constituted in relation to its opposite; and in so doing the two constitute the terms of their association. The structuralist theory of society shares with linguistic anthropology this same perspective on the capacity of thought to make oppositions as a means to know about the world. Much structuralist work ends in the study of myth, neither as misunderstood science nor as primitive unsophisticated philosophy. Instead, the anthropologist makes unequivocal judgements about the relations of myth and as a mature elaboration of human thought.

This chapter examines the structuralist theory of social difference by discussing the various critiques of Lévi-Strauss's theory that focused principally on women, not as a biological substantive entity, but as the locus of social relationships and as a signifier of the interrelated ways people act with each other. Some of the earliest endorsements of structuralism understood its associations both with the linguistic theories of Saussure and with the theory that kinship forms alliances between groups. Many have criticized structuralism for giving too much attention to human thought processes over and above the substance of human relationships, as if these could be separate things. Instead, it would be preferable to unite the theory of kinship with the theory of myth and knowledge. In turn, I examine the substantive aspects of the theory of knowledge to address the matter of feminist ideology, a body of thought which the structuralist theory of difference engaged enigmatically. By focusing on the exchange of persons, particularly women, I will show that structuralism could not encompass theoretically the political and social project of analysing gender relations.

Reason and society

Understanding the inequalities of either substance or form in society begins with an early essay that speculates on the social and intellectual habit of classification. The earlier essay, *Primitive Classification* by Durkheim and Mauss (1963 [1903]), established many of the same issues as those of the structuralist theory of society. In that account, Durkheim and Mauss assess the character of social organizations. They seek evidence of the character of human knowledge and its extensions in the organizations of social life. They consider whether the patterns of residence, arrangements of marriage (both its inclusions and exclusions) and plan of social organization can be considered social expressions of human knowledge, and if so how they come to be different in different places. I think that Needham's introduction fails the bigger project that Durkheim and Mauss introduced because he proclaims the evolutionary argument as a dominant feature of their argument, when it is not. While Durkheim and Mauss make some claims for the evolution of human thought and human social organization, they also cast doubts on the general claims that societies evolve. Their deeper contemplations betray their argument. It is a study in hesitation and reconsiderations about the links between human knowledge and human social organization. One begins to wonder if a later editing introduced some revisions that exposed the doubts of Mauss about the evolutionary claims he first argued with Durkheim. In *Primitive Classification* it is possible to consider how people plan the world and live in accordance with a design of social life that nearly eludes them. They might certainly begin with how they classify the social world, the world of relatives as moieties, as clans, as kin.

Sometimes society can be 'seen' in the formation and interaction of distinct social groups, such as the moiety or the clan which works together in ceremonies. In the film *Ongka's Big Moka*, the Melpa people of the New Guinea Highlands stand ready to exchange the pigs they have prepared (Figure 5.1). The clans stand ready, each about to enjoin the other in the exchange of pigs.

Figure 5.1 The ceremonial exchange of pigs brings the clans together in one place and thereby establishes the great prestige of the host. Charlie Nairn took this still photograph in the mid-1970s at the time of the filming of *Ongka's Big Moka* (Granada TV, 1976), first reprinted in *Disappearing World: Television and Anthropology*, edited by André Singer and Leslie Woodhead (1988), Manchester: Granada TV and Boxtree.

A viewer can see how the social organization appears by reason of the work of ceremonial exchange, just as Durkheim and Mauss had discussed adroitly for the general cases of Aboriginal Australian society.

Structuralists later would grasp at this underlying design of society and call it structure, eliding more superficial classification of the natural and social world as indigenous accounts. Godelier (1986) remarks on how structuralists gave their attention to the underlying knowledge rather than that local account. He proposed that the structuralist theory of society, especially as elaborated by Lévi-Strauss in *Elementary Structures of Kinship*, depends on an intriguing innovation upon Mauss's theory of why people feel obligated to reciprocate what they receive. As I discussed in the previous chapter, Mauss answered his questions about the feeling of obligation to reciprocate the gift by illuminating the effects of the spirit of the person. According to the Maori interpretation, which Mauss accepted, the spirit animated the gift. A structuralist theory of society addressed the important observation that the gift could be a person, and took up a general question. What difference does the gift of a woman make to an understanding of social relations? I argue that these are not simply questions about kinship. They are questions about what people claim to know about what they do.

Asking these questions leads to a reconsideration of human knowledge about social life and the grounds of that knowledge. But this is not a new concern. Turning to Mauss helps a contemporary anthropologist to think more clearly about the definition of human subjectivity, with reference to the deep structures that delimit it. Mauss's work poses the possibility that the exchange of objects works as a system of communication by enchaining one person to another through processes that signified their spiritual or immaterial relationships with material goods, given as gifts. The gift of an object signified the relationship. How does it make a difference then that the gift of a woman across clans would come to signify a relationship? How kinship could work as communicative system perhaps fascinated Lévi-Strauss from his earliest research, which he published in 1949 as *Elementary Structures of Kinship*.

In thinking about the question, what difference the gender of the gift makes to a theory of social relations, I have followed two different critiques of the structuralist theory of society. In making these critiques I have taken direction from the anthropologist Schneider (1970), who conjoined Lévi-Strauss's work on kinship with his study of myth, rather than dividing it into separate topics. Schneider argues that kinship itself can be a system of knowledge, very much like a myth corpus. Reflections upon the social habit of naming or recognizing those people you know can be the most interesting starting point for research into kin and relations. In this way, kinship can be understood as a kind of communicative practice, laying out a network of meaningful association. My second guide in this is Strathern. Her feminist analysis of the exchange of women shows that women's subjectivity is more than a position within a social structure. Rather than describe structuralism directly, this chapter will analyse some of the theory's assumptions by drawing on these two critical perspectives.

What difference does the gift of a person make?

Structuralist anthropology is introduced with *Elementary Structures of Kinship* (Lévi-Strauss 1963 [1949]). In this text, cross-cultural examples of kinship are analysed in terms of the kinds of alliances that people make between clans and villages. In the example of the Amazon, Lévi-Strauss shows that villages in conflict with each other can resolve their differences and agree to make a peaceful future. The agreement is confirmed with the exchange of women, demonstrating the alliance between the villages. The alliance is possible because the principle of reciprocity is understood implicitly. That is, the structure of social life flows from the acknowledgement that social relationships simply require the return of the gift of a woman, by the group who received it, underlying any kind of negotiation of how or why that might be right.

Let me return to the New Guinea Highlands to illustrate this point a bit better. In viewing the film *Ongka's Big Moka*, students often find themselves a bit disturbed by the equation of women with pigs, in the exchange of bride wealth (Figure 5.2). While they quickly readjust their judgements so that they accept the custom as a significant and respectful ritual in the region, they sometimes ask how a woman might be given to one clan, while many pigs are returned. The mistake would be to think that a woman comes to be substituted with a pig, as if the pig was a form of currency for her purchase when it is not. The better way to grasp the ceremonial exchange of women, pigs and pearl shells in bride wealth exchange is to think of it as a form of communication.

Women become a central point of concern in understanding kinship as a system of communication. The gift of a woman suggests many things to those who receive her and to those who offer her. Notably, the first arguments about this exchange begin with the observations that some men give a sister, while another man receives a wife. It is important to understand that the alliance made by marriage does not limit itself to the couple alone, but extends to the parties involved more broadly in the marriage. Most commonly the marriage creates relationships between the kin of the bride and of the husband, elaborating more ties between the extended families that are now connected by the new marriage. In societies where the clan organizes everyday political life, such as in the Amazon or in Papua New Guinea (as is the case even at the time when I am writing this), the marriage creates relationships between clans. What does it mean to give a sister and receive a wife? What transpires between humans that shapes their understanding of the transaction?

Lévi-Strauss refers to this basic transaction of the gift of a sister as the principle of reciprocity. He insists that, because the woman leaves as a sister and arrives as a wife, the exchange opens longer negotiations over the relationships between the two groups of men, who are now relatives by marriage. In subsequent comings and goings, ceremonial exchanges, and political alliances between them, the men elaborate the 'pathways' of communication between them as kin. As to why a sister is given in marriage, he explains that people

Figure 5.2 A mature woman will raise and tend pigs that are used as a form of bride wealth to be given by her clansmen at marriage to the clansmen of a woman from another clan. Still photograph by Charlie Nairn, first reprinted in *Disappearing World: Television and Anthropology*, edited by André Singer and Leslie Woodhead (1988), Manchester: Granada TV and Boxtree.

universally honour the rule of exogamy and the prohibition of incest, even where those rules might be practised at superficially different degrees of relationship. The point is that it is the rule that marriage must be made outside the intimacy of the natal family, and it is the rule that offspring of sibling or filial relations violate social sensibilities in all societies because they give evidence to the fact of an incestuous relationship. The reasons for the rule against incest can be various, and should generally be understood as the concerns of any specific society; however, structuralists argue that the principle of exogamy is a human universal that can inform a general theory of how society is organized, works, and differs from other societies.

How does the gift of a sister become significant in making society? Some would argue that asking about the significance of the gift did not concern the structuralists. Struturalists were interested in how the gift of a sister would be received and used. The gift of a woman is certainly negotiated, representing at once the fastening of agreements between men and the opening of new negotiations between them. This becomes even more apparent after the woman gives birth to children and becomes a mother, as well as wife. When a woman and man bear children in the marriage, those negotiations take on new importance. The arrival of children shows that the woman possesses the ability to nurture the children, as well as to grow the clan to whom the children belong. Sometimes a series of subsequent gifts are made to assure the clansmen of the husband and of the wife that they recognize the children as relatives. Once again, gifts can be used to recognize the relationships among the clans, and the new relative of the mother's and father's clans.

There are important differences to be understood from the gift of a sister, especially as the practice of marriage exists so differently in different societies. In many cases, when a woman marries, it is common practice for those who receive the woman to offer another gift in return. One possibility is to offer a sister in return. In some places this might be called a preferential habit of sending a woman to 'marry back' into the clan of those who gave a woman. This habit might reflect the principle of reciprocity as 'restricted exchange'. This means that the gift of a woman can be remembered by many people, and will be honoured or reciprocated within living memory by creating another marriage between the same clans.

Another possibility is to offer bride wealth to the kin of a woman, out of respect for the gift that they have made of her as their sister. This wealth represents or signifies the marriage, and its dispersal among her male relatives makes the marriage secure, and perhaps very difficult to break. This unrestricted exchange makes the various uses of ceremonial wealth more complex. When men use bride wealth to supplant the gift of another woman in marriage, back into the first clan who gave their sister to them, the significance of the gifts varies much more widely than in the case of restricted exchange. Whereas, in restricted exchange, men give women as sisters and receive wives in return, in unrestricted exchange, men give women as sisters and receive ceremonial wealth in return. The uses, the significance of the ceremonial gifts, open negotiations between the men even wider than in the former case. The social values that inhere in gift giving in the latter example might be more negotiable and variable and possibly open ways for more exploitation between men. Transactions at marriage open the possibility, if not the necessity, of discussion and negotiation. In the smallest sense, the exchange of women in marriage can be understood as a communicative act, and a transaction that makes social relationships into a matter of concern over which people a person might recognize as relatives. In the biggest sense, the exchange of women can be understood as a form of communication because a woman is a slippery signifier, both of the natural and of the social life. In receiving a woman as wife, a man and his kin understand that they have new political associations, as well as the ability to add children to their own daily lives, with the offspring of the marriage.

What does a person give to another when making the gift of a sister to become a wife? Some scholars argued that women possessed capacities both to work for the domestic household and to bear children. These capabilities were exchanges with the women themselves, as if they were aspects of their person as much as skills they could use. Many scholars addressed women's work as a capacity of their persons that can be measured and valued for its potential to produce wealth in the forms of food, children and material goods. In feminist analyses of these, women's work was understood as if it were an object that could also be valued in material terms, or given a price. Those feminists criticizing the concept of women's work as a resource traded between men argued that the attribution of the material value to women's work could never succeed in freeing them from the drudgery of homemaking. In this condition, women found out that men exploited women's work for its products of children, food and wealth.

In *Elementary Structures of Kinship* (1949) Lévi-Strauss describes woman as the supreme gift. Later feminist theorists find the comment inspiring, but in different ways than Lévi-Strauss meant it to be. In analysing matrimonial exchanges, the efforts to identify the gift of a woman as the supreme gift led to the development of a general theory of society. Feminist critics took issue with Lévi-Strauss's statement in order to clarify the ways in which women were objects in ceremonial exchange. Further, this also opened a discussion of the subjectivity of those women, and the extent to which the exchange of a person compromised the woman's subjectivity.

Are women the supreme gift for social reproduction and history?

Both the followers and the critics of structuralism find Lévi-Strauss compelling on the same point, that 'woman is the supreme gift'. The followers of his argument agree that the gift of a sister in exchange for a wife establishes the centrality to society of the principle of reciprocity, rather than the repression of Oedipal desires. Women remain luminous in the imagination of the exchange partners, as if a man looking at a woman sees her as a manifestation of and reference to the principle of reciprocal exchange. The critics follow two different pathways of thought. One avenue leads through the problematic question of inequality, social reproduction and history; the other pathway opens up the enigma of inequality, social reproduction and gender (which I will turn to later).

One point might be raised in the defence of structuralist theory; that is, anthropologists did not approach the study of social change as a concern of special interest because they worked to create a different kind of account of human variation than did the evolutionist historians of the nineteenth and early twentieth centuries. To criticize structuralism for its failure to address history is to ask it to do something it cannot, or to take up different questions than it is prepared to ask.

There is a puzzle or an enigma here because a structuralist theory of history is played out in the reproduction of social relations in one of two ways. I think Gell is correct to say that structuralism did engage with the question of history, and did so in a rather interesting and sophisticated way in order to dismiss the false history of evolutionism (Gell 1992b). The distinction between hot and cold societies remains useful for understanding history and social reproduction most generally. The terms hot and cold distinguish those societies on the basis of how people understand themselves against their past. Cold societies live out the continuities with the past. Hot societies live out changes with the past, and thereby come to know it. Historical or 'hot' societies are those societies in which enduring values seem to reproduce while social changes escalate. These societies tend to take social changes into consideration and regenerate old values to hold the changes. Mythical or 'cold' societies are those in which myths elaborate and ideologies complicate human knowledge, while society remains much the same as it always has been. Such societies tend to keep social forms intact as the social expression of the logic of society, while allowing the efflorescence of myth, knowledge and legend throughout years of interaction. It is as if feet, hands and minds ran fast, while staying in one place.

These ideas about the way in which people perceive the passing of time, which are expressed beautifully in *The Savage Mind*, can also be found in another form in *Elementary Structures of Kinship*. In the earlier work Lévi-Strauss shows that societies which practise generalized exchange of women over the long cycles of reciprocity play out their mutual obligations over a long period of time. This habit has an enormous effect on the importance of social reproduction, and localized understandings of it. I hope to demonstrate this argument differently than did Gell, by focusing on the gift of a woman between clans.

People in some societies exchange women over the long cycle of reciprocal obligations, and these extend over generations. The people of these societies do so with the awareness that ambiguities are introduced to the relations of prestige or of equality between the clans. This is done with the sense that over time the differences will be equalized because the underlying principle of reciprocity will endure. In the other case, where women are exchanged for women, egalitarian relations endure across clans; but this is not true in all ways, as we shall see. How people assess their relationships with each other affects the ways in which they keep or sustain an egalitarian society. The obligation to return a woman remains self-evident in men's memories, especially when they must keep that obligation in one generation. The capacity to account for the differentials of the transaction lies within human memory.

Godelier has discussed elegantly much of the complexity entailed in the restricted and generalized exchange of women. He emphasizes that the exchange of women for wealth and the exchange of women for women simply imply contrary dynamics of historical consciousness. The compelling argument holds for examples of contemporary societies that practise different forms of matrimonial exchange. None the less, I remain uncomfortable with the idea that some forms of society have evolved from the other. The authors of the compilation of arguments in *Big Men and Great Men* (Godelier and Strathern 1991) have wrestled with this idea and abstracted core concepts of use to the creation of a better theory of society, at least one that focuses both on the strategies by which men create their own prestige and on those by which they create equitable relations with women.

Feminist critics try to develop a better analysis of processes of creation of social reproduction. The friendliest of these tried to make the terms of social reproduction clearer and therefore chose to examine the logic of society in detail. Critics think that the work of exchange of women might provide an insight into wider processes by which inequality works in social life. I address this in the next section.

Woman as subject, woman as object

What difference does the gift of a person make? In answering this question, anthropologists came to elaborate more fully a structuralist theory of society, and extend important reflections on that theory in their work. Alliance theory could answer the question of what difference the gift of a woman made, for any given society or at least in the ethnography of the Amazon. But the question has grander implications than this for the development of structuralism. The exchange of women between men, the giving of a sister and the accepting of a wife, necessarily must be understood in the round, both ethnographically and conceptually. If I am to understand kinship, then I must also understand the nature of women's experience as objects and, by implication, their subjectivity. Structuralist anthropologists did not aim in the first instance to address women's subjectivity, nor did they propose a feminist project. But women's subjectivity is inseparable from understanding the objects of the exchange. I think that by interrogating these limits of the structuralist's ability to address subjectivity it is possible to expose some of the most interesting assumptions of the theory. I pursue a deeper understanding of structuralism's assumptions through a review of the feminist critiques of the theory. These remain somewhat closer to the structuralist understanding of the problem than they first appear.

Some anthropologists understand society as a system of communication where 'women' represent different social capacities than do men. The exchange of women did create channels or means for communication between men, quite literally enabling them to make agreements with each other about contemporary and future conduct between their kin, clans and villages. But, in even more sophisticated understandings, transactions of bride wealth and women are considered as signs or as signifiers of the social relations. Women could both represent the social relationships between clans and be the medium through which the relationships could be made.

I make intentional comparisons between women in exchange systems and signs in communication systems. I want to emphasize that in either case, of exchange relations or of communicative relations, it is not so much the women or the image that is important to the analysis. Structuralism seeks the deep structures of relationships. In kinship the woman simply represents them; in communication the image represents the cognitive structures that make it possible to create meaningful utterance.

By considering society as similar to communication, structuralism created grounds for thinking about human action as the expression of social values; that is, the exchange of women enabled the discussion of what people believed about social life in general and the ways in which people should live. Other scholars considered women's subjectivity and their objectification of the problem. It is hard not to address immediately the ideological concern that subjective experiences can be objectified, and lost or misunderstood by the individual. Instead, if we first address where women stand as subjects and as objects, it might provide a clearer understanding of women's position in society. Then a better account of how women's experience is objectified can be made before discussing the limits on their subjectivity.

When exchanged as an object between men, many critics raised doubts about women's subjectivity because the woman seemed muted. The anthropologist can be left unable to understand why women accept subordinate positions, or why they believe they are compelled to enter into relationships that can be oppressive or become increasingly exploitive over time. Yet, when an anthropologist asks questions about women's subjective understandings of their experience in matrimonial exchanges, the answers can be confusing. What women say might not be indicative of what a feminine or even a feminist point of view might entail. As much as in any other circumstance or with any other subject, it is likely that the meaning of her answers and commentaries will remain inscrutable. 'Giving voice', as later cultural anthropologists came to say, to the woman in matrimonial exchanges will not expose a better understanding of the nature of subjectivity.

A critical review can be made of the status of women when women are viewed as the subject of the exchange. Here, as I have already shown, a number of anthropologists addressed women's work and the alienation of women's labours in exchange of bride wealth gifts to their brothers from their husbands. These analyses begin by confirming the basic fact of women's subjectivity as inherently valuable, but proceed by analysing the transformation of subjectivity into her objective value to other people. Women then become nothing more than the value of their labours to others.

An anthropologist might ask a question of both sides of the problem. If women are given as objects, then how does giving a woman for marriage cause and sustain social relationships? The answers to these questions differ greatly, and take anthropology into different directions. That is because the concept of woman vacillates between objective and subjective definitions. If marriage alters a woman's subjectivity from the time she leaves her clan as one of its sisters to the day she marries into another clan as a wife, then what is the significance of the act for her and for those around her? The important matter here is this: in structuralist theory a considerable ambiguity exists in the category of woman, the woman can be subject or object. The category shifts around in different anthropological analysis. Just as the play of woman in structuralist theories of society opens the thought to different possibilities for society, so too does the play of the sign – as when the word can mean several things at once – it opens thought to critical insights about social conventions of communication.

What difference does the gender of the gift make?

Asking about the gender of the gift becomes an enormous task. Some people analysed exchange as if women could only 'signify' social relationships and they thereby establish society as communicative practice. Others analysed women as objects of exchange, marrying models of production and models of exchange into comprehensible wholes. Women were at once producer and product, exchange object and the subject of exchange. The exchange of women could open a wider discussion of the whole of social reproduction into more provocative and wider reaching analysis than had existed before. But these were feminist questions as well as anthropological ones.

A further, and more provocative, line of enquiry focuses on the fact that it is a woman (and not a man) that is the gift made at marriage. Accordingly, the most important fact of social life lies in the recognition of gender difference. That recognition enables discussion of the facts of life in more abstract forms, allowing informants to talk as they did in Malinowski's day about a 'father's love' and 'the rule of the mother's clan'. This is similar to the anthropologist's efforts to recognize gender difference by addressing the facts of life as 'natural symbols' of fatherly love and the jural authority of the men of the matrilineage.

Alternatively, the recognition of gender difference can work as a symbolic expression, or symbolic operator. That is, the gender differences work as a marker of meaning across different societies, and across different eras of our own society in quite different ways. Gender does not mean the same thing in all circumstances of its use. One of the simple cases might be the situations in which to be womanly might mean to bear up to social responsibility, whereas in other circumstances it means to be feminine in frivolous and decorative ways. Media images often show these differences rather graphically, but one might also consider how the role of the wife or mother differs from one family to the next. The current BBC reality television show, *Wife Swap*, while suggestively titled, does more than suggest. As a programme based on the exchange of women between households, the dynamics of the plot simply unwinds with a little time, ten days to be exact. In that time each woman learns the rules of the other's household, the families expose and come to terms with the underlying assumptions about those 'rules', and the implied capacities of women as subjects are re-addressed in each marriage as the importance of the woman's beliefs and personality. *Wife Swap* makes explicit the full load of extra associations that might be borne by women in their capacities as wives and mothers. The reality television genre engenders *real* discussion about women's work as housewives, as the viewers continue to analyse the implicit assumptions that the TV families held about women's work. Conversations about the work of a wife continue on radio commentary, on television, in casual office conversations and among neighbours. But the debate points towards a different kind of question about the substance of exchanges.

Can there be a danger in making over-rigorous divisions between the domestic world of women and the public world of men? Is it more appropriate to analyse historical transformation by addressing the changes in social reproduction as they might be exposed in the private spaces of the home? Does Lévi-Strauss's structuralist theory of social variation permit a fuller understanding of human history, one that does not assume that the great events of any society are made by men in wars, public policy and government, and in international trade? Does the exchange of women turn attention to the most important locations of social transformation in society?

Feminists have doubts about all of this

Lévi-Strauss's attention to the exchange of women by men appears to address the matter of how to think about gender inequality in society a bit more fully than earlier anthropologists had done, in so far as he discusses directly women's role in ceremonial exchanges. This arises from a change in emphasis in theoretical orientation. Functionalists considered the rules of social life, whereas structuralists examined principles of society. For example, Malinowski had focused on the Trobriands by thinking about the trade-off between the rules of the relationship between the natural affection men regularly held for their children and the customary law of women's matrilineal concerns for the clan; but the structuralists addressed the gift of a woman as a reflection of the principle of reciprocity in kin relations.

The claim that the gift of a woman can be the supreme gift causes some concern especially among those who see this as an ideological claim. Of course, to claim the gift of a woman as a supreme gift was ideological, but structuralism aimed to reach past the mask of ideology to deeper social knowledge. The structuralists argue that the gift of a woman expresses a pre-ideological position; the grounds of knowledge that makes the world work as it does makes women into the supreme gift in many instances of matrimonial exchange.

Feminists contemporary with Lévi-Strauss's structuralism take issue with his claim about women and his claim about the grounds of belief about women. Most famously, Gayle Rubin (1975) recorded her dissatisfaction with the ways in which structuralism understood 'deep' knowledge. She believed that the capacity to make oppositions, to distinguish and divide entities knowing light from dark, did not determine human reasoning. Rather, she argued that the nature of the unconscious mind propelled particular versions of reality to consciousness and so found expression in human social relations. She asks what the role of repression is in the unconscious knowledge which shapes social action. This is an intriguing alternative to Lévi-Strauss's work, and it is worth returning to Rousseau, as much as to Morgan and Marx.

Rousseau believed that gender inequality was different from inequality among men who marked their differences according to their degree of access to enjoy private property. He claimed that women were substantively different from men by nature, but men were different from each other because of the inequalities they formed. This first judgement, perhaps this first error of judgement, invited further critical analysis by subsequent generations of scholars, especially feminists of the mid- to late twentieth century. In particular, the claim met criticism by those scholars seeking to understand the relationship between the powers of the state in the generation of class as a social hierarchy by comparison with its power in the generation of patriarchy. In this section we will discuss the way in which feminist anthropologists used their legacy from Rousseau, the concept of the Noble Savage.

Many anthropologists of the mid-twentieth century tried to redress the elision of the analysis of gender inequality from the rest of social and political life. Some took seriously the claim that the kind of inequality suffered by women differed from the kind experienced in class relations. Others insisted that women's deep implication in their work in the everyday economy inextricably tied them into the processes of class formation and reproduction, such that women's inequality could not be uncoupled from socio-economic differences. One question pressed forward some of the best of this early work; that is, how did women come to be considered the property of men, bound in marriage and subject to the authority of the head of the family? The pervasive use of dowry and bride wealth across most marriage rituals confused the issue even more. Was marriage everywhere a form of exchange of commodities, with money and goods going to the family of the woman in exchange for her reproductive capacity and her potential contributions of her labour to the new husband's household? By contrast to such arrangements that subordinated women's individual interests to those of the husband and his wider family, the earliest feminist anthropologists described the limited powers that a woman could express in non-state society. Some challenged the idea that women held inferior status to men in such societies, and argued that women's sphere of power in the non-state society complemented men's domains. Leacock's historical study of the Cree of northern Quebec suggested that men and women held separate and complementary spheres of power, mutually dependent upon each other in non-state society (Leacock 1953). She discusses the power of women shaman to be intermediaries with the supernatural world and thereby threaten men's control of social life. But, most importantly, she described the ways in which women could organize their own work to limit the actions of men. For example, Cree women could refuse to plant and harvest the crops that warring men needed in order to go into battle. Women's inequality to men could be measured only in relation to men's capacities to act in their own sphere of influence; outside that sphere women exercised kinds of power substantively different from men's. The earliest work questioned how women lost their complementary powers in non-state society to become men's subordinates in state society.

Ortner, much later (1974), insisted that men's domination of women occurred universally, whether in state or non-state society. Just how women could be universally dominated remained something of a problem for anthropologists. Ortner answered this by declaring that women's sphere of influence generally included the domains of procreation, nurture, and food production and preparation for the household. These activities put them in close proximity to the natural world, and more importantly emphasized the natural capacity of women's bodies. She argued that women's power lay in affinity with nature. By contrast, men's power belonged to the social and cultural spheres of experience. Men sought to control and dominate nature by establishing and maintaining social institutions and culturally acquired habits. Men enjoyed superiority over women, because they exercised male power in the social and cultural world to dominate and shape the natural world. These powers might be better balanced in non-state society, but state society built itself upon men's domination of women. Here, Ortner comes to a different conclusion than earlier feminists; inequality between men and women was the same as inequality among humans. Gender inequality predicted the extensions of that inequality to relationships between men made according to social and economic hierarchical distinctions.

Ortner's conclusions suggest that her reader consider how women's lives might be different without the corruptions of patriarchy in state society. Revolutionary change to gender relations entailed revolutionary changes to the state. Anthropologists swallowed this heady cocktail of analysis with ideological prescription for change because it echoed the political arguments of the generation of feminists who sought a total and full transformation of social life, but they took it with disquiet if not alarm. Ortner's argument challenged feminist anthropology to reassess how it might work across cultures. Should anthropologists assume that women's subordinate positions could be the same everywhere? If so, did they understand (even recognize) how men dominated women in the field site, whether in Morocco or Melanesia? Were men's actions towards and against women always best understood as domination, even when they appeared to be like gender domination in American and European society? In Ortner's hands, the generation of forms of inequality by which men came to dominate other men came to be only one version of the substantive inequality by which men overpowered and dominated women's lives.

A radical analysis of men's domination of women needed a fuller appreciation of what a woman is. In the first instance, Marilyn Strathern challenged Ortner's claims that over history men weld women's power into the natural world, extolling women's reproductive capacities. Strathern argues, first, that nature differs across the world, being 'wilderness' in the New Guinea Highlands, and the frontier in the nineteenth-century American west – each landscape suggests different associations of power. Hence, to be associated with the powers of the natural sphere did not predict that a woman should hold a subordinate position to a man. Second, society did not always harness the natural world in order to produce new people, wealth, or material forms of prestige and power. In some locales, the social and natural spheres of power complemented each other and the social did not subordinate the natural to its cause. Third, Strathern reminded other feminists that people used the language of gender to accomplish other kinds of social and political outcomes. People in many places could speak and think about gender differences among them, as did many people across state and non-state societies in initiation and puberty rituals. The anthropologists could use gender as a code or a language for understanding how people analysed social differences among themselves.

The legacy of the Noble Savage in arguments about gender inequality complicated Rousseau's old assumption that women suffered inequality under men, differently than men suffered inequality under other men. In Strathern's hands, the legacy of the Noble Savage enabled her to make a breakthrough in an old question about substantive inequality and formal inequality. Women's substantive differences from men appeared to be substantive only if the anthropologist did not analyse the ways in which people used gender to explain power relations to each other. Strathern's call for cross-cultural analysis of the generation or perhaps the cultivation of gender difference posed the possibility of a new era of social and political anthropology, enabled to describe and explain gender inequality as a culturally constructed form of social relationship.

Conclusions of the critics of structuralism

Consider the social value of structuralism to its times, whether in Europe, North America or the Amazon and Melanesia. Structuralist anthropologists explained the problem of social difference within society and across different societies by exposing the deeper grounds for their common similarities. In most of the world this scientific argument reinforced the efforts towards a reasonable response to modernity, or at least the social processes which people defined and interpreted as modernity.

The feminist critics of structuralism anticipate the limitations of the theory's value for explaining the world of the post-Second World War era. Some criticism both from the postcolonial intellectual movement within academic life and from the feminist movements can be heeded, but not in order to pursue an ideological project as these movements suggest. Instead, the critics of structuralism reframe several larger questions about the nature of society. These concerns are first, power; and second, subjectivity. By power, I mean the historical conditions in which society is made and regenerated. By subjectivity, I mean the concepts of being human and human being in which people in any society come to act out their hopes as agents and as persons. Theorists committed to the anthropological project continued to find the way forward by reflecting upon many of the primary assumptions of the theories of modernist anthropology. I address these two concerns over four chapters in the next section of this book.

Summary of chapter 5

As an attempt to grasp the totality of social life, some anthropologists have examined giving gifts as evidence of deeper social structural principles of human association. Consider how the very possibility of cross-cultural understanding depends upon the acceptance that the other person, otherwise a stranger, can communicate meaningfully with you because they assume you understand how social relationships do work. Earliest works, especially *Primitive Classification*, cannot show that the social life flowers from reasoned thought, or vice versa. It is a chicken and egg question that links deep structures of communication to social structure. Ceremonial gift exchange is considered a kind of communication between groups of people. Consider then how the substance of ceremonial gifts affects the constitution of society more widely. What difference does it make that the ceremonial gift is a person, especially a woman as in matrimonial exchanges? Lévi-Strauss called the gift of a woman a supreme gift, combining both natural and social capacities of reproduction in the same event of exchange. If that is considered further, then the woman is at once the subject and the object of the exchange. The 'supreme gift' of a woman is at once a person who is related to one group who give her away as a sister, and related to another group who receive her as a wife. The gender of the woman is not a matter of her nature, or her substance. Instead, gender is created as a kind of relationship created with the gift of a woman because men come to know themselves as siblings or as marital partners through such exchanges, just as do women. What difference does recognizing the gender of the gift make? It raises a feminist debate about what is the feminine. In that ensuing debate a number of Euro-American ideological assumptions are exposed in the study of matrimonial exchange about women's work, about marriage and sexuality and about status vis à vis men and social institutions.

Part II

POSTMODERN REFLECTIONS

Historical criticism

6

DEBT IN POSTCOLONIAL SOCIETY

Postcolonial exchanges

Postcolonial anthropology analyses the debts that societies owe each other as a result of their shared history. This is an awkward proposition that anthropologists cannot explore fully within their own discipline. It requires historical investigation to complement ethnographic insight. In the case of the Pacific Islands, Thomas, the scholar of postcolonial society, observed how the anthropological object was entangled in historical and cultural processes of the exploration and colonization of the region. An interdisciplinary approach to postcolonial history was needed if anthropologists were to assess how those historical and cultural processes created alienation of wealth from societies there. How did misunderstandings about gift exchange become a fulcrum from which to lever out wealth from Pacific Island societies? While some anthropologists have described the history of colonial and postcolonial relations in terms of specific transactions, many other anthropologists study the context of those postcolonial transactions. The language of debt and the idiom of indebtedness pervade much of the writing about the postcolonial world. By examining several cases of mutual misunderstandings about debt and obligation in colonial and postcolonial encounters, I outline the various ways that anthropologists have used 'historical context' as a concept. Historical context in each of these case studies provides a motor that turns the processes of cultural transformation: sometimes with brutal force, sometimes with good intentions directed towards bad ends, and other times to codify living processes into meaningless forms.

Living in a postcolonial world is part of shared conventional knowledge, but not easily or transparently so to everyone. Even while people remember the colonial past, significant features of the postcolonial present can be forgotten, including a cosmopolitan city's powerful ties to distant places in a wider postcolonial world. It is possible to analyse the nature of contemporary exchanges without acknowledging the contexts in which they are made. For example, the destruction of the World Trade Center in New York City as a symbol of international business transaction is differently understood in the context of the wider network of relations between American capital and the rest of the world than it can be understood in the context of a single violent interchange between acquisitive capitalists of the American business world and a terrorist group acting in the name of Islam. Not clarifying the context, leaving it vaguely as postcolonial dissent, makes it more difficult both to understand power relations within those exchanges, and to explain why history takes the course that it does. How anthropologists analyse the postcolonial context matters to their understanding of the relations made across society, especially when those relations are misunderstood for what they are.

Alienation typifies the postcolonial condition: not only the alienation of land from people, but also the separation of people from their past and their present. If alienation is the condition in which humans came to see their creative capacities falsely turned into substantive forms, then they can only be deceived into believing in those entities as valuable accounts. The perception of loss, whether material or spiritual, inheres in such discourses of alienation, just as it does in the postcolonial condition. I address these questions by looking into three cases in which shifts in the relations of gift exchange seemingly lead to the dispiriting of the collective interests of the different peoples involved. Those cases are the uses of wampum (bead money) in the Iroquois confederacy, the substitution of rice with money in the votive gifts to Asian landlords in colonial countryside near Calcutta, and the habit of 'begging' in Fijian trade relations in the nineteenth-century Pacific.

Anthropologists who examine the colonial legacy by focusing on the modality of interaction known as gift exchange have to address particular problems that enlighten broader disciplinary issues. The basic problem is how to describe the colonial encounter as more than an unfair deal cut between trading partners. A solution to this rather limiting analysis would be to take seriously Mauss's critical claims that Europeans accepted only recently the idea that humans were first and foremost economically minded beings. Analyses of the exchange of gifts in the early colonial encounter give a broader insight into the issues.

In this chapter I address the work of anthropologists in the postcolonial era, asking how their arguments use a critical theory of gift exchange. First, I point to an error that can be easily made by conflating European or Western common wisdom about the primacy of economic rationality in everyday life with the analytic approach to the exchanges made in the early colonial encounter. Then, in the rest of this chapter I outline the approach that assumes that the exchange of gifts in early colonial encounters is more than an economic exchange. This opens the analysis to the wider problem of assessing the colonial encounter: namely, how did it lead to the condition of alienation? The conclusions assess what the anthropologist working in today's postcolonial era can say about the history of colonial relations and the role of anthropology in creating the postcolonial legacy.

The transfer of Manhattan

Any school child in the United States can tell you that the Manhattan Indians sold the island of Manhattan for the contemporary equivalent of 24 US dollars in wampum. They may present the story mythically. The Indians received wampum beads for the transfer of their claims to residence on Manhattan Island to the white community, and the transfer of their name to the land area that is bounded by the Hudson River on the west coast and the Atlantic Ocean on the east coast. A wampum is a coloured shell bead woven artfully into patterned necklaces or belts. It was common to the north-east seaboard region because it was used as currency in fur trade and in tributary payments among English, French, Dutch and Indian groups in the area. Part of the story's interest to most people in North America comes from the fact that New York City spreads wholly over Manhattan Island, which now hosts the head offices of many multinational corporations. During the autumn festival of Thanksgiving when families congregate for feasts with their kin and their friends, it is common to reflect whimsically on the story. Sometimes people reflect on the contemporary social conditions of the island, and comment on the different fates of the Manhattan Indians, the Iroquois Indians and the early white settlers on that island. It is hard to say why some people recall it at this time and what it means, but that is another story.

The anthropologist Graeber (2001) looks closely at the north-east United States to analyse how the transfer of Manhattan Island put both the Iroquois and Algonquin-speaking peoples into debt with the white settlers. Is there a kind of duplicity on the part of the purchasers, or at least a misunderstanding on the part of both parties about the nature of the transaction? As Graeber notes, although the Europeans may well have thought they had bought the land by contractual agreement, the Manhattan Indians probably thought they were confirming the peaceful arrangements for a beneficial association with the Europeans that would continue into the future. That may be so, but how does it lead the indigenous people of North America wholly into indebtedness?

This story offers a sage insight into the events of the colonial past for the postcolonial present. For some, perhaps the poets, knowledge of that tragedy fosters humility about the contemporary period. And in the postcolonial time, the history foreshadows the end of the progress of political and economic expansion by hinting at the possibility of apocalyptic change. The postcolonial situation often finds more intimate terms of expression. Postcolonial ramifications are felt in the face-to-face relationships that challenge humans to reconsider the terms of their existence. A poet uses the postcolonial to express an intimate experience of loss by drawing on the image of the colonial conquest of North America that exists in common knowledge. 'Man who fears death, how many acres do you need to lengthen your shadow under the endless sky?' (Duffy 1987). The school child's history class gives her reasons to believe conventional wisdoms about the history she shares or does not share with the rest of the region or country. Somehow early encounters lead people into more than they bargained for. The school child and the poets' empathetic insight into the early encounter of European with the indigenous community share a common wisdom that exchanges between European and the American Indian engendered their difference. This chapter examines how exchange in early colonial encounters – whether capitalist market exchanges or honorific exchanges – exposes the process of alienation that created misunderstandings about human relationships. As we shall see, the kernel of the problem for understanding alienation in the postcolonial era is that exchanges made to open new relationships open each party to 'more than they bargained for' in the trade.

The legacy of the Manhattan purchase (an example of an inequitable exchange) poses at least two conceptual issues for anthropologists before they explain what happened in the colonial encounter. These two issues are culture and value. Indians and the early Americans misunderstood who and what they were looking at, as they peered at each other through different viewfinders. Graeber presses his fellow anthropologists to consider the assumptions and logic used by all parties to the trade in determining the value of the objects used in it, such that each believes that they made a fair trade. A collaborative effort to analyse alienation in the colonial encounters provides an opportunity for anthropologists to work with historians. Historians persuaded anthropologists to consider wider questions of historical change as they occur in social relationships made and unmade between very different people. And similarly, anthropologists encouraged historians to acknowledge that colonialism entailed more than an economic relationship between peoples or nations in which one group forced the other into subordinations. Together, researchers in the disciplines of anthropology and history can address the problem of explaining human alienation in the colonial encounter.

So, how do colonial relations alienate human beings from each other? The documents remark on the lifestyles of the indigenous communities in extraordinary detail. Historians record the decline of the communities, destroyed by warfare and disease. I check my own understanding of their analysis as I read through the well-documented history of colonial America in the seventeenth, eighteenth and nineteenth centuries, and the sixteenth- and seventeenth-century writings of the *Jesuit Relations*, published from the discussions of the missions in the region of the Great Lakes and Quebec, or as I can check on the details of the archaeological record of the Huron Indian communities in the fifteenth and sixteenth centuries (following the historian, Trigger 1969). Finally, an ethnohistorian can research more deeply into the world inhabited by the Huron, or Wyandot as they called themselves, until the disappearance of their villages in the eighteenth century.

Writing of the wars of the Iroquois, the early anthropologist Morgan (1878) tells us of the extraordinary conflict that damaged the matrilineal clan system by destroying the process by which the Iroquois transferred names across the generations. War erupted with the need to replace the dead into the names of the clan, and the captives would be adopted or captured as to the wish of the clanspersons. The early reports carry disturbing details about violence and torture as aspects of the custom of the Iroquois and the Huron. Recently, an anthropologist has highlighted the visceral images of the indigenous custom throughout the ethnography.

Some of the most interesting reports of the peace made at the end of warfare refer to the uses of belts of wampum. The wampum belts are beautifully beaded and bear the marks and pictures that refer to the history of agreements between the giver and the persons who receive the belt. For example, one beaded belt marked agreements between the Huron and the Jesuit Fathers that a mission named St Marie should be built there. The markers and pictures, in this case the pictures of the church steeples, work as mnemonics for the events at which people gave the belts. They work as aids to the recollection of memories about the history and agreements.

More than anyone else, Graeber made the aesthetic value of the wampum and axe heads the central problem of his reports. There are two sensibilities for decorating the body with material objects. One is the expansion of the spiritual life with the gift of the wampum belt, like a shawl around the neck and back to the prisoner of war adopted into the clan. The second sensibility complements this. The second is the contraction of the body; a physic of the loss of life as when war prisoners found a torturous death with strings of red-hot axe heads around the shoulders and breasts. Without the colonial European presence, the two sensibilities seem to work like a thermostat, a dynamic control on the swings between peace and war.

That thermostatic control between expansion and contraction should have been effective, had there been harmony between Dutch, French and English interests in the region. But attempts to control the fur trade complicated the treaties made between the Iroquois and the colonists. Graeber writes confidently about the confused and violent encounter of the American colonies with the Indians of the region and particularly with the split of the Iroquoian confederacy. Graeber's account of the sale of Manhattan explains the alienation of the Indian nations in the story of violent oppression and conflict. Understanding the value of the beads, we learn of an interesting dynamic between the contraction of the body into depression, death and violent anger against the outward expansion of human vision into peace, treaties and the afterlife of the spirit.

This case only partially answers two questions of concern to postcolonial anthropologists. Despite Graeber's best attention to aesthetic dimensions of the value of wampum beads, this analysis of aesthetics does not explain how humans came to be alienated from each other in the colonial period. Instead, violence itself became the mechanism creating social and material alienation, the means of expressing alienation of spirit. An anthropological account that took seriously the role of aesthetics in creating values that alienated humans from each other would potentially discuss violence as the outcome of such forces. Graeber resorts to an aphorism, or a common folk wisdom to ground his anthropological theory of alienation through the colonial era: 'the boot always comes down'.

There is another concern that somehow the move to model the colonial administration and government upon indigenous political structures enabled the further destruction of the Iroquoian nations. The confederacy, as it was called, constituted itself a council to negotiate a system of treaties that the different nations or bands held among them. As a system of government, it substantiated a more egalitarian model that used negotiation and discussion of the history of agreements that kept the peace. The story shows us that the early American colonists first admired the confederacy in which Iroquoian political treaties made up their 'system of government'. Early American colonists admired it so much that they adopted it for their own federal system. But, perhaps their admiration proved to be more dangerous for the Iroquois than the earliest record of the most sensational violent aspects of their lives. Once they abstracted and copied the ideal form of the confederacy for their own purposes of independent government, the colonists then fought a number of wars against its living members, and moved some tribes to the regions to the north of the United States borders. Other Iroquoian nations fell into warfare with each other. The confederacy no longer existed, except on the paper that outlined the confederate system.

In Graeber's final analysis, European economic interests in acquiring capital destroyed the Iroquoian confederacy. In the light of later developments in the protection of trade and democracy through warfare, contemporary readers might think these events a bit ironic. The desire to control the trade in furs for the financial benefit of the European settlers and trading companies led early Americans to send armies against the Iroquoian tribes. Seeking control of trade from the hands of the French and the Indians, American colonial governments thus destroyed the complex chain of treaties that made up the peaceful Iroquoian confederacy, the idealized model for the federal system of democratic government in the new United States of America.

What then is the role of anthropologists in the pacification of the Great Lakes and north-eastern seaboard region of the North American continent? How did those carrying out anthropological research contribute to the colonial powers that dominated the Iroquois? These are hard questions to answer in this case, largely because the discipline of anthropology came to these issues well after the destruction of the Iroquoian confederacy and in the period of Iroquoian cultural revival in the nineteenth century. Morgan's researches into Iroquoian kinship, and those of Wallace who tried to construct a theory of the ritual life of the Iroquois, presented a rich picture of the cultural life of the communities at the end of the nineteenth century. They aimed to fill in the picture or close the gap of understanding about the confederacy by getting into the inner details of the political and spiritual life of its members. Because their ethnographic studies presented the last remnants of a disappearing world, they completed full studies to the best of their abilities. Whereas the earlier writers addressed the most spectacular and exotic aspects of the Iroquois, Huron and Algonquin life, later writers portraying a pacified and conquered people described them with textbook-style clarity. Certainly conventions of anthropology had changed by this time, and the styles of the later age matched with the growing status of the new discipline as it sought recognition as a science. Graeber, or any analyst who finds out that American colonial communities overpowered the indigenous American tribes by force, warfare and violence, does not incriminate anthropology too easily in its accounts.

The democratic experiment that built a government on the relations between the Iroquoian confederacy and the federal system in the early American democracy misunderstood the wampum belts as a kind of contract, an abstract document to which people attach no history. The contract depends upon a complex set of assumptions about the natural rights of a natural man; it is as if the image of the Noble Savage appears to haunt the formation of democratic government. The founders of the federal system of American democracy used the abstract model of the Iroquoian confederacy in ways a bit more akin to a contract, rather than the treaty system that it was. Graeber shows that people exchanged wampum beads in order to make a treaty rather than a social contract, using the aesthetics of the beads as a way of recalling the history leading up to the treaty. The beaded images woven into a belt and worn around the neck at the time of the agreement keep in the foreground of everyone's minds both the reasons for violent conflict and those for the making of a peace. The treaty works because signatory parties can recall a history of events leading up to its writing and agreement among them. The contract fails when the memory of the treaty's history is erased by negotiations for future action.

South Asian indenture

Success and failure in colonial administration became lessons to the work of empire. Most famously, Macaulay's notebooks from the administration of policy in British India show that he and others aimed to prevent a repetition of the earlier failures of colonial administrators elsewhere (Said 1977). They agreed that the misanalysis of cultural relations has deleterious effects on the livelihood of people who live with the after-effects of policies developed from misunderstandings about cultural practice and from mistakes made in implementing the policy.

Take the example offered by Prakash (1988) of the colonial administration's attempt to erase debt bondage at the beginning of the twentieth century in the countryside near Calcutta. Throughout the nineteenth and early twentieth centuries, British colonial administrators worked to free the farmers from relationships with landowners, which administrators believed were fundamentally abusive because farmers were trapped by relationships of debt to the landlords. The action to interfere in local politics departed from the conventional habits of the administration, which sought to let people rule locally while the colonial administration managed wider business interests. Historically, British colonial administration aimed to respect or preserve the different traditions rather than eradicate them. Most interventions had aimed to modify cultural habits towards a better quality of life in the future; that is, a lifestyle enabled to meet the challenges of a changing economy across the empire.

In the countryside landlords collected a tax from farmers in exchange for protection. The farmers gave the tax as part of their offerings within the 'Jajmani' system, in which the gifts made to people of higher caste helped to establish a hierarchy of social order. Many administrators felt that the social hierarchy of the Jajmani system enabled the long-term functioning of politics in the region; but they were increasingly uncomfortable with the excesses of privilege that landlords chose in the later decades of the empire.

A new relationship between landlords and farmers developed with the wider extension of business opportunities across the region. With business employment and the rise of international trade that affected the area, money could be used for the purchase of a number of different things, including the payment of taxes to the landlord. Landlords delighted in the farmers' gifts of money because they could use it to buy prestige goods. Farmers who substituted money for the gifts of rice from the crops were freed from the obligations of farming and maintaining the land, and from the anxiety of working against crop failure. Throughout the nineteenth century, the landlords had substituted money as payment for the normal collection of rice because it created agreeable relations between the two groups. The traditional use of a tariff on rice could no longer be used against the landless farm-workers. Administrators' economic plans had disrupted tradition, but had created a better livelihood for the majority of the population.

In order to break the debt cycle between landlord and farmer, the administrators persuaded landlords that farmers should have the possibility of buying the land. They agreed, but by the last decade of the nineteenth century a new development changed the impetus of the original policy. An agricultural depression which lasted from the 1890s through to the First World War created an alarming new situation. The value of rice increased dramatically, while the purchasing power of money fell. Landlords now appealed to customary habits of paying fealties in rice, not money. Some farmers could not meet the landlord's demands. Other farmers sought other means of paying the landlord for the land and thereby escaping the changing demands of fealty offerings. They entered into labour contracts away from the countryside, so some left with the intent to return with cash to pay off the landlord or buy their land, and others left with the intention to find a new start.

Some people left to enter into a new kind of labour relationship, that of bonded indenture. The flow of labourers from the countryside into Calcutta presented an awkward social and economic problem to the British administration in India. The colonial administration had facilitated the end of 'feudal' systems of land tenure in the countryside, for the benefit of freeing the Indian peasant from unjust taxation by feudal lords. The end of the system of votive offerings and feudal taxation also eroded the symbolic aspects of precolonial status in the countryside. Now, in the countryside where old feudal lords finally gave way to the rule of colonial social and economic policy, the offer to work abroad on a fixed contract made it possible for people to escape otherwise insurmountable hardships. The historian Prakash (1988) tells us how a system ended, and how most colonial administrators thought it good that it had because they believed (somewhat erroneously) that it entailed servitude and bondage. The problem remained: what could the former farmers and workers do now that they no longer could depend on the regional lord for the organization of social, economic and political life? Obviously many of the lower caste farmers found themselves readily employed in making a better life, but others chose to work in the Pacific for a few years in order to make some money to return to India. The indentured labourers chose to sign on with companies who supplied workers to plantations in the Pacific. These were the labourers who came to develop Fiji's sugar plantations.

Early Fijian trade

The third case through which I examine the modality of gift exchange as constitutive of the processes of colonization is that of Fiji. Fiji's violent exchanges happened in the early twentieth century on plantations, and the events of open violent conflict came just over ten years after independence, in the postcolonial period. None the less they bear great similarity to the history of the North American conquest.

The Fijian islands became a territory under British control only in the twentieth century. Kelly tells us that colonialism was very much an economic project, undertaken on behalf of the Fijians so as to make the financing of a government of the islands possible. This would give benefit by creating political stability in the region which had suffered from the competitive rush by European and American nations to control it. Several West European countries rushed to own colonies in the late nineteenth century and the United States entered the early twentieth century with a plan for economic development and military control of the Pacific region, especially after establishing new relations in the small islands of Micronesia, including the Philippines and Hawai'i. The British plan had been to develop a local sugar industry for the export trade, so that the Fijian islands might have sufficient finances to support their own administration. It is possible to say that self-government, if not independence, was already in the minds of the early policy makers working in Fiji.

This period must be understood as the end of the imperial era of global control. The administration of the Fijian colony followed upon the changing plans for the south Asian colonies. Each colony's administration drew upon the lessons of the past, trying not to recreate the mistakes of the previous administrators. The corrections cast much of the political landscape into a confusion of ideologies and beliefs about what the value of the administration might be. Coming under control so late in the colonial days, the Fijians perhaps benefited from wisdom learned from the mistakes made elsewhere, but the administrators inadvertently infused layers of policy with misconceived ideas and ill-hatched theories about the nature of indigenous politics and the possibility of indigenous rule. This monstrous postcolonial bird comes home to roost in the administration of Fiji and in its postcolonial politics.

Things came apart first on a decision to find labour for the plantations from outside Fiji itself. According to Kaplan, there were two reasons for this. One lay in the fact that many of the administrators wanted to protect the integrity and nobility of the Fijian lifestyle, its chiefs and systems of honorific gifts. The administrators argued that this lifestyle would be corrupted and wholly undermined by the plantation work. Further, some administrators argued that Fijians already held responsibilities for the garden work that supported customary life and therefore should not be busy with plantation agriculture where it cost clans and families the labourers and work needed to support the production of their own food.

The second reason for the use of labourers from distant India was applied in a more hopeful rather than protective spirit. Administrators believed that the development of the Fijian colony could be undertaken as an effort to solve the labour problem in the Calcutta countryside, which I described in the previous section.

Does the history of trade across other cultural groups in other areas, in Fiji for example, predict that conflicts in understanding should lead to alienation and violent conflict? What is the story of alienation where violent and oppressive warfare does not explain the whole of the conflict between the trading partners? Does trade in Fiji, for example, hide different violations of trust of spirit and of obligation that lead to the same end? Sahlins, Thomas, Kaplan and Kelly can speak at great length about how to assess the exchanges between Fijians, European traders and South Asian migrants in the early colony. What they aim to describe remains a subtle cultural practice. In each case of the Fijian and the Indian, the anthropologists are confronted with the importance of assessing a habitual or ritual activity, undertaken in new contexts or with new people who might not understand it nearly as well as the practitioners hope. Getting the descriptions right can mean everything to the way in which the story unfolds, and if the earlier anthropologists had it all wrong then the postcolonial anthropologist must not only get it right but also expose the record of error and the implications of others following that record.

Perhaps history does imitate myth and legend. Or perhaps certain structures of colonial power resonate through time and in different places because they are adapted and used to fit new locations. The contemporary conditions of life in the Fijian islands echo the mythic story of the colonial relations between the Iroquois and the Thirteen Colonies. Here, first the colonial administration, and then later the independent national government, provided the same legal arrangements to the citizenry. Indigenous Fijians emerged as the rightful property holders on the basis of their long-term residence on the islands, whereas the immigrant community of labourers from India could not claim ownership of the Fijian land. In the second half of the twentieth century this half of the population of Fiji, whose ancestors came from India only two and three generations ago, could not buy land and had restricted rights in economic activity in the nation. How does the Fijian government continue to insist on the propriety of such arrangements for democratic rule, especially after the Commonwealth of Nations ousted the small nation of less than a million people in the late 1980s as a new democracy failing to keep its obligations to protect good government?

Assessments of Fijian Kerekere Vakavidi (or begging)

In order to understand the habit of begging in Fiji, I will turn to the many descriptions of the practice that are provided in the colonial record. In the first instances, the record of begging in Fiji seemingly invited the reader to enjoy the somewhat raunchy-sounding terms used to describe it. 'Kerekere Vakavidi' is a Fijian term that the European traders learned to use in order to describe the plaintive and ingratiating approach made to them when they arrived in the harbour. If I understand the practice correctly, the traders felt a bit uncomfortable with the forthright manner in which most Fijians approached them. The trading began with a request for the sailor to give particular objects to the Fijian person. This initiated trade because the sailors and traders then could express a liking for what they felt were equivalent objects of value, particularly objects of the luxury trade with east Asia and back home in Western Europe, objects such as bêche-de-mer (sea cucumbers which were highly prized in China for their medicinal and invigorating qualities) and sandalwood. There emerged a small trade in a local shell currency and sharks' teeth, both of which had uses in the ritual exchanges of the Fijians. Most Fijians and Europeans entered into these exchanges with good will and lively excitement at the process. If there could be a complaint on either side it simply came from the European sailors who felt that the Fijians did not really have very good trade goods, and the sailors often gave currency for goods that they could find elsewhere, where the goods would be of better quality and in greater quantity. These accounts by Sahlins relied upon his reading of both missionary texts and sailor stories.

What then can anthropologists know about such kinds of trade prior to the colonial encounter? Sahlins uses the science of archaeology and of linguistics to answer that question to his satisfaction, but we will see that his answer did not satisfy everyone! As for the archaeological record, he tells us simply that the region had been a crossroads of trade for centuries, including times before the European colonization when Pacific islanders used the Fijian islands as a stopping point in their gradual migrations into the eastern Pacific, where they first settled as recently as 600 years ago. Sahlins shows his readers that the linguistic record is somewhat more complex in interesting ways. As speakers of an Austronesian language, the Fijians enjoyed the ability to communicate with many other island peoples who were involved in similarly far-flung journeys for ceremonial trade in different parts of the Pacific. The word 'kerekere' means to request (something). 'Vaka' is of the (Fijian) people and 'viti' is a suffix that designates the conventional form of the noted practice. Hence, the word that the Fijian traders taught to their European counterparts simply meant to ask (for something) in the manner of a Fijian. I am tempted to imagine that the Fijian trader bore the same skills of flexibility with translation and cultural styles that an experienced anthropologist might develop.

The assessments lead Sahlins to propose that Fijian culture might be something as simple as these codified forms of it, but that would understate the significance or power of such a thing in human life. He reckons that anthropologists should be attuned to the devices by which indigenous people come to see themselves as possessing cultural institution and social forms in need of interpretation to strangers. This would bring them closer to the project of understanding how culture can be transformed in the process of colonization, and how it comes to be thought of as something that exists outside the social relationships in which people make it. But for Sahlins this is a creative process of shared and mutual transformations, affecting the colonizer and the colonized equally.

Critics of Sahlins (and the structuralist school of anthropology that they claim he represents) argue that his anthropological project is confused. Thomas understands these creative processes by which people reflect on their cultural practice and name it as a code of practice as alienation of people from the roots of meaningful life. Instead of understanding custom as an innovation in practice that allows for its codification, they see it as a failing of the discipline that colludes with the colonial power to apologize for the triumph of administrative control. In the strongest claims of his argument, Thomas (1992a) makes the claim that most of the description of the gift exchange errs in the direction of assuming that it could ever have been a practice untainted by European habit or thought.

Sahlins makes an equally extreme response to this. He argues that the flourishing of indigenous cultural practices need not be seen as a failing of the imagination. Instead he argues that the inventive capacities of social relationships sustain humans in making cultural life, albeit somewhat differently, but still driving towards a meaningful expression of their regular daily experience. For Sahlins, especially in his later work (1992, 1994, 1995), the study of cultural life led him deeply into how people practised it innovatively to the end of finding meaning in vicissitudes and hope in its alterations and transformations.

Assessments of Indian votive sacrifice: Holi to Diwali

Sahlins's insights into the processes of making cultural life meaningful in new ways resonate through many circumstances of postcolonial politics, but one significant development has been addressed by his student Kelly. Kelly writes of the rituals of the Indian labourers in Fiji, the labourers whose lives changed irrevocably when they left India for the sugar plantations of the small colony in the late nineteenth and early twentieth centuries. The departures from India created new difficulties among the Hindu community who wished to maintain the habits by which caste might be sustained and remade. They made some attempts to renew and purify caste relations with ritual celebrations, especially after the ship's passage to Fiji and the work on the plantations made the observance of caste and the pollution of social life almost unavoidable. Early in the years of the colony, the Fiji-Indians (as they then called themselves or the Indo-Fijians as others more politely came to call them in later years) practised the ritual of Holi, a renewal ritual that sought to lift the rigid status markers of wealth and caste for a short period of time. In days of licence and celebration, the community tore apart and rebuilt the status system they sought to regenerate in their lives away from India.

Later years altered that story. After the Second World War, the Indo-Fijians bore different allegiances. No longer certain that they would leave their colonial bosses and return to a newly independent India, they sought to make a life in the small Fijian colony. The decision to remain in Fiji led them into a series of decisions: to leave the countryside for the town, to quit plantation work and to open small businesses, to plan marriages with each other across the country. This meant that they found new release to create religious life in the new context where their future did not mean returning to their past. They abandoned many distinctions of caste, enlivening only the differences of Brahmin and 'lower' people in their daily lives. But, more than before, they practised a daily life infused with rituals of devotion, and many of the Indo-Fijian community became practitioners of votive rituals in the Bhakti sect of Hinduism. Through these rituals they sought to purify life and thereby open their social relationships, and hence their lives, to new possibilities. With Fijian independence in 1970, the Indo-Fijian community made a show of commitment to the new nation and showed its solidarity with it by naming the ritual of 'Diwali', the festival of lights, the national ritual of celebration. Kelly observes that the festival of lights, like the votive rituals of daily life in 'Bhakti', suits the new lives of urban dwellers with small businesses, a kind of work ethic and devotional practice that wholly supported the new relations of labour and capitalist enterprise.

Conclusions: postcolonial history as the context for the study of exchange

I have approached the study of the colonial encounter, and what it has meant for the people described by the anthropologist, by examining the nature of trade and exchange in the early period of anthropological research. It is common enough to consider that anthropologists travelled with other Europeans to distant places, but the nature of their relationships to the colonial project varies greatly. The problems of understanding human history make it wholly necessary to deal with what people understand about what they are doing when they encounter each other and make an effort to open pathways of trade between them. One way of explaining the impoverishment of the villages and clans that anthropologists describe in their early monographs would focus on the commodity exchanges between Europeans and people living on the periphery of state society, in colonized territories. The wisdom taken from careful histories of these encounters could point out the mutual misunderstandings between the two. If anthropologists made this kind of assessment, then they could focus on the cultural elaborations of a basically economic encounter by giving primary importance to the social values of the figure that Mauss once called 'Homo economicus', when describing the economic rationalist whose decisions are informed by self-interest in maximizing wealth. But this judgement would be wrong.

I can recall an older warning from Mauss, introduced in the section about the limits of using economic man as a modern term in all societies. Is it dangerous to assume in all colonial encounters that the persons involved share a belief in the primacy of homoeconomicus, of the rationalist economic person? This assumption that all individuals work towards maximizing material wealth, in their own self interest, sometimes led early anthropologists to misunderstand the world around them, and more often led traders to err against the best interests of the people with whom they were trading. The examination of the history of trade makes that clearer.

Here, I looked at an example in which it can be shown that while it has been important to underline that many anthropologists first assume a common humanity with their research subjects, it remains the case that assuming that all humans are primarily concerned with economic well-being leads to a misunderstanding of just what can be transacted between them. The effect of assuming that a common wisdom about the nature of humanity prevails sometimes leads to error, when the specifics of that theory might be informed by the subtle ideological preferences of anthropologists.

Anthropology, as the discipline that made a virtue of difference and theorized social variation among humans, now finds itself with doubts about the effects of that project on the lives of people around the world. A history of misunderstanding is blamed, but surely that begs for better understanding? One of the points of departure must be a re-conceptualization of historical context. Some new efforts to understand context are already under way (see Dilley 1999), and they point to the need to think of anthropology as an investigation into the totality of human experience and exchanges as evidence of the total social fact. The analysis of anthropology in the postcolonial period could begin by assuming that humans were fundamentally social people, rather than simply economic beings. If so, it would be possible to explain how alienation creates and regenerates misunderstanding, rather than originates in it. That will be the focus of my attention in the next chapter.

Summary of chapter 6

Postcolonial anthropology explains how inequality emerges in colonial encounters through misunderstandings (often mutual) across different societies. Often anthropologists aim to describe the colonial context of historical encounters in order to clarify that domination and exploitation begin in the earliest days of the colony and continue to the present. This chapter examines three different early colonial encounters to investigate how some societies become indebted to colonial powers. First, we look at the alienation of the society of indigenous people of North America from their land by early American settlers who misunderstood the trade of wampum as something like a social contract and a political constitution, when in fact it was neither from the Manhattan Indian point of view. Second we examine the alienation of the labour of farm workers from their wider role in the south Asian religious and economic system by allegedly well-intentioned colonial administrators who sought to free them from economic exploitation likened to 'enslavement' in caste relations, but instead separated them from the jati system of society and the means to make a life in the subcontinent. Perversely, the migration and economic dependence of south Asians on the sale of their labour indenture contracts became complete as a result of colonial policy. Third, we examine the case of Fiji, the destination of the same labourers from south Asia whose caste relations and social identity had been destroyed by misplaced administrative policy. The mutual misunderstandings between early English traders and indigenous Fijians seeking exchange relationships with them do not explain the creation of indebtedness and poverty without accounting for the misperceptions of resident south Asians who remained concerned with the sacrifice of their labour. In summary, the Fijian case exposes best the analytical assumption underlying all the cases, namely that the 'colonial context' is defined as a background of forcible action by colonial powers, thereby reducing social relations to pre-social dominating forces. A better analysis of the 'colonial context' is required to expose how egalitarian relations across different societies are lost through negotiations and transactions of specific social relations.

7

MISTAKING HOW AND WHEN TO GIVE

In the last decades of the twentieth century, anthropologists began enquiries into how to account for the ways in which human history was played out through the practices of give and take, especially as used in the everyday lives of people. There had been increasing concern in the last part of the twentieth century to reflect upon the ways in which routine habits were weighted with meaning. It was especially the case that the habits of everyday life seemed inflected with the experiences of the past, even when those experiences might have held only small meaning to the immediacy of the present. The American anthropologist Margaret Mead wrote in an article for the popular journal *Redbook Magazine* about how the habits of a woman's domestic work in the 1960s household often imitated patterns set by her grandmothers. For example, routine tasks that would have been necessary with the household technologies of the early twentieth century – such as ironing linens to dry the faint dampness and to smooth them – did not arise out of necessity by the late part of the twentieth century when new household heating technology removed the worry of finding mildew forming in the laundry closet. By the 1970s a generation of suburban women proclaimed that they did not iron linens and thereby voiced some part of their freedom from domestic drudgery! Mead and her colleague Rhoda Métraux, with whom she wrote many articles, argued that dramatic modern social changes against the past might occur with the alteration of everyday and conventional practices, even among isolated groups of people. She proposed a more provocative alteration to American marriage practices, suggesting that marriage might be contracted for companionship and economic collaboration prior to child rearing, for the work of child rearing and even for companionship and social support after child rearing – a kind of two- or even three-step marriage would be arranged with the purpose of the union clearly in the mind of all the participants. Habits and laws of matrimonial transactions would thus move within the ken of the times. While many would dispute the 'real' revolutionary force of Mead's proposals for lower-middle-class women readers of a popular fashion and lifestyle magazine, they remain good examples of the new awareness of the widespread testing of habits and conventions of social life in the late twentieth century. Like marriage and household work, the habits of give and take are especially interesting for the anthropologist seeking to understand the force of historical experience in everyday life. The problem in all of this has been to describe in what ways historical experiences can lade habitual social action as non-conscious expressions of the past.

How are gifts given and received and what does the analysis of the practice, rather than the rules or the deep patterns of reciprocity, tell about social life? The answer to that question requires a theory of social action that goes beyond the analysis of ceremonial exchange to encompass small personal exchanges, thereby offering an even more broadly defined theory of exchange. A practice theory of gift exchange claims that anthropologists can raise a historical critique that would trace the legacy of powerful relationships through to the immediate era because analysis focuses on the 'how' of giving; that is the modes, strategies and deployments of gifts. The basic aim of practice theory is to expose the human subject's agency as aspiration that is demonstrated in hopeful social action. This is how the gift works to create the social agent in the matrix of a relational social hierarchy. Practice theorists' aims to expose the ambitious agent are fundamentally modernist: however their efforts to launch a new kind of historical critique that reflects back upon its own premises move them beyond modernist social theory. Practice theorists' effort to develop a reflexive sociology raises the potential for practice theory to escape modernist assumptions that might underlie or encage the theory, thereby pressing it into the creation of social hierarchy.

The sociologist Bourdieu, and somewhat differently the anthropologists Sahlins and Ortner, and even more profoundly differently, Strathern (who would reject the label of practice theory) argued that gift exchange was more than the transaction of objects: it was a knowledge practice. By calling gift exchange a knowledge practice, anthropologists understood that people understood both ceremonial exchange and little acts of give and take to be social acts that expressed conscious and non-conscious belief, and made social relationships at the same time as it recreated social structure. For the most part these anthropologists, especially the sociologist Bourdieu, focused on the work of culture as the playing out of non-conscious processes in everyday life. Bourdieu named this constellation of non-conscious social action 'habitus', using the label first developed by Mauss for routine behaviour, which has been shaped over years of experience as habits might be. Habitus is a mnemonic device for encoding generations of historical experience within a single person's body and acts, or within the shared acts of a number of people.

What difference does it make to think about the *practice* of gift exchange, 'the how of the gift', as a kind of argument about the shared human experience of history? How does thinking about the practice of giving and taking expose the work of reconciliation that people do in order to make sense of their experiences of the past? What memory or knowledge does the exchange of gifts hide from the consciousness of the participants in the exchange?

Power and misunderstanding in modernity

Passing time is an idiom that people use to let others know that they are waiting for more important matters which will be decided in the future. A person might wait for another to arrive, thereby passing the time; but the sense of the terms suggests that getting the time correct does matter to the effectiveness of our actions. When used idiomatically, it suggests that the actions of the present do not matter so much to what is yet to come. The timing of the gift changes everything about human exchanges because it makes people reflect and act upon their reflections. What people understand about the gift changes as they reflect upon it, and in turn changes the way they create their relationships with each other. The timing of the gift alters the power as it is played out in human relationships.

What does the study of the gift contribute to any analysis of power in human relationships? Of the ways in which power relationships can be established through giving gifts, perhaps the most significant would be the sense of timing that people use in gift giving. Although I have already described some uses of spiritual power in the example of the hau, there may be other ways to discuss power in the exchange of gifts. In this chapter, I will discuss how the timing of the gift changes everything about its implications for establishing power in human relations.

Careful timing serves the best ends of the giver of the gift, even if that is an anxious kind of situation. To be the host of the feast, or to be giving the dinner sets a claim or an obligation over the guests either to return the hospitality and keep the relationship, or not. You might think about the feasts that you might participate in at different seasonal holidays. Often there can be considerable consternation about where and with whom a holiday feast might be celebrated. In a different example, as in shared student households, it can be common for housemates to share the cooking, alternating responsibility for cooking dinners. If one housemate brings a spontaneous gift of wine to the table, others will think of responding with a gift of a similar kind. Unfortunately, if they mistakenly give a bottle too soon, perhaps the next night, the gift smacks of a 'pay-back' or an insult to the friend who made the first gesture of generosity.

In the largest picture, a question arises: How do people mutely play out the continuation of traditional habits into modern times? This question introduces the central problems of practice theory: How do non-conscious beliefs play out in society? How do human agents reproduce society? How does the use of knowledge succeed in creating the power dynamics of social hierarchy? How does misunderstanding contribute to the continuation of social relations?

Some of these questions expose the failures of modernity; that is, they show how the problems of the older more traditional society continue into modern times. The description of continuing traditional beliefs in modern times poses the possibility of a powerful criticism of modernity. However, another contribution of this work arises. That is, the opportunity to reflect upon the nature of unconscious and unspoken knowledge in social relationships. Here, the case that Bourdieu elaborates for Algeria becomes interesting for what it can tell about the character of unspoken knowledge in the social imaginary.

The Berber case

Throughout this chapter, I will draw primarily upon discussions of the gift in North Africa. Although the history of exchange in the region had been examined carefully in the work of Polyani, who drew attention to the local (and internal) mechanisms of capital formation as they surfaced in cultural idioms of exchange and barter, I take his work to be largely historical, and not ethnographic except for his argument to give attention to cultural features of history. Although North Africa famously presents anthropologists of law and religion with the compelling example of the differential force of rule in the practice of Islamic belief (for early work see Gellner 1973, 1981 and more recently Messick 1993), some of the most interesting concerns for anthropological methods and ethnography come out of research into marriage customs and feasting in the region. My concerns here will be with everyday practice and belief, and the extents and limits of its flexibility in the region. Most of my references in this chapter are drawn from anthropological work conducted in Algeria and Morocco. I examine the research of Bourdieu (1979), Geertz *et al.* (1979), Rosen (2002) and to a lesser extent, Gellner (1973, 1981) for what it explains about the relationship between power, the conjectures of belief, and the dissemblance of exchange practice. Bourdieu, more than the rest, addressed directly the practice of giving and receiving gifts in North Africa, and also made the most extensive commitment to the people of the region, especially the Berbers who lived nomadically throughout the different nation states. By comparison, Gellner, and the collection edited by Geertz *et al.* (1979) made the character of rationality the matter of concern. These anthropologists found that disentangling economic rationality from philosophical rationality would prove enlightening, not only for the fuller understanding of the region, but also for the process of doing anthropology.

North African anthropology holds the attention of the ethnographers of gift exchange, as well as the regional ethnographers I have mentioned, because in that cultural region economic rationality can seemingly overwhelm all other explanation of human transactions, and at the same time efforts to establish the rule of that rationality can turn quickly to farce. There always exists a double or triple or quadruple level of understanding to which all social relations turn. Bourdieu describes this as *misconnaissance*. His translator names it 'misrecognition'. Social relations are not governed by the rule of recognition; instead, misrecognition generates the social life of the group. But, in general, ethnographers of gift exchange are challenged with how to account for misrecognition.

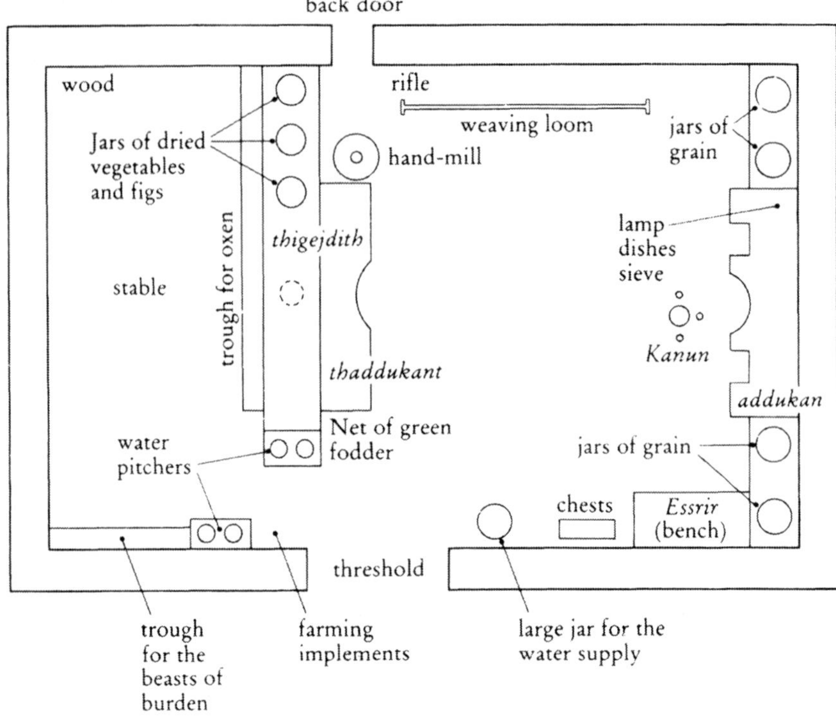

Figure 7.1 The Kabyle house plan shows the routine organization of household space through which men and women move every day. Bourdieu shows that the space works as a mnemonic for the history of men and women's shared experience and identity. From *The Logic of Practice* by Pierre Bourdieu 1980 (1990), translated by Richard Nice, copyright Polity Press, Cambridge, UK; Stanford University Press, Palo Alto, CA. First published in French 1980 by Les Éditions de Minuit as *Le Sens Pratique.*

The historical record of Bourdieu's research work in Algeria shows him to strengthen his commitments to understanding how people reproduce social inequalities, even while they aim for social equality. Consider first the honorary feasts in the Berber communities, which Bourdieu described during his sojourn there as a French soldier in the period of the Algerian wars on the eve of independence. Most commonly the feasts celebrated the marriage of a woman and man from the same region, creating relationships that could be consolidated with the rhetorical language of 'blood' and honour. These marriages of cousins and close acquaintances sustained community sentiments as they shared similar values and beliefs. Speeches addressed the history of trade, exchange and alliance between the different families, sometimes envisioned as well-worn pathways or roads of exchange along which women and wealth flowed routinely. Reinterpreting Bourdieu's concern with social reproduction and power into a concern with the sentiments of the collectivity, Hildred Geertz explained that the event of the wedding feast and the speeches in honour of the hosts served to create a sense of felt community that reproduced its interests and its futures in well-travelled pathways of exchange relations.

Berber households located the sensibility of order in everyday life, dividing men's and women's labour to different purposes for the social and economic sustenance of the household. Berber households included extended kin and the women worked together (and not as a single housewife as in the nuclear family). Women exerted considerable power in the choice of a wife for the son. This wife would be a member of the household for some years, and the women claimed that they did not want to tolerate an individual who could not share the domestic work and routines of the household. Perhaps it is not surprising that Bourdieu had been able to show the design of a Berber house as a blueprint for the organization of memory and the regulation of social behaviour. His illustration of Berber households becomes a model of the non-conscious practice and belief, made all the more apparent in circumstances in which the rules of its operation might be threatened. The organization of the Berber house is illustrated in Figure 7.1.

On occasions when women married into the group from greater distances, the very presence of the newcomers and their undisciplined habits posed a problem to the community's sense of well-being and cohesion. At marriage feasts, the arrival of a bride from a more distant place required the recognition of an honourable history of association across that distance, and speech givers recalled longer pathways of exchange over a deeper history. Distant or foreign women marrying into Berber households posed considerable concern, such that it became necessary to create stronger claims for the honour of the match. Conversely, with the more powerful claims to honour came more serious injunctions against the defamation of that ideology. For example, the regulation of women's sexuality became a matter of wider societal concern, rather than the concern of the women of the household alone.

Bourdieu aimed throughout his career to create opportunities for reasonable discussion between North African and European scholars, by establishing a journal for intellectual collaboration as well as study and research positions for students from the region. In the first years when Bourdieu lived in Algiers, he spent his days in the rural villages in order to describe the political life of the community as it was made and reproduced in ceremonial feasts as well as in everyday life. In later years, he took a post at the university as a young man, and continued to support Algerian researchers and students throughout his career. Much of Bourdieu's work supporting the North African community was not made public, yet his interests in these people did move him into a new development in his scholarship overall. At the very end of his career, he wrote about the suffering in the livelihood of the poor and the immigrants who had been excluded socially from the normal pathways and moved to the hidden quarters of the European city.

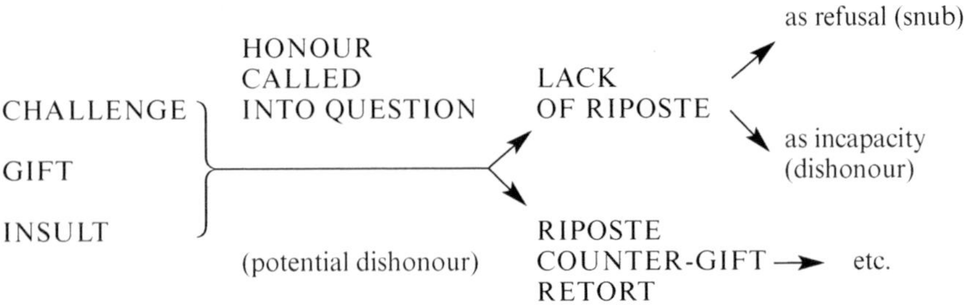

Figure 7.2 Bourdieu's model of challenge and riposte shows the dynamic structure of feasting. A Berber leader wins prestige by demonstrating his ability to be generous by giving the most wonderful feast of recent memory, at just the right time. From *The Logic of Practice* by Pierre Bourdieu 1980 (1990), translated by Richard Nice, copyright Polity Press, Cambridge, UK; Stanford University Press, Palo Alto, CA. First published in French 1980 by Les Éditions de Minuit as *Le Sens Pratique.*

His biographers tell us that as a soldier of the end of the colonial period, Bourdieu became an ethnographer more by accident than by plan, although he long harboured a fascination for the contemporary debates in anthropology. Bourdieu's intellectual biographer, Jenkins (1992), reminds us that as a researcher of social hierarchy and power in France and in social life most generally, the Algerian experience disturbed Bourdieu and changed his overall career dramatically. Reed-Danahay (2004) in her intellectual biography argued that these years radicalized the young Bourdieu, but in personal ways that had remained unexpressed until the end of his career when he theorized just what autobiography should be (see Bourdieu 2004). While in the Berber village Bourdieu recorded the means by which the Berber leaders established power in the community simply by wining the respect of the rest of the villagers. The festive events follow one upon the other, enhancing the reputation or prestige of those hosts of each feast who surpassed the last. Often, these were marriage feasts which all of the village attended. Not only did the feasters celebrate the marriage of the couple, but they also enjoyed the speeches, jokes, banter and displays of generosity by the hosts. On these occasions a host could establish his reputation as an honourable man, well able to treat his guests in grand style. Leaders could draw others together with them in acts of generous hospitality; yet, Bourdieu's analysis shows that hospitality could also be a suitable modality for the generation of powerful new alliances and the creation of dominant and subordinate partners across the households of the village. Consider Bourdieu's model for the competitive exchange and competitive hospitality of feast giving, shown in Figure 7.2 above.

To ask about the timing of exchanges is to consider that giving the gift might not be a straightforward act of generosity, but a self-conscious and self-interested act of power. Of course, there has been ample evidence of the way in which a person can enter into competitions or tournaments of giving wealth away. It allows for the deploying of the gift in many different ways: as a challenge to another person to respond in kind, a request for future relations with a new partner, and perhaps the pacification of raw feelings. But the timing of the gift opens up different meanings for its use. The timing of the gift changes everything about its significance, just as when a gift of appreciation is given too soon. How do people misunderstand each other? If an anthropologist gives attention to the timing of exchanges, then how does that enable better arguments about how to live? Anthropologists did that by making a distinction between what people said they knew and what they did.

A comparison between Bourdieu's and Lévi-Strauss's timing of gift exchange

Chapter 6 examined the importance of alliance theory in the period after the Second World War by thinking most carefully about the substance of the gift. This chapter looks at a complementary approach that builds upon alliance theory and critiques it by examining the role of time in either of the theories.

I compare practice approaches with structuralist ones to show that the work of time in the two cases is remarkably different. On the one hand, time either collapses or unfolds in the structuralist project. On the other hand, in approaching the study of practice, anthropologists did not give much attention to its ambiguities, mysteries or uncertainties of social relations. First, I will go back to concerns raised in the previous chapter because so much of what follows here criticizes some basic concepts and explanations worked out by Lévi-Strauss in his structural theory of social variation. While Lévi-Strauss's alliance theory aimed to expose the principle of reciprocity underlying all of human society, other scholars aimed to explain the implications of mistaking the grounds of social life for ideology and belief about society.

Lévi-Strauss explains that the course of time passes in two different forms of reciprocity across the generations: the short cycle of exchange between clans and the long cycle of exchange. In the short cycle, clans gift back the gift of a woman within a generation of time. The clansmen whose sister leaves them to marry a man of another clan will receive the gift of a wife from the women who are sisters of the other clan. That is, a Clan A woman leaves her brothers to marry a Clan B man. Soon, within the same or in one generation, a Clan B woman leaves her brothers to marry a Clan A man. This preferential marriage rule, or the principle of marrying back into the other clan, mirrors the short cycle of reciprocity and the marriage of cross-cousins. For a man in a patrilineal society, that would mean he would seek to marry one of his mother's brother's several daughters. Lévi-Strauss diagrammed it as shown in Figure 7.3a.

In other marriage arrangements, a longer time passed before a clan recovered a bride from the same clan to whom they had given a bride. These longer

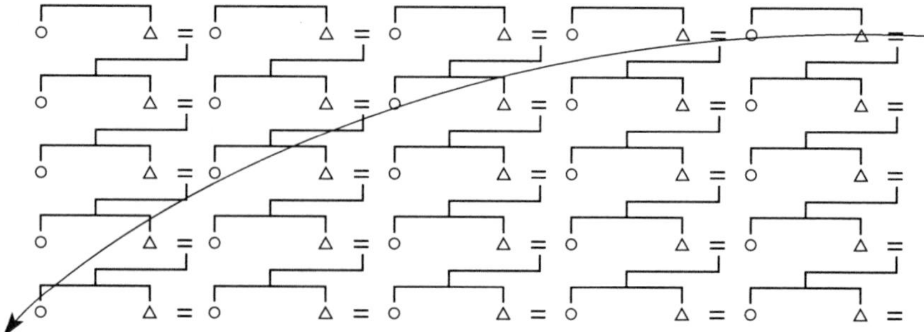

(a) Cycle of reciprocity. Marriage with the mother's brother's daughter (long cycle).

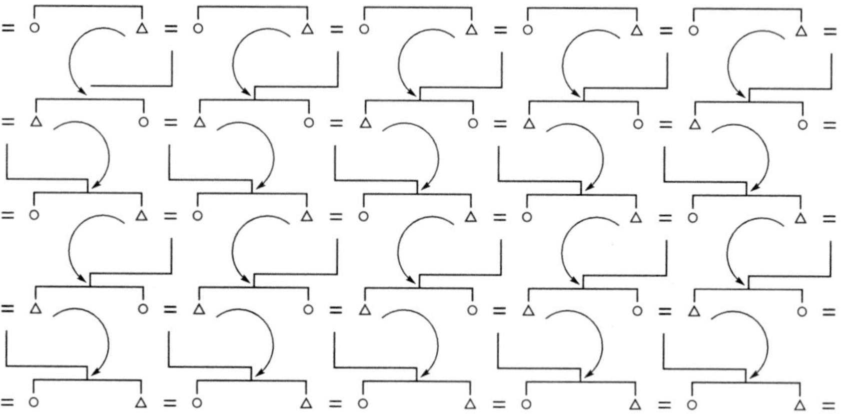

(b) Cycle of reciprocity. Marriage with the father's sister's daughter (short cycle).

Figure 7.3 Cycles of reciprocity (long and short) over several generations show that the passing of time is marked from one generation to the next by each moiety. Men of one moiety return a sister for a wife received from the opposite moiety in an older generation, thereby preserving the structure of social organization over time. From *Elementary Structures of Kinship* by Claude Lévi-Strauss 1967 (1949), first published in France under the title, *Les Structures élémentaires de la parenté* in 1949. A revised edition was published under the same title in France in 1967. Translation copyright by Beacon Press. Reprinted by permission of Beacon Press, Boston.

cycles most commonly included a preference for arranging a marriage with a cross-cousin. For a man in a patrilineal society, that would mean he might seek to marry one of his father's sister's daughters. Lévi-Strauss diagrammed it as shown in Figure 7.3b.

I am fascinated by Lévi-Strauss's uses of the alliances made across clans, as they spell out over several generations to achieve the literal accomplishment of the reciprocal exchange of women between clans. This accomplishment within living memory of the clans (that is, within five generations) allows them to observe their own success in keeping reciprocal relationships. Often the ritual event could be diagrammed to show the success of the work.

Other anthropologists, for example Leach and Godelier, each argued this a little bit differently in their attempt to understand social inequality within systems of reciprocal exchange and marriage alliances. Leach tried to show the complexities of an ideological political system with a sociological reality of marriage alliances. Godelier demonstrated the alternative forms of inequality generated in those societies in which wives were welcomed and reciprocated with bride-wealth, and those societies in which men reciprocated with other women, usually their own sisters and clanswomen.

Leach's (1954) study in Burma showed that alternative systems of marriage – a system of keeping reciprocity in short cycles and a system of keeping it in longer ones – might co-exist within the same villages. He argues that hierarchy in Burma becomes a very interesting problem because the exchange of women succeeds in differentiating men to greater and greater degrees of hierarchy over several generations. In a frustrating attempt to explain how reciprocal exchange in marriage alliances could foster hierarchy rather than equality, Leach ultimately surrenders to the older argument. The social differences collapse as the interaction between the two systems of marriage leads to the point where the simplest work of alliance making succeeds: giving your sister to men from whom you have received a wife. At this point, the structural principle becomes the same as an ideological conviction.

Godelier's (1986) study in Highland New Guinea looked at how men used knowledge to establish systems of prestige based on the differentiation of expertise in warfare, sorcery, or ritual and cosmological knowledge. In this research, Godelier compared the ritual exchanges at marriage. He pointed out that in many New Guinea Highland societies, such as that of the Kawelka Big Man described by Andrew and Marilyn Strathern, when a man married a woman he gave away bride wealth to her brothers. By comparison, in some New Guinea Highland societies, when a man married a woman, he immediately gave a sister to his wife's clan's men in order for her to be a wife to one of them. The simple focus for Godelier's analysis is the fact that bride wealth could represent, or signify, a woman in some societies, whereas in other societies a woman represented, or could stand for, nothing else but another woman. Again the simple focus for Godelier was that a woman was exchanged for a woman. A very neat and tidy paradox emerges: where wealth can signify the gift of a woman, the extremes of variation of hierarchy among men could be achieved through gift exchange and ceremonial feasting; but where women can only signify the need for another woman, men's hierarchy emerges more fixedly.

The researchers each address the larger problem of this chapter: just what is the relationship between ideology and sociological fact of relationships? Each of them addresses the problem of inequality as a function of timing of exchanges, in relation to the signification of exchange, but in different ways.

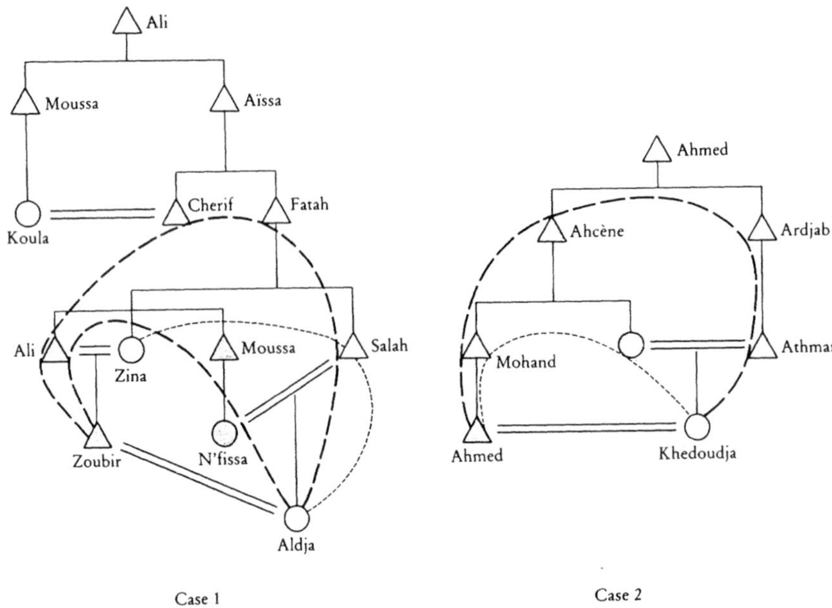

Figure 7.4 Matrimonial exchange 'misrecognizes' the central importance of the ideological purpose of the marriage (shown as the dotted lines) thereby hiding the structures behind the union (shown as the solid lines). From *The Logic of Practice* by Pierre Bourdieu 1980 (1990), translated by Richard Nice, copyright Polity Press, Cambridge, UK; Stanford University Press, Palo Alto, CA. First published in French 1980 by Les Éditions de Minuit as *Le Sens Pratique.*

The principal theorist to address the timing of exchange is Bourdieu, but in order to think about his argument more clearly, I will turn again to the Berber research on the eve of Algerian independence.

The kinship diagrams drawn by Bourdieu (Figure 7.4) trace the explanation for the marriage and the history of exchanges between the clans. What he outlines better than most is the ways in which patterns of marriage emulate basic rules of exogamy, even where the households involved do not hold the principles by which they plan marriages up to scrutiny and discussion. The claims for the work of marriage might run ultimately in the same direction as the claims for the honours of marriage, but a more superficial analysis would have assumed that other arrangements for marriage would prevail. For Bourdieu's analysis, it is helpful to recall the new illustration of the genealogical chart in Figure 7.4. The illustration provides the reader with a visual image of Bourdieu's argument that the reciprocal exchange of sisters in a marriage alliance is misrecognized as the outcome of histories of men's honour.

Intriguingly, this 'marriage' of principles of exogamy (to parallel cousins) with ideology of honours and households and their overt alliances leads to the elaboration of a new theory. The conjunction of local explanation and acts with the regulating rules and habit of interaction draws attention wholly to the work of how people practise their social relations. Bourdieu argues that by giving attention to the timing of exchange, rather than seeking the hidden principles of it, the anthropologist can give a fuller account of power.

Pathways of exchange

Practice theorists show that the exercise of power in exchanges coerces people into gradually altering the habits of generations into new forms. It remained common enough for all present to realize that the long-term habits of marrying women from adjacent villages could gradually change to include marriage with other women. Over years the agreements between kin came to include consultations with the new wife's kin, and thus new ways became routines. As people told and retold the links and connections that made them relatives, they learned the stories and genealogies very well. New pathways through the memory of associations soon became habitual pathways. It is this play of power, strategizing and association that fixated Bourdieu's attention to the lifestyle of the Berbers. Although Bourdieu pays little obvious tribute to either Durkheim's or Mauss's work, he undertakes a new elaboration of Mauss's claim: that the gift constitutes and concentrates social processes and thereby uses the analysis of gift exchange as an instance of the total social fact. He does this by examining the dynamics of the uses of time in exchange relations in ceremonial life, in the everyday life of the household, and in the small personal exchanges of daily life.

In extending the work of ceremonial exchange to everyday life, Bourdieu notes the uses of small gifts to mark how the personal exchanges of the Berber household move its members to fuller realizations of the orthodoxy of their relationships. In this, his study underlines the exhaustive role that exchange plays in daily life. Although he does not conceptualize his problem following Mauss's concepts, his careful empirical description of the pervasive habit of give and take in everyday life sustains the claims of Mauss that some habits constitute a total social fact.

How do people exchange small gifts, or even ceremonial ones, to make social life more hazardous or challenging? Could there be pleasure in agonistic exchanges, such as the competitive feasting in North Africa? It might be wise to doubt the clarity and order of Bourdieu's account of the Berber lifestyle, given other studies of the region that emphasize its fluidity and peripatetic knowledge structures. Perhaps Bourdieu's emphasis on embedded tradition of everyday life resonates throughout the book. This is a virtue in many respects, because finding the details of life to bear out some sense of meaning has been the hallmark of much anthropology.

The difficulty of accepting Bourdieu's account as an account of the totality of life arises from a number of other ethnographic accounts that make duplicity and dissemblance the problem of the day. Theft and trickery remain one of the more common details of transactions in the Berber social networks. A debate about the importance of conjecture and theft emerged. No ethnographer would claim that sheep stealing is a definitive characteristic of the Berber villages, but the question is how to reconcile this habit with the routines and traditionalism described by Bourdieu.

Second, it is important to consider how the disruptions of daily life under colonialism might be considered more fully in the account of how Berber villagers exchange gifts with each other, and how they exchange across villages. Bourdieu certainly takes criticism for isolating his account of Berber life, as if it were a kind of pre-modern existence. I think that this claim needs scrutiny under fuller consideration of the problems of dissemblance and disruption of meaningful communication in the early or late colonial period.

Translation of customary and colonial trade law

Geertz retells a joke shared with him by a Jewish informant (notably after the expulsion of the Jews from Morocco), recorded in his field notes in 1968, to illustrate just how difficult it is to record empirical examples of the extent to which historical knowledge is shared among a group of people and the record of an informant's commentary can be indicative of a system of belief. The fact that the joke has disturbed later generations of anthropologists because it presents the manipulations of social memory and stereotypes as indexes to collective memory makes it all the more compelling as an example of the complex problem of how to translate fieldwork experience into anthropological knowledge. Geertz tells the story from the early colonial period of 1912, of how a Jewish trader named Cohen uses and manipulates Berber law and colonial French law in order to win back legal compensation for his loss of trading goods in a house raid against him during his visit to Berber territories. After an initial failure to rob the armed Cohen, the Berber thieves (who came from a tribe different from that tribe with whom Cohen had his trading agreement) dressed as Jewish women in order to enter the house by trickery. Cohen's companions die in the raid, but he hides and escapes with only his life, to avoid his death in the house fire that the thieves planned to set. Cohen secures the agreement of the French captain that he may seek compensation under customary law, but at his own risk. Cohen does seek his "ar', the customary compensation, with the help of armed Berber Marmushans, of a different tribe to the robbers. They kidnap a shepherd of the robber tribe and take the tribe's sheep as their compensation. This theft is recognized by the robber tribe as judicious appropriation under the trade-pact system, and they ask Cohen to make a fair-minded selection of sheep to meet the demands of his 'ar against their earlier theft of his goods. Cohen makes a selection and returns to the colonial fort to show the success of his journey. The incredulous French captain in charge of the fort imprisons him as a suspected Berber spy and impounds his sheep.

The story shows that the early attempts by colonial authorities failed to erase a customary trading law that gave access by Jewish traders, especially those fluent in Berber, like Cohen, to Berber tribes. Cohen, entering into trading with Berber tribes under the system of trade pact, 'mizrag', also had recourse to compensation, 'ar, if the system broke down. While colonial law would respond normally with punitive action against the Berber thieves who made the house-raids on Cohen during his trading journey to Marmusha, in this case the militia could not protect Cohen or find him justice because the territory fell beyond their reach, as a geopolitical area, its people out of the control of colonial administrative forts. Customary laws of political and trade relations remained effective where new colonial laws could not be enforced. But success in customary trading law brings Cohen no joy because it does not make sense to the colonial officials. In the imagination of administrative officers the success of customary law appears as collusion between Berber and Jew, an impossible situation in a Berber area where the French military worked in order to protect the Jewish residents.

The story also shows that the irreconcilable stereotype of deep conflict between Jew, Berber, and French does not apply to the event. The anthropologist records explications of other people's explications. As Geertz writes,

> Here, in our text, sorting out would begin with distinguishing the three unalike frames of interpretation ingredient in the situation, Jewish, Berber, and French, and would then move on to show how (and why) at that time, in that place, their co-presence produced a situation in which systematic misunderstanding reduced traditional form to social farce. What tripped Cohen up, and with him the whole ancient pattern of social and economic relationships within which he functioned, was a confusion of tongues.
>
> (Geertz 1973: 9)

These contingencies in the work of exchange, especially the deployment of customary laws of exchange, can never escape the work of ethnography. Code is not conduct. The event might have unfolded in so many different ways, perhaps with the Berbers resisting both the motive to continue the trade pact and the subjection to French colonial law. Perhaps they would have murdered Cohen and his friends instead of negotiating over the cull of the sheep. Geertz would remind Bourdieu that ethnographers must struggle to keep ethnography alive to the gist of the events, to the sense of the communication, or risk reducing it to a private joke.

Geertz provides readers with an interesting conjunction between the vague and misunderstood: ambiguous uses of customary trade law within Berber social relations converge with the confusion of colonial relations. Geertz considers the events as a farce, generated by a 'confusion of tongues', not by the imminence of orthodoxy of knowledge practice. Past madness is bound up in the figurative Jew, becomes reasonable as told by the Jewish Cohen. It is retold as a fable for the present, but it is a fable told as a joke. In this case the joke, albeit a poor joke, suggests that anthropologists might be a bit suspicious of the orthodoxy of colonialists' knowledge. He shares notes from his field book, which show readers how sheep stealing is also a kind of law.

Geertz's story poses an unusual question about relations of power, exchange and debt by reference to an example of sheep stealing as a case in which a man's exchanges are easily misunderstood and affect the plans for his timely delivery of the wealth of sheep as legal compensation into the hands of the rightful recipient. Deeply agonistic exchange appears as collusion between enemies in this difficult and unpleasant joke from the earliest part of the century. Yet more than 50 years later, informants remember the shambles of colonial relations and the strange playing out of power within them.

Consider Geertz's claim that it matters that people mistranslate different versions of how to exchange. Here, the story might make sense of past madness by exposing it. The misrecognition of Cohen who has been robbed by Berbers disguised as Jewish women; as a Berber who has recourse to action through an exchange relation known as 'mizrag'; as a legal plaintiff who can appeal to the French colonial soldiers, presents a problem to practice theory's claims. What evidence shows that there is intentional miscalculation in making a virtue of confusion in power relations? Fifty years after the earliest colonial occupation of Morocco, what distinguishes misrecognition from camp humour and from social farce?

A question to pursue for better understanding of misrecognition might be: How does a person recognize the historical and structural limitations on their habits and change them? Practice theory can claim that history repeats itself as farce because the misrecognition of power in social relationships can certainly lead to continuities of inequality in society. But Geertz's example suggests that history repeats itself as farce when people know that they make a travesty of those relations as a means to setting a different course from the one authored by events of the past.

Conjecture, strategy and misrecognition as problems of collective memory

A consideration of deception and conjecture in social relations can help anthropologists to clarify the ways people make social relationships work over time. Some of those working in this new approach followed the projects of those philosophers who argued that there was no structure to society. Further, they proposed that human society was a historical product and not informed by deeper meanings than those that pertained in the present. They argued that a person was no more than the sum of his public social acts. Of course, the rejoinder to this included the complaint that a person could be deluded about the structures that moved him or her to act as he or she did. One of the concerns raised in this critique must be whether the focus on immediate daily existence actually raised new questions about the importance of agency in shaping social relationships.

Recalling three decades of research experience in Morocco, and reflecting upon movements of people across North Africa more generally, Rosen (2002) poses a number of important questions about the nature of collective memory in the region. It might be judicious to say that in his reflections on the ways in which people come to shared understanding of the past, he has posed an important contribution to the problem left unsolved by Bourdieu's practice theory: namely, how do people make explicit and change the assumptions and beliefs by which they live? Rosen recounts how when 'asked to relate their own historical memories people would often refer to moments when the existing sets of dominant relationships were in a state of uncertainty or upheaval' (Rosen 2002: 90). Taking the work of the timing of power relations as a kind of social game that people played, Rosen tells us how people understood change as a reconfiguring of social relations, a recognition that a possibility existed for 'the board to be swept clean' so that 'a new round of the game could begin' (p. 90). The costs of that reconfiguring of collective memory can be intriguing for scholars. Anthropologists might ask how memories of whole groups (not simply individuals) disappear from the collective history. Here's one example. What does an anthropologist make of a collective history that insists on a memory of a past that has no continuing connection with the present? He takes the case of a public garden built by French administrators in the colonial period, which continues to be accessed intermittently by the public and admired for its 'pathways, plantings and benches' (p. 94). As a physical space, collective concern for it gives it a conceptual significance to felt relationships that could be made through it as a location of memory. Does it underscore the fact that the possibility of a shared public space existed once in the past, but cannot exist again with any certainty? In a second example, Rosen asks us to consider what precisely does an anthropologist make of the absence of the official memory of the Jews in shared narrative of Moroccan history? Or more difficult still, what does an anthropologist make of a collective memory of Jewish folksongs, sung by Muslims (some of them Jewish converts to Islam) with nostalgia for a people who are all but gone?

Conclusions: history as misrecognitions of exchange relations

In this chapter, I have examined the ways in which gift exchange engendered misunderstandings, by showing how competitive individuals used the ambiguities of the meaning and reason of exchange to differentiate people into hierarchical relations with each other. I have also examined two cases in which the participants in exchange knowingly submit themselves to playing with ambiguity in the games of establishing themselves in differential power relations with each other. What does it mean to recognize that all the tricks in the game are being played against you, or that you are using all the tricks of the trade to establish your prestige vis à vis your exchange partners?

In an assessment of the playing out of gender ideology (rather than men's hierarchy) in the Pacific, Marilyn Strathern offers respect and caution for Bourdieu's theory of knowledge in the coining of the term misrecognition. In Bourdieu's practice theory she reminds us that he offers an important insight that humans bear a double consciousness. It is Bourdieu's fundamental insight that people give great importance to the overt discussion of their agency within the conventionally accepted terms of their lives, at the same time that they operate with conscious awareness of less overt reasons for being.

> If the system is to work, the agents must not be entirely unaware of the truth of their exchanges, which is made explicit in the anthropologist's model, while at the same time they must refuse to know and above all to recognize it.
>
> (Strathern 1988: 304)

The relationship between the different orders of knowledge, the openly discussed account and the hidden knowledge receives my attention here because Strathern makes important points about practice theory in general, but not for Melanesia alone.

In Strathern's terms, the hiding or purposeful refusal to recognize the knowledge makes potent use of its role for determining action. But she points out that yet another situation occurs. Sometimes people aim to make clear the basis of what they know; for example, Melanesians aim to expose the gender of things and presumably know when they conceal it. This would fit with many aspects of Bourdieu's model of misrecognition, if there were not yet another kind of problem of misunderstanding that deserves discussion. Strathern writes, 'the habit of finding the generative dynamic of relationships in the gender of things remains important. People cannot hide what they do not know' (1988: 304). Such a statement opens the possibility that a total coherent system remains a fantasy of the social scientist, rather than of the informants. Do informants remain less concerned with the efforts to explain life in its totality and more concerned to acknowledge the relational basis of what they know and do?

The history of anthropology in the modern period provides few answers to the question of whether the informant's perspective on their history can ever be a total one. Many scholars claim that only the anthropologist carries the distinctly total view, and that is a critical project in its best forms. The evolutionists examined the environmental adaptations and the technological innovations made by societies allegedly made in transition to states of more advanced civilization. Functionalists rejected the false history of the evolutionists for its privileging of European values. They described the uses people made of their social institutions in creating specific, holistic understandings of the world in which they lived. Comparativists sought insights from the juxtaposition of local understandings with European interrogations. Some of these analyses, Mauss's included, suggest a return to evolutionist accounts but do not fully embrace the evolutionary model of history. Structuralists sought a general theory of social variation that opened out the possibility of explaining social variation across the world, without resorting to false history or racist ideology. But the analysis of the structuring principles of society did not account for how people might change the conditions in which they lived. That entailed envisioning their subjectivity at the nexus of many social relationships. In the next two chapters, I will examine the ways in which people visualize who they are and how they should keep relationships to each other through exchanges of wealth.

Summary of chapter 7

Practice theorists argue that a total account of social relations within one society can be made through analysing the ways in which both ceremonial and small everyday gifts are expressions of a shared historical consciousness. This shared consciousness is complex, being a product of forgetting the conflicts and negotiations of the past so that it is empowered to work non-consciously in the present. Bourdieu called shared consciousness 'habitus' because it embraced actions and beliefs that non-consciously shaped daily bodily behaviour and social actions, but he also made misrecognition a central aspect of habitus. Misrecognition is a shared mistake of understanding about how the social processes of one society work to reproduce social differences. For example, some people manage the passing of time in manipulative strategies to create prestige and power. A comparison of the work of time in the kinship diagrams of Lévi-Strauss and Bourdieu aims to clarify the way in which it is differently bound to structure by theories of practice and by theories of structuralism. A question is how do people recognize the sleight of hand in the workings of habitus and change them? A comic and provocative example comes from Geertz. Working in North African society, as did Bourdieu, Geertz asks what sense should anthropologists make of the meaning of past events retold as a self-deprecating ethnic joke that intentionally points up the confusions of exchanges as theft and as customary compensation payments? Strathern, hailing Bourdieu's self-assessment, points out that misrecognition works to reproduce social hierarchies only if people know at some level that they should expect to be duped by others. The challenge to anthropologists would be to provide a total explanation of social processes in one society that describe how people hide some relationships from themselves even as they pursue connections with others.

Part II

POSTMODERN REFLECTIONS

Critiques of subjectivity

8

ENVISIONING BOURGEOIS SUBJECTS

In this chapter I ask what the bourgeois subject knows as a result of visualizing his or her subjectivity in and through acts of exchange with other people. I continue an enquiry into false consciousness that I began in the previous chapter; here I ask how people come to see their relationships with each other through the practice of exchanging wealth. More than that, I ask how the visualization of the subjectivity of the participants can change the meaning of their gift exchange. In turn, I ask what is perhaps an unpleasant question: how far is it possible to claim that the bourgeois subject is alienated from full knowledge of his or her conditions of existence?

In the introduction to this book, I discussed anthropological argument in connection with the Enlightenment fascination with human reason, and further, its testing or its trial in the essay. In this chapter I will discuss what visualizing subjectivity might mean for understanding the human subject as a reasoning person. How does a reasonable person make moral decisions and exert judgements about the obligations he or she keeps and does not keep, if that person can visualize the different kinds of relationships he or she holds with other people?

There are numerous models for the human subject as a thinking and reasoning being. In the most common sense in west European scholarship humans are sentient beings, and therefore different from animals, but the difference between humans and animals (or between the brain and the mind) is not my concern here. In the first part of this book I wrote about the legacy of the Noble Savage in anthropology, the attempts to understand the world directly through experiencing it, the ways in which comparison made it intelligible, and the principles that anthropologists enlisted in a social science of human variation. Sceptical understanding is common to all of these developments of modernist anthropology. For its intellectual inspirations, the discipline owes a great deal to the philosophy of Descartes, who showed scholars that they possessed both minds and bodies. His philosophy has helped anthropologists to see that because they were both minds and bodies, they could know things by either medium of intellect or sense. The two capacities for acquiring knowledge led people to question what they perceive through their body and senses, or what they assume to be true by calculation. This constitutes a modernist project in anthropology, which affirms the importance of reason as a kind of rational argument expressed in language, especially writing.

Maussian scholars critiqued the Cartesian distinction between mind and body by recalling that the individual is not natural, but social as demonstrated by the history of ways of being a person. Dumont, for one, discussed thoughtfully the various models or icons of personhood that emerged in the Western Enlightenment tradition (Dumont 1970). He addressed the idea of the possessive individual, a concept distinguished in the Hobbesian and Lockean traditions. By possessive individual he means the person as the proprietor of the self (Macpherson 1963). For example, the possessive individual is a person who believes he or she possesses a self, or sometimes more explicitly a private conscience. The political theorist Macpherson showed that the concept endured and dominated for centuries because the education of the possessive individual becomes a matter of political and personal responsibility to the whole of society, even when the possessive individual emerged in Adam Smith's theory as the economic rationalist and champion of free trade.

Dumont and later anthropologists draw on the insights of Mauss about the interpolated nature of the person, a category that emerges with the articulation of two aspects of human subjectivity to critique the concept of possessive individualism. Mauss showed how the sense that the human subject holds or bears a private self emerged at the same time with the different sense that the human subject must also enact a public persona. Mauss made an early and important contribution to this debate, one that might go unnoticed because it depends on analysing a very brief and convoluted essay written close to the end of his career. His essay on *The Category of the Person* (Carruthers, *et al.* 1985) stimulates further discussion, at least because it remained incomplete at his death. His notes for the essay remained, but the essay itself had disappeared into the ether of the classroom. Although he lectured to his students on the essay, there had been no copy. As a gesture showing their regard for their teacher, Mauss's students and colleagues brought together the various bits of notes from lectures to construct a text that outlined his thoughts. Consider what an extraordinary thing this is then, a personal essay written by the people who heard it! Mauss, the person who delivered it as a lecture, is long dead; but he is reconstructed as the category of the person, as the lecturer who spoke on these matters. Even when delivering a lecture, even in the moment when a person might be most clearly a focused singular reasoning subject, Mauss's ideas become the material of what others make of those thoughts.

Postmodernists accepted the arguments posed by anthropologists, that historical and cultural processes constituted the human subject. On the one hand, they agree with the many anthropologists who argue that there is nothing 'natural' about human reason, yet they do not know how to advise a scholar about the choices ahead of him or her as they submit to the vicissitudes of the social construction of reason in their work. Many anthropologists feel that the postmodernist critical project is successful in exposing the baseless claim that human nature is rational, but nihilistic because it cannot carry forward a political project in which others join (Hutcheon 1989; Yeatman 1994). In order to make that critique work effectively to the ends of political change, new researchers argue that the postmodernist needs to return to the anthropological project. In order to show the importance of this, I discuss the bourgeois individual, as a concept critiqued differently in the visual or literary arts. For example, it is helpful to consider what images of the bourgeois individual come to us from the arts and literature of the mid-nineteenth-century industrial city.

The Counterfeit Coin

The example of the gift of a counterfeit coin might be considered a bit more deeply than I have examined it to this point. There is a story by Baudelaire, which Derrida exhausts for its teachings on the gift. It tells of an encounter of two friends with a beggar on the street in the late nineteenth century. The events take place after the gentlemen friends buy tobacco from a tobacconist to enjoy for the afternoon, a privilege of a middle-class individual. The commodity exchange complete, the two friends hold the change from their purchase of tobacco, and in Baudelaire's day the transaction is already marked by modernity – the shop, the gentlemen, the fresh tobacco. The entire issue develops because they encounter the beggar with change in their pockets.

The dilemma arises because one of the friends holds a counterfeit coin of a high denomination. It is a coin that will be of no value to future transactions if it is found to be counterfeit. He passes the coin to the beggar, who is overwhelmed at the generosity, but unwitting to the gentleman's mockery of largesse. At the knowledge that one of them has passed the counterfeit coin to a less fortunate man, the two friends confront each other in new ways. The relationship is risked on the exposure of the knowledge of the deceit.

Looking at more intimate or interpersonal aspects of pleasure and work in the creation of the bourgeois subject, it helps to change the focus to a common material transacted between people. Tobacco use is both personal and widely distributed. Its use transcends different social milieus and changes persons into individuals and friends. Baudelaire addresses this fully in his accounts of the uses of tobacco between two friends. Tobacco is a luxury gift in this story. The friends share it as a matter of course because they are peers. Tobacco is also a prestige gift. The friends give it in order to show charity and largesse. The beggar is not an individual, but an object of their attention. He is an event in their lives, not a person with whom they hold a personal relationship.

The question at the end of the story would be: what has transpired in the human relationships? Two answers can be given. First, Derrida is concerned with the nature of altruism and the authenticity of the concept of generous free gifts, as introduced by ethnographers with hopes of finding moral fables for better lives. Second, the reader of Baudelaire's story must question the ethics of exchange more deeply. Friendship is lost in the witting transaction of false coin in the place of charitable gift. Here we find an account of stupid cruelty; a gentleman passing a false coin to a beggar in the hopes of making an event in his life, and in hopes of achieving a measure of self-satisfaction that he had discharged his duty to demonstrate his charitable character. This is important. Derrida interprets Baudelaire's story as a meditation on the impossibility of making a gift that costs nothing to the giver. Baudelaire's narrator continues to value altruism, but loses his relationship with his selfish friend. The narrator can sustain his friendship only if the gentlemen's selfish motivations remain unacknowledged and unseen. He cannot sustain the friendship once the gentleman makes evident his knowledge of his selfishness. The literary art of Baudelaire's short story about the counterfeit coin affects something more than Derrida discusses. Baudelaire exposes the fragility of friendships and human relationships in which people risk appearing as individuals to each other.

Poststructuralists pose one of the most powerful critiques of subjectivity in anthropology. They do this first by casting doubt on scientific rationalism. They show the readers that the words that a researcher uses as signifiers of action do not adhere firmly to the reality that the anthropologist seeks to describe. Hence, the representative quality of written language fails the earnest scientist in the effort to describe the society in which he or she lives or studies. Poststructuralists argue that human words fail if they are meant to describe the reality of the world. In turn, these failures cast doubt on the powers of the sentient being facing the creative task of naming, classifying and describing the world. Curiously, the poststructuralist critique does not end with an assault on scientific rationalism. Derrida seeks in his later work to extend his critique of subjectivity to economic rationalism. In *Specters of Marx*, Derrida conjoined ideas about economic rationalism with ideas about scientific rationalism to form an interesting conclusion. This interesting marriage of different forms of rationalism in relation to the bourgeois subject appears to the reader as an even more problematic form of human subjectivity than the critique first suggests.

The Manchester Man

The Manchester Man is a nineteenth-century novel describing the human side of events of industrialization of Manchester throughout the eighteenth century (Banks 1876). It explores the division of society into men of privilege who win reputations and independence by their own efforts, and men of bad fortune whose well-being is compromised by poverty and hard blows of life. By the nineteenth century, when Mrs Linnaeus Banks wrote *The Manchester Man*, the middle classes hoped to understand the nature of their relationship to the growing number of poor people in the city. What is a reasonable man of character to do if he is to live in the same coenobium of villages as did the working poor and those who had fallen on hard times and did not work? What charitable dispositions should he hold? What obligations to the poor should he keep?

The Manchester Man belongs to the history of the north west of England in more ways than its place in a middle-class inspirational literature would indicate. Any Mancunian (a resident of Manchester) could hold Manchester Man's virtues as his own moral values; integrity and industry, *concilio et labore* as the council adopted them for the motto of the city. And though the city adopted the bee as a civic image, the emblematic character of Manchester Man, obsequious throughout the city as Jabez Clegg, holds the values of the late nineteenth century fast in the time for the people of the present to understand. His story follows a familiar narrative. As a foundling from the canals of central Manchester, he is raised in a humble home. He studies on scholarship, but finds his way in the world independently. He becomes a respectable citizen of Manchester and a man of influence and wealth in its commercial life.

The figure of the self-made Manchester Man found its way into two different kinds of scholarly debate about political economy. On the one hand, Adam Smith and later the advocates of the free-trade movement of the 1830s used Manchester Man as the figure of the ideal man in order to argue for the relaxing of trade restrictions on the transport of corn and cloth between England and its colonies (and to link the ideal figure of the self-made man to their fragile arguments about Chartism and the need for parliamentary reform). Henceforth, Manchester Man is embraced by the Manchester School of Political Economy, famous for its critique of the entanglements of early capital in pre-capitalist social relations and the need to extricate capitalist exchange from the older elitist and conservative political structures. In the examples contemporary to the late nineteenth century, Smith and others argued that capitalist relations should be extricated from politics. If traders were freed from politics, then too there would be changes to relations with the colonies. One example is the repeal of the preferential agreements for trade with colonial elites in Canada (before 1867, the provinces of Upper and Lower Canada) under the parliamentary bill of legislation that detailed the Corn Laws, a repeal made with the partial aim to thwart colonial revolution (such as that in the Thirteen Colonies). Colonial rebellions by disenfranchised farmers and businessmen against the political privileges of British colonial elites had made painfully visible the corrupt machinations of formal politics in the health of both economic and social relations.

On the other hand, the critics of emerging industrial capital relations understood that the heroic values of the 'ideal figure' of the bourgeois individual could be a fiction. Critics of the middle-class ethos (which was shared throughout the society of professionals and factory owners in the north of England) argued that great danger lay in mistaking the values that the Manchester Man espoused in relation to his poorer brothers for virtues held by his character. The Manchester Man could suffer the conditions of alienation as easily as the urban poor of the city because he misunderstood the grounds of his moral action. The danger lay in perceiving the bourgeois subject, the Manchester Man, to be a reservoir of moral judgement and thereby losing sight of the importance of the obligations to others as he kept them for the support for his thought, ethics and action. As an ideal construct, the Manchester Man needed to be turned upside down, not only to empty his pockets of the accruements of his lifestyle, but also to clarify the complexity of the relationships by which his image appeared to hang clear of the frame of his times.

Envisioning bourgeois subjects

Not everyone would entertain the idea that the poststructuralist Derrida introduced anthropologists to a new critique of the bourgeois subject. Most would argue that he introduced the idea of the inventive 'play of meaning' across structures, rendering it impossible to isolate or define the truth of any representation of the world. A few people might think that this slippery condition of meaning deconstructs the subject of anthropology, making the world of the informant forever elusive to the ethnographer. A very few now assume that deconstructive renderings of the subject ended anthropological science because they reduce subjects to the forms of their relations. These assumptions leave us with an old idea of mystification: that the condition of anthropological knowledge is such that it serves to obscure the world from the eyes of researchers and informants alike.

The deconstructionist's attention to knowledge forms that play with human sensibilities echoes a much older concern about the work of enchantment and mystification. An insight made by Marx in the critique of capital led him to expose the fact that humans alienated each other neither with money nor with capital per se, but in the ways in which they apprehended and misapprehended the relationships in which currency and commodities were exchanged. His critique extended deep into social life, and argued that people created behavioural conventions out of false knowledge of each other. Social interactions, such as manners, habits and informal social institutions, constituted an alienated world that challenged the possibility of direct meaningful experience.

Bourgeois subjects misapprehend the world less as individuals, and more so as people enmeshed in alienating forms of relationships. Marx uses the illusory world of light projections of images as an illustration for his argument. He points out that the world around the person enlightens the person as much as the reflections of light on a screen. He argues that anyone who tries to understand the festishization of commodities and vision of the bourgeois individual must grapple with the fantastic link between the camera obscura and the real world. The camera obscura is not so familiar to present-day readers, but it was a marvel of the nineteenth century. Not privileged to be part of a world of moving images, as most of the people born in the twentieth century have been, Marx wrote of the ways in which the vision of the bourgeois person could see only a world of fetishes, a world of refracted light on a concave screen. The bourgeois subject had grown so accustomed to his or her world of images that he could no longer recognize the complex processes by which it appeared to be real. Thinking a bit about the camera obscura helps in this case.

The device, the camera obscura, was itself something of a spectacle in nineteenth-century England and Europe when it appeared in exhibitions and public parks. I saw one renovated on Eastbourne Pier, and although I have no information to confirm it, I am tempted to consider that this is one that might have been viewed by Marx himself, on some unusual holiday excursion with the other educated Victorians of his era. Now, a hundred years on, in the centre of the tower room at the top of a spiral staircase I stood with friends to look at the concave disc bearing a reflected image of the pier stretching out below us. Through a very narrow hole, and reflected downward by a mirror, the outdoor light struck the concave disc. Quiet at first, our eyes adjusted to the luminous images on the curvature of disc lying in the dark grey light of the room. We learned to see the images, and awoke to the fact that we understood what we saw only after a few mute minutes while speechless viewers struggled to take in what they saw. The camera obscura showed us how easily we could construct a verisimilitude between the movements on the pier and the movements on the screen; but that too deceived. The problem was that the screen looked real in ways in which the world was not, imposing a concave disc in such a way as to make us come away with the sense of having seen a flat image. All this worked, in spite of the fact that the viewer can certainly take in the world of the camera obscura, but neither as a two-dimensional space nor as a flat image stretched against a page or a wall. The idea is that we see the world as a painting or two-dimensional image, rather than as a summary of knowledge won by rapidly scanning the eye across the curvature of the horizon, the same vault of sky imitated in the curvature of the concave disc.

The bourgeois subject eludes researchers who live in a world of images that are mistaken for reality because it is easy to forget that the images are just that: the effects of processes of representations and misrepresentations of humans to each other. Unfortunately for anthropologists, the bourgeois subject has the odd habit of appearing reasonable, just at the moment when the researcher least expects to be thinking critically about it. This confusion lies in the fact that the bourgeois world is as much inside the mind of the researcher as the researcher dwells within the creations of that world. Deconstructionists working towards a critique of the bourgeois subject can show how that is so.

The spectacle of the camera obscura displaces its opposite – that is, the greying or the paling of the conscious world or experience which is the world in which viewers learn to watch the refracted lights. In general, putting some aspects of experience into spectacular form causes the disappearance of other processes, which must be remembered if the network of meaningful signification is to be recalled. If the world of representation and spectacle obscures some processes – the mechanism of the camera obscura, a room darkened to be illuminated by a narrow beam of light that refracts on the wall, or the conscious learning of how to adjust the human vision to the spectacle – then humans can alienate each other.

Think of the relationship that many people have with their television, the programmes or 'shows' that are necessary watching, or the relationships that the watcher makes with the people of the screen. In the corner of many living rooms stands a television screen. It is a small space that transmits images into the private, even personal spaces of lives. Often people forget that television was called 'the box' when it first arrived to add to the panoply of objects that a middle-class home might contain. It is an aperture through which light arrives in the room and we find an image in front of us. Although the television seems light-years distant from the technological work of the camera obscura – an ancient effect of light in the dark, made into a nineteenth-century technological mystery – we often forget that it shows us visions of our own lives, but as if at a distance. Recognizing the differences that exist between a lived world, a world of images, and a world lived with the real effects of images invigorates a critique of ourselves, and in particular of the bourgeois subject.

Perhaps, as an example, I can note two different television shows currently being broadcast in Manchester. One is the long-running soap opera, *Coronation Street*. It is set on a fictitious but typical street in the city, and details the daily lives of a community of neighbours whose problems are dealt with in daily episodes, many of which are situated in the local pub known as 'The Rover's Return'. Its changing story lines address concerns of the day in a kind of morality play that is watched by many people across the city. At the time of the writing of this, the working-class neighbourhood on *Coronation Street* is struggling to come to terms with the same-sex romance between two lads in the neighbourhood. The second programme, *The Royle Family*, focuses the camera on a series of conversations among a family sitting around a television set. Middle-aged parents, their daughter and her husband entertain the grandmother and other neighbours from time to time in front of the television. We do not know which programme is being broadcast on their TV, nor do we get any sense of it from their commentary. The camera views the family from the location of the TV screen, making the viewer feel as if they could be the subject of the programme that is always running on the Royle family screen. The name of the show – a pun on the word royal – already suggests that the sovereignty of the viewer's gaze should be questioned. On the screen, the characters in the programme seem to invite the TV viewers to see themselves as actors who play with real life as if it were artistic form. The aesthetic form of the programme underscores its themes, which play with the odd convergence between the iron-grasp of family relationships in Manchester and, simultaneously the fragility of those relationships. Common wisdom and philosophy from the armchair flows from the set as the family tries to solve the same problems that every other family needs to address: for example, can the household budget sustain the extra expenditure for satellite TV programming?

Tricks of vision and efforts to learn to see differently had as important a place in the early anthropology of the nineteenth century as they do in the late twentieth and early twenty-first century. One example comes from the historians' effort to describe the social conditions of the working poor in northern England. Engels famously described Manchester streets with small diagrams of the bricks of houses to show the shoddy construction of the homes of the poor by contrast with those of the rich. In other passages he takes his reader to the Royal Manchester Infirmary to 'see' the waiting room, filled with people seeking medical treatment. In the midst of this account he writes of the uses of small pills to boost energy and vitality, pure medical quackery in the midst of modernizing practices. He asks his readers to learn to see the conditions of social life around them. Learning to see the poor, to see poverty and its causes, meant attending to the minutiae of life. In the ethnographic dimensions of the work of Engels, the ethnographer learned to expose what the participants could not. Here Engels the social historian championed the descriptive efforts of social science, in a common effort with the early ethnographer to create the foundations of moral reasoning.

To compare this envisioning of social relations by Engels with the effort made by the anthropologist Rivers at a somewhat later time is most interesting. Rivers aimed to expose how people visualized relationships. In the Torres Straits research undertaken in the 1890s, he undertook to sketch kinship relations, by drawing genealogies based on marriage and birth. His diagrams form the first examples of kinship systems. Most importantly, he provides the anthropologist with the extraordinarily powerful visual images of relationships. An example of the diagram used to map the relations of the Torres Straits people to each other shows the possibilities of organizing large amounts of knowledge, simply by writing down accounts of people's lives in relation to each other (Grimshaw 2001).

Both Engels and Rivers raise questions as to how human subjectivity can be made in solitude, when it is evident that such complex cross-cutting networks of social relationships remain part of the individual's life, whether they are immediately visible or must be exposed to sight. The end result is a document that can be used to establish the significance of the legacy in modern Australia of the residential claims of Torres Straits' people to the islands. In the well-documented Mabo decision of the late twentieth century, legal officials in the courts could consult the diagrams of Rivers's work and find exact reference to the claimants' ancestors. The fact that ethnographic notes could be powerful also relied upon the visual power of the images. The images of kinship became the measure of the implicit ground of relationship in which contemporary Aboriginal people walked. Establishing a judicious claim to land depended upon making the relationships appear in the eye of the court. Diagrams of kinship, such as the ones I used in the previous chapter, became exposures of implied or otherwise hidden connections. Where Engels tried to make class relations appear in the details of a city, Rivers attempted to make relationships appear in his diagrams of the connections between people based on birth and marriage.

Flipping the image: the aesthetics of representation

Can anthropology use the distinctions between the real and the imaginary successfully in the critique of the bourgeois individual? Does this make it possible to expose the implicit connections, as if they were the ground of the existence of the individual? Earlier in this chapter, I discussed the camera obscura on Eastbourne Pier, and the way in which the people in the room learned to see the images of the world outside now reflected on the concave screen. Learning to see those images required us to talk and to teach each other about how to see the images. This included how to think about the images in relation to the 'real' world, the importance of the very narrow aperture for the light. In the machinery of the camera obscura at Eastbourne is a pulley that turns the apparatus 360 degrees for all of us to see. The image of the outside 'real' world can be viewed at any angle from where the person might be standing. The visitor is invited to consider an upside down world and to play with the presentation of the view. Given that some people learn to manipulate adroitly their personal view on the world, and to exchange their perspective for another person's, how should anthropologists consider the views that the informants might have of the conditions of their own times?

Here is a comparison to consider, made by two men working in the same period and addressing similar ideas: George Orwell and L.S. Lowry. Orwell ignited the political imagination of British Socialists with the publication of his short book, *Down and Out in Paris and London*. The account of life as an impoverished and casual worker in both cities left an indelible mark on the minds of the radical vanguard. Until then, much of their efforts went to the organization of the worker, to making the factory worker and the miner understand the importance of collective work and collective argument. Orwell's book exposed another victim of the capitalist political economy, but this time it was the victim of the bourgeois capitalist whose pleasures were taken by consumption of finery and the pleasures of the world of theatre and entertainment. After a year as a dishwasher and helper in the restaurants of Paris, Orwell admonishes his reader never to eat without thinking of the fate of the worker who lives below in the kitchen. Showing how it seemed almost impossible to escape from such employment, given its hours and its irregularity of treatments and pay, Orwell exposes a group of people whose labour supports and is exploited by capitalist political economy; yet these people have few opportunities to meet to change it. The hotel workers are hardly attractive characters, and I do not think that Orwell holds too many fantasies about the romantic image of the worker in the hospitality industry; the bourgeois individual comes out much less attractive still because he is the ignorant consumer of his pleasures of restaurant meals and stylish entertainments. Orwell, in a powerful Marxist tradition, used wit and personable story telling to write a realist account of the poverty of casual workers in two different cities.

The effect of the book on the radical left was so great that the owners of the

Figure 8.1a Miners' cottages at Coatbridge (photographer unknown). The photograph is reproduced here as an example of the many used in the first publication of George Orwell's *The Road to Wigan Pier* (1937), London: Victor Gollancz Publishers. An extensive photographic report on northern working-class housing had been made by socialist journalists of the time. I chose to reprint this photograph from that period as an example of the uses of the English documentary tradition in photography. All efforts have been made to find the copyright-holder of this photograph, but neither the original photographs nor the names of the photographers can be found.

Red Press, decided to send Orwell to the north of England to examine the unemployed in the mining towns where the pits had been closed by the economic depression. He shows the life of the unemployed miner in a number of photographs that cut bare the situation for the subjects. *The Road to Wigan Pier* takes its title from a jest; the miners call the structure that delivers coal across the heap of tailings by the name used for the broad walkways to the ships that come into a seaside town. The workers do not elaborate upon the picture they see, and it is possible that many had not visited a pier. From Wigan, an inland town, workers might be most likely to spend their seaside holidays in Blackpool with its carnival attractions. Who made it to the seaside from among the families that Orwell photographed is impossible to tell, even at a time when workers took opportunities for seaside visits when they could. But the hopes of a bourgeois lifestyle might include more frequent seaside holidays, and walks on grander, more stylish piers than Blackpool.

Orwell contributed realistic photographs of working conditions and family life in the north of England to a general knowledge of the region. His work is

Figure 8.1b Accommodation for mine workers and families. The caption from this 1937 plate reads, 'Outside Newcastle: Whole families of miners live in these tiny and unsanitary dwellings, for which a rent of seven shillings is charged'. As with the previous photograph from Orwell's book, the photographer is unknown.

part of the genre of socialist realism that sought to study everyday life through the visual and use the camera to see more honestly or more truly all those aspects of life that might otherwise be hidden. The realist photograph assumes that the real might be there, except that the eye had been trained to choose selectively between different sites of social life. The apparatus of the camera did not allow the person to exercise his or her preferences to view some images over others. The social context existed in the frame as much as the featured practices and faces. Take for example the details of the impoverished lifestyle depicted in each photograph (Figures 8.1a and b). Not only do we have the faces of people who work in the mines, but also the nature of the household's composition, state of repair of the dwelling and the resources from which the family might make a home. The account is difficult to address here. Only the framing of each image could be considered important to limiting or defining the scope of the realist project, and that is a considerable issue of concern that I do not fully address here.

By contrast, Lowry's paintings emerge from a different kind of attention than Orwell's photography. As one of the first serious landscape painters to use the urban setting in landscape painting, Lowry abstracts the impoverishment of urban lifestyles, and the mechanistic everyday routines of urban living. Consider the painting, *Coming from the Mill*, which is reproduced here in black and white in Figure 8.2. Although the original is in colour, Lowry greyed the shades of red brick buildings and low yellow light, so that the urban landscape

Figure 8.2 *Coming from the Mill* (L.S. Lowry) © The Lowry Foundation, The City of Salford. The painting shows figures walking as if in mechanized movement, even after they leave work.

appears to be heavy with industrial grime. In Lowry's painting Mancunians walk in the same way on the street as they might move on the textile mill floors. Another painting, which is not reproduced in this chapter, currently hangs on the wall at Old Trafford, the football stadium that is home to one of the regional teams, Manchester United. Here Mancunians can see Lowry's representation of an earlier generation of football fans in *Going to the Match*, as it is titled. As with *Coming from the Mill*, *Going to the Match* shows the way the posture and movement of bodies records a memory of arriving at work in the textile mills, even at a weekend leisure activity. The artist's aerial and distant point of view unnerves the viewer into seeing themselves as the subject of the painting, and as a product of the historical processes depicted. Many people in Manchester commonly say that they do not like Lowry's 'stick figures' because they deplete the kind of life that is lived in the region.

The significance of these paintings can be understood in their ability to portray the effects of historical processes, and to effect viewers of the painting, better than in their representational qualities. Lowry painted people working in industrial Manchester, at a time when that period was ending or had finished. His works distil the sensibility of an age that had passed, and perhaps the abstraction of the qualities of that life imitate the memories that Lowry had of the family elders, the men and women he recalled from his childhood that had been drawn out by the experiences he recorded. Was Lowry's painting a fantasy of greyed colour and image that sought to recapture the processes that had made the people he knew into the images that they were?

His critics express a certain kind of dislike for his stick men, a dislike that is difficult to name as discomfort with the themes, or as dislike of the aesthetics. This is not realist art in the way in which Orwell's writing composes the realist image of the worker. Instead, Lowry's art evinces an insight from the viewer that contrives a sense of the problem. If the art critic, the viewer, feels diminished by the viewing of Lowry's masterpieces of urban painting, perhaps this is because Lowry's painting has affected him or her in a way that Lowry intended.

I am struck, when I compare Orwell and Lowry, by the ways in which they use the aesthetic of their art to evoke and portray the bourgeois subject's unconscious collusion with the oppression of the worker. Orwell writes to expose workers and unemployed men, hidden from the eyes of the bourgeois. He also exposes the workers to the eyes of the intellectual left who keep their own bourgeois habits as part of their radical lifestyle; they are a group whose motives he suspects. The respective imaginings of the worker bear shadows. In one sense the shadow of the bourgeois subject can be seen in the mechanistic lives of Lowry's workers. They are followers of routines designed by bourgeois persons, or designed to feed the interests of bourgeois persons. In Lowry's painting the world of the worker is not hidden from the bourgeois world and then exposed in the images. Instead, Lowry shows the shadows of the bourgeois subject as they are cast in the world of the worker.

I have focused on visual knowledge about the north west of England, including the image or bourgeois figure of the self-made 'Manchester Man' and the record of two different attempts to depict his counterpart, the working poor. The relationship between these two figures can be explored further; that is, the relations between the self-made success and the less materially fortunate worker or even the homeless poor receive little mention in 'Manchester Man', or in the work of political economic theorists of the day.

In order to think about the nature of the obligations between the bourgeois 'Manchester Man' and the homeless, I can return to considerations posed by poststructuralist analysis discussed at the beginning of the chapter. I uncovered considerations of Derrida's work on the nature of the gift, but I do not take up Derrida's concern to interrogate the possibilities that determine whether there can or cannot be a free gift, a selfless gift. I think that to argue about whether gifts are or are not free requires the anthropologist to make some fundamental assertion about human nature, or at least presumes ontological concerns to underlie all giving. For example, to be able to give a coin freely assumes that the coin is already separate from the self and ready to be given away. This suggests that, to some degree, the alienation of the 'Manchester Man', or the 'Torres Straits Man' from this network of clan or personal relations has already taken

Figure 8.3 *Business as Usual* (Lucile Pardee 2002) © The University of Manchester. The street trader sells pamphlets describing the tragedy of the collapse of the two towers of the World Trade Center, at the site of the disaster where the iconic building once stood.

place. I think that the question is less one of looking about for the absence of free gifts, and I will turn instead to the work that Strathern conducted on the problem of keeping obligations. In Melanesia the keeping of relationships certainly matters more than liberating oneself from social relations in order to give freely.

Conclusions: envisioning bourgeois subjects

In comparing the values of the bourgeois subject with the values sustaining the lifestyles of the workers and the unemployed, Lowry and Orwell provide a meditation on the problem of alienation, simply by exposing a visual subtext. When I turn to look at Derrida's treatment of alienation, I find that the poststructuralist's account exposes the deceits of the bourgeois subject. In deconstructing values, the poststructuralist critique of bourgeois subject echoes the concept of alienation in the Marxist critique of capital. Whereas for Marxist critics alienation entailed the loss of meaningful social relationships based on something like 'authentic' understandings of experience, for poststructuralist critics the play of meaning across structures makes and remakes social relationships. In deconstructing value in economic rationality, there is no loss of meaning and economic rationality continues in another form – as business as usual.

In deconstructing the meaningful matrix of symbol and structure there is no truth that becomes clear, except that it is possible to measure a critical distance from one image to its after-image. This is the 'difference that makes all the difference' to their respective criticisms of the bourgeois subject. Such a measure of after-images is a point worth considering before the end of this chapter. I have been fortunate in recent years to know and work with a number of students who study for Master's degrees in visual anthropology and ethnographic film making in Manchester. In the summer of 2002, Lucile Pardee filmed the business conducted around the base of the destroyed World Trade Center (Figure 8.3). In her film, *Business as Usual*, she helps us to see that business continues as usual around the site of the destruction. The street vendors who worked in the vicinity before the collapse of the buildings in September 2001, continue to work on most of the same street corners only a year later.

The film exposes something we would not grasp quite so easily in speech or conversations. Pardee films what she can capture on film, and what remains after the buildings' collapse. She cannot film what is not there. The modern image of world trade, as represented by the twin towers as standing twin monoliths at the south end of Manhattan Island, is gone. Neither can she film what is there, the business with the vendors, except by negotiating her rights to film. It is an awkward film to watch because the negotiations of the film maker and the vendors must become transparent throughout. She engages in business as usual as a part of filming vendors around the base of the towers. Her own negotiations enhance the film's aesthetic effect. She shows us that the transactions of business continue, and that street businesses flourish with the flood of visitors, mourners and tourists who come to the site of the destruction that was once the towers of the World Trade Center. It is grittier capitalism than that which had been practised in earlier years in the offices that stood high above the ground. Pardee shows us that business as usual at 'Ground Zero' of the World Trade Center disaster grows, in the rubble, on the street or in the after-image of the buildings as a symbol of world trade.

Similarly, the early Free Trade movement of the nineteenth century finds new life in the twenty-first. In Manchester, the Free Trade Hall, the Italianate building of the Victorian era, was once a grand site for the exchange of commodities. In 1999 it stood with a 'For Sale' sign on its façade (Figure 8.4). Do Manchester estate agents who trade in bricks and mortar (as well as in palisades and gilt) now trade too on the symbols of exchange, creating a new value in rapidly escalating property prices for the image (or the after-image) of the symbol of free trade? Is it 'Free Trade' or the building that is for sale? Business as usual indeed!

Figure 8.4 'Manchester Free Trade Hall – For Sale' (1998 © Aidan O'Rourke). The Free Trade Hall was perhaps one of the earliest buildings to be named after a political movement. Members of the Manchester School of Political Economy and other followers of Adam Smith's theory led the Free Trade Movement throughout the early nineteenth century. Since its construction in 1856, it has been used principally as a location for musical entertainment.

Sometimes arguments about the bourgeois subject hit us in the face because they can be seen, as well as read and heard. Perhaps this insight comes from beyond the poststructuralist project that plays with the world of text, but makes room for the oral or the visual only as that elusive knowledge of human experience that can be brought fully into conscious discussion and speech. Does the visual medium help to expose how subjectivity can be unfolded or drawn aesthetically out of the conventional form? It has been my intention in this chapter to show one place where an anthropologist might begin.

Summary of chapter 8

Can an account of social processes, values and structure be given from the viewpoint of some members of society over and above others? Dumont, Macpherson and Mauss ask interesting questions about the social construction of the individual. One of these might be: what social processes enable the individual to assume insight into the workings of the whole, given that he or she is the product of that society? Does the individual ever have a privileged insight into the workings of the total society, as say did the free trader upon whom Adam Smith modelled his economic man? This chapter has examined the case of Manchester capitalism. Here, common knowledge of the nineteenth century suggested that the allegedly self-made man understood perfectly how to live by values for the social good, and by processes of that bettered society, and so too his own situation. We might ask: how do members of one society come to envision that an individual might be the prime-mover of social change for them all? Understanding this entails an examination of how people hide the very social relations that made them from others and from their own consciousness. Critics of the bourgeois subject, including Engels, argued that this was bourgeois fantasy and showed how researchers could learn to see the city differently as the material effect of capitalist exploitation. Later, journalists' analyses of bourgeois subjectivity, such as George Orwell's, argued that the poor had privileged insight into the total society because they experienced the effects of the same processes that others had to hide from themselves. Artistic representations by Lowry can show the effects of capitalism in the city landscape and the bodies of individuals. Does capitalism submerge some social relationships only to privilege visual evidence of its effects in other relationships? Consider the recent history of the uses of the symbols of capitalism, in processes ranging from small enterprise to warfare; for example, the sale of the Free Trade Hall in Manchester for use as luxury accommodation and hospitality. To what extent can we say that people transact primarily in a virtual economy by forming social relationships by reference to the fantasy or images of free trade?

9

GIVING BEYOND REASON

This chapter considers how anthropologists have answered charges that gift exchange entails irrational behaviour. Whereas some people argued that largesse is rational because it builds the middle class person's prestigious reputation (Veblen 1967 [1899]), other scholars (especially Bataille 1967 in Bataille 1994) insisted that some people acted with excessive generosity towards others in order to release fellow humans from the misery of poverty, and thereby return the totality of society to a moral and ethical condition of material and spiritual equality. Although many (especially Wolf 1999) have criticized Bataille because he believed that habitually generous uses of material wealth would create an ideal and utopian social state, I will return to Bataille's arguments in this chapter because largesse is common to many different places. Largesse is irrational only in so far as generous acts cannot be understood within the terms of self-interested giving. How can an anthropologist explain why some people give too much to other people? One way forward would be to ask what kind of sense other people in other societies make of those parts of social life that seem ambiguous, enigmatic and irrational.

In this chapter I will go beyond the limits of the previous chapter, which considered the aesthetics of the 'bourgeois subject', to investigate how transgressions of rational action and of rational thought constitute human subjectivity. How does an anthropologist explain the excesses of emotion, action or thought in acts of gift exchange? Are some issues simply too dense to think about, or does focusing on the excesses of gift exchange enable interpretive analysis of the more irrational aspects of human consciousness? Can you give too much? What is at stake in giving it all away? This chapter explores further the problem of dealing with what the surrealist essayist Bataille once called 'economies of excess'.

In addition I will examine several attempts to explain why people do give too much, investigating answers to several questions about why people give beyond reason. What should an anthropologist do when the otherwise rational subjects of his or her research suddenly act with munificence – perhaps comic, perhaps violent, and indubitably excessive? For example, does parental love move adults to give unrestrictedly? If so, then what kind of 'motive' is parental

Figure 9.1 'Yam house' (Plate XXXVIII, *Argonauts of the Western Pacific* by Bronislaw Malinowski, first published in London in 1922, and under the same title in 1978, reprinted 1991 © London School of Economics and Political Science). Malinowski tells us that Kaouta'ua, one of the chiefs of Sineketa stands in front of his beautifully decorated yam house, his lisige (own dwelling) in the background.

love such that affection belongs to kin relationships (rather than inside the mind of an individual)? If love goes without saying (as is the reported case when some Trobriand men give to their children), then what should anthropology make of it? What has been said of the social effects of such giving? If a person has been fortunate enough to receive such intangible gifts as renown or affection, can he or she ever give the gift away? Can people give too much, if the end of most relationships will certainly be physical separation from those people that they know?

The beauty of symbolic exchange

Some of the earliest efforts to address the habits of giving too much claimed that it made symbolic meanings for economic transactions possible. Consider the example of the Trobriand yam house; it has no functional purpose in sustaining the diet of men and women in the village. Summarizing Malinowski, the ethnographer Young (1979) reminds us that men and women in the Trobriand islands think that yam houses are beautiful, and that the gardens in which they stand are places of pleasure and works of art. A man builds a yam house for the purpose of holding yams that he receives from the brothers of his wife. The houses tower above the earth, great silos of agricultural wealth, and paradoxically the contents are seldom used. These houses hold more than enough yams for eating, and more than enough for ceremonial work. The yams contained within them remain until they rot; so unhappy are their owners to actually give out yams from them that they will take yams directly from their gardens and go hungry themselves so that they can keep the abundance of the yam house at full capacity (Figure 9.1).

Most importantly, the yam houses simply show that the man has relatives, men to whom he is related by marriage and upon whom he can count to look after him with food. The abundant garden wealth can be retained in a yam house as a mark of capacity and ability to respond in full to any request for food for feasting, or for kula transactions. They represent the capacity of a man to respond to the requests of his affined relatives. They represent the success of a man's magical abilities to cultivate a garden. A successful Trobriand man, especially a chief, holds all these relationships together in good form.

The yam houses, houses of excessive wealth in yams, are beautifully carved and imbued with magic. Do the yam houses, which hold such extraordinary wealth, stand as simple symbols of the power of men to hold all their relationships together in one place? That might be a rational interpretation of such a fascinating symbol as the yam house, but I wonder if that grapples fully with the problem of understanding why men need to demonstrate that ability with a yam house as an artwork. More importantly, why should a chief be seen to hold too many yams for his own consumption? People give too much to some relatives or to some friends. How can we know when giving too much must be addressed as more than a rational act? Take for example the excesses of gestures of affection.

Excesses of affection

Take the example of the Trobriander father as an example of behaviour that has no rational explanation that can be grounded simply in self-interest. He simply gives too much to his children because he loves them, showing his affection for the child as a member of another clan, with the matrilineage of his wife and her brothers. I have written at length about the work of making mapula gifts, the work that a Trobriand father does in order to succeed in giving his child and wife a lifetime of small gifts. What seems most extraordinary of all of this effort to keep on giving the mapula is that a father can never exhaust his obligations to give. Weiner recorded the words of the Trobriander, pointing to his trees, which are evidence of his father's mapula. The man said that if the wind blows down the tree and it dies, then his father simply replaces the tree, unlike the trade storeowner who will not replace the kerosene lamp if it breaks while the purchaser has been using it (Weiner 1992: 25). The mapula is not exhaustible, and there is no point in time when the father can finally meet, once and for all, the obligations to give to his children and to his wife. At the father's death, the child, who is by now an adult, will give the fruit of the tree and an additional gift back to them. The gift made in acknowledgement of the father's work marks a lifetime of giving small gifts. The child acknowledges the father's generosity with ceremonial gifts at his funeral, rather than calculating the value of his largesse during his lifetime.

Fathers insist that they give small gifts to their children out of affection and fatherly love, although mapula gifts might exhaust a father. They press him to find the resources to keep the obligation, but he continues to give the mapula. Malinowski had been puzzled in his early work. Just what overt or manifest motives could move the father to keep the mapula gifts? It seems that only deep motives to connect with his wife and child, perhaps reasons of which the father remained unconscious, could cause him to give mapula continuously, generously and complacently. At this disjuncture of understanding, Malinowski introduced a theory of Trobriand unconscious that articulated with Freudian beliefs. The appreciation expressed by Parsons of Malinowski's struggle to understand the complex of social relations that psychoanalytic anthropologists refer to as the Oedipal complex grasped the nature of the kinship problem that lies at the heart of Malinowski's question: namely, how to account for the playing out of power as an effect of the basic affectionate intimacy of brother and sister in matrilineal society.

The surfeit of gifts from a father puzzles anthropologists, who ask how they should understand the excessive gifts that a man makes in the action of giving to children who will always be his children, although they will be supported jurally and customarily by men from another clan. Malinowski's version of Trobriand psychology turns most questions of the excessive generosity of fathers around into questions of personal power legitimated by jural authority, as socially defined by matrilineal society. He sidelines the questions of erotic 'power' as the provenance of garden magicians and the shady world of love magic. In the example of Trobriand kinship, the mother's brother remains the person who holds jural authority over the affairs of the matrilineage. Children learn of the mother's brother's power, from an early age forward to the present, and the dismantling of the power and authority of the maternal uncle (the mother's father's brother) can be as intense as the undressing of the authority of the father. Parsons proposes that the Trobriand case insists on a twist on the classic schema: that a young man should come to envy the father as the symbol of authority and desire the mother as the embodiment of intimacy and love. A long debate ensues (Jones 1925, Parsons 1964, Spiro 1982) as to why it is that a youth should be moved to usurp the power from the mother's brother as senior member of his own clan and come to see that man as a block upon receiving his mother's affection. Malinowski's interpretation aimed to provide an accurate account of the power relations of the Trobriand family and opened the way for Schneider and Gough in *Matrilineal Kinship* (1964) to propose a general schema for matrilineal society; that is, where the bond between sister and brother is strong, then the bond between husband and wife could be fragile or weak. The nature of the bond is very much in question.

In Malinowksi's appraisal, the question is how to understand the father's habit of excessive giving if the outcome of his actions amounts to the reinforcement of customary law. Let me recapitulate this point. Malinowski argues that the father aims to make the mapula work for his best interests, both as a father and within the customary law of the islands. He aims to secure his children as his own, and to limit the power of their mother's brother in the life of the family. He makes mapula gifts because by doing so he is recognized by custom as the parent and indebts his wife's brother to assist with reciprocal ceremonial gifts at his death, which in turn builds his reputation as a senior man in his own clan. On his own reputation he is able to make customary law effective in his own matrilineal clan.

Anthropologists debated the many motivations for the mapula gift only to discover both a rational and an irrational cause for a father to give to his children. A father participates in two forms of economy at once, an ideal or symbolic one that brings him prestige, and a material one that brings back to him the tangible effects of his affection. In his old age, he will reap the benefits of what he has sown. His material expenditure on his children's behalf will be rewarded. Children will acknowledge him as 'father' and will care for him in his last years. Beyond these two 'rational' motivations for a man to give excessively to his children is another irrational motive; that is, his parental love for them, which is not irrational at all.

Understanding excess in the case of potlatch

Let me turn from the apparent inscrutability of the excesses of filial and parental affection because it is hard to analyse anthropologically just what people do with the excesses of affection. An anthropologist might consider the problem of the 'waste' and surplus of exchange by analysing what people do with the leftovers of their work, their trade, and the extraneous bits of what they know. Bataille focuses upon the excesses, the 'accursed share' that anthropologists sometime mistakenly try to ignore. Instead, just as an archaeologist learns much from the middens, the refuse pits, used by the people of an ancient village, an anthropologist can learn a great deal by studying the knowledge, goods and actions that informants discount as unimportant. A society can do many things with its excesses of wealth. It can give its wealth back to the natural elements, as did the Kwakiutl of north-west Canada, who discarded embossed and decorated copper shields into the sea, or burned them into the air. It can create magnificent artistic creations at great expenditure of labour, time and care, as do the Melanesians of New Ireland who make funereal sculptures that must be displayed and destroyed. After the destruction, they remember the ephemeral beauty of the carvings and of the memory of the corporal presence of their deceased kin. It can expend its excessive wealth in a war of conquest, such as the wars of aggression waged by National Socialist Germany against its neighbours in the middle of the twentieth century. It can disperse this excess with a massive movement of non-production, such as the mortuary practices of Thai Buddhism, and thereby gamble with its future.

What do people do with excess? This is a first question for anthropologists to ask if they are to understand the economies of excess or the habit of giving too much. In some conditions, the uses of excessive wealth, or the displays of wealth and its literal destruction, succeed in challenging the spread of market social relations. The problem in all of this lies in recognizing that material excess represents a measure of exploitation, on the part of the person who holds it now. What does an anthropologist understand about excess in society that is neither capitalist nor fully transformed into capitalism? Recall from my description in chapter 4 of the ceremonial exchange known as potlatch. In British Columbia, the First Nation peoples (that is people resident before the arrival of settlers from European nations) of the Bella Coola, Coast Salish, the Haida, the Kwakiutl, the Nootka, Tlingit and the Tsimshian participate in a system of ritual exchange. Although each of these groups uses a specific collective name from their own language, rather than the colonial versions of their names, I will discuss the Kwakawaka'wakw speakers as 'Kwakiutl' to create coherence throughout the history of ethnographic texts written about them. What can an anthropologist understand about the display and destruction of an excessive amount of wealth without reducing the action to the judgement that it is simply irrational?

How the chiefs of matrilineal clans disposed of wealth became important to just about everything in ceremonial and everyday life, and, despite the most insistent efforts of the Canadian government to ban it from 1885 though to the 1920s, the potlatch continued. The earliest work on potlatch, by Boas, aimed to demonstrate that prestige of north-west coast chiefs was based on ideas about their largesse. Like many of their neighbours, the Kwakiutl acknowledged that the receipt of a gift from a man in ceremonial exchange signalled the power of the man giving away all of his wealth. Each chief could win his prestige by giving too much, impoverishing himself of resources and capturing the imagination of the entire village with displays of selflessness. In the first investigations of potlatch undertaken by Boas at the turn of the century, he argued that these exchanges were driven by competitions for power between chiefs. The event of a potlatch grew out of a kind of personal desire to perform largesse better than anyone else in the village and imitated the competitive struggles of capitalists of the era.

It is hard to rectify Boas's ethnography by referring to the rest of anthropological work on gift exchange because his work is resolutely descriptive, offering no larger claims for a theory or critique of political economy. His studies in the north-west coast (Boas 1897, 1966), which I described in chapter 4, were undertaken earlier than much of Malinowski's studies. He attempted to record the life of the indigenous people of the north-west coast in advance of the disappearance of the lifestyles of the different language groups. With an enormous amount of help from George Hunt, an anthropologist who was the son of a First Nation woman and an English father as well as having married into the north-west coast communities, Boas set about the work of recording the life ways of indigenous people, which seemingly remained vital even with the advances of modern American society. The ethnographers provide richly descriptive work without the unnecessary explanation of the habits of the people whose lives they recorded.

Boas's best intentions to free ethnographic descriptions from the corruptions of Western theory or philosophy left many puzzles about potlatch. After his death, Codere completed Boas's unpublished manuscripts and tried to fill in the gaps with a careful account of the particulars of history and belief concurrent with his research. Boas described the ceremony of potlatch, but never grasped the nature of the social totality. Did north-west societies organize their social relationships by kinship, or by degrees of differential access to material and symbolic wealth, by ritual performances; or what?

If the extraordinary ceremonies of potlatch were to be understood in terms that mattered to the peoples of the north west, then an anthropologist should understand several key social terms of Kwakiutl life. First, each Kwakiutl person knew that he or she was a member of a matrilineal clan with a specific totem, such as the salmon, bear or eagle among others; but the clan membership did not predict anything in particular about prestige. Birth order distinguished the first four children as 'elite', and subsequent children as 'common', but the birth order itself did not solidify the prestige of a person. If a person was born into the elite, then participation in secret societies brought prestige to the person. Some individuals joined secret societies to acquire a special 'name' but others joined in order to participate in the winter festival known as Hamatsa (which had been outlawed by the Canadian government in the nineteenth century.) If a person was born common, then he or she was servant to the elite and joined a 'house' as a satellite of the elite who led that form of association. Common people did not marry elite, and over time, the common people grew in number and became proportionally more numerous by far than the elite. In a later review of Boas's work, Lévi-Strauss decided that north-west coast society was not based in any form of kinship that made clans, but instead in a basic form of marriage exchange that made the house and its traditions. The house was a social form more similar to the medieval house than to the clan. In his assessment of Hunt and Boas's and Lévi-Strauss's understanding of the house traditions, Wolf (1999) assumes that only for a very few decades is it possible to view Kwakiutl life in its totality by examining the activities of the elite members of the house, who for a time organized the ritual, political, economic and social life of the rest of the society.

Among the elite, prestige was won through competition, after it was first ascribed by birth order. The elite of each house belonged to one of several 'numayn', that is, a 'group of fellows of the same kind'. The numayn joined and organized potlatch rituals, and entreated the others of their clans, common and elite members alike, to aid them with the events. The numayn is the central form of association of Kwakiutl society, and its internal organization and structure is debated. The numayn is the social location of the most important changes happening to the everyday and ceremonial life of the people of the region, and therefore is difficult to describe. Friendly, but intense, competition between members of the numayn escalated with colonization when some men (and women) found casual or part-time employment for wage in the settler towns nearby. As time passed, the numayn used wages to buy goods for potlatch, and the ceremony increasingly included gifts of blankets bought from trade stores, as well as the ceremonially decorated copper shields of earliest years. As common members of the clan increasingly found work in the settler towns nearby or joined in the wage economy by starting their own businesses in salmon fishing and canning, the elite increasingly entreated them to participate as individuals, rather than as clansmen. In the twentieth century, a potlatch succeeded because an individual man cajoled a network of acquaintances into assisting him.

Consider what is left now of the material arts of the north-west coast. Copper shields were so highly valued in potlatch rituals because the participants destroyed them; few shields can be seen. Instead, the European imagination can play with the images of the totem pole, which was made to be a permanent installation in the forest or at the site of a house of an elite man. They stand in museums, as primary examples of north-west coast art, but their provenance is colonial. The totem pole is a distinct new artistic form that emerged as people drew increasingly upon the disparate associations of kin and acquaintances to create personal prestige in ceremonial displays of wealth. Each post records the totem of each participant in the host's feast, the loosely constructed network of matrilineal clans that came together for a few days to complete the ritual, often the burial of a senior man. The totem pole is an invention of the nineteenth century that records the failure of the numayn and the rise of the network of clan associations. Its presence depends on the participation of the many clans, not on the singular host; and hence it is a multiply owned object as much as the post of a single prestigious man.

Looking back on it all, many recent anthropologists and theorists believe that Mauss approached the potlatch as the greatest enigma in his theory of the gift. Certainly, in recent years more attention has fallen to it than to the hau as an indigenous form of gift giving. One reason for the discussion lies in the claim that potlatch valuables were not given away exactly as Mauss thought they had been. The distinction between ceremonial and everyday valuables matters a great deal to the analysis of potlatch. The ceremonial valuables, embossed copper images, can be seen at potlatch events only momentarily. For most of the time, a potlatch copper will be hidden away and not shown until it is time for it to be 'potlatched'. At the time when the copper is displayed it is then destroyed, usually by throwing it into the sea. Later ethnographers described some copper valuables as too precious to be given away, and so these were held back and not given away in ritual.

I do not know if there are some copper images that are excluded from destruction because they are of a category of wealth that is inalienable, and therefore too sacred to be destroyed; or if these are only being saved from destruction on this occasion because they are too sacred to destroy in a feast with these particular clans and leaders. Godelier and Weiner argued that the good is held back because it belongs to a category of sacred objects that never enter circulation among the villages and clans along the north-west coast. These valuables can only be given across generations so as to keep them within the same clan. If some ceremonial copper images are so special that they cannot be given away or destroyed, then people demonstrate such extraordinary generosity in the potlatch ritual because they know they are keeping true to what that wealth symbolizes. Clans can own wealth among themselves, and it is sacrosanct and not given away without risking collective loss. Perhaps then the generosity of clan leaders appears rational if they keep their sacred valuables, while enabling each other to give other valuables. The ethics of such giving confirms that the principle of the communal is sacred to human social life and the transactions that sustain it.

Among the other more common interpretations of potlatch, that ceremony in which too much is given, anthropologists have argued that people exceed reasonable limits on potlatch because they are making gifts to the spirits of the dead, not to other living humans. Not just any gods, but simply the spirits of their ancestors. The chiefs sought benevolence from the ancestors so that they might avoid misfortune. They believed that the ancestral spirits might be jealous of the fact that they had bodies and lives. That fact, that the spirits are relatives, is the most important issue here. The spiritual and immaterial world does not exist apart from the living world. It is part of it.

There remains the question of whether the goods were in fact given in generosity, or given for public destruction. If it is the latter, then potlatch raises some compelling questions about the nature of exchange when people seemingly give too much. And more seriously it raises the compelling question of whether or not one can give too much. Does holding the most sacred potlatch copper images back signal that no one is fool enough to rid themselves of true valuables? Economies of sacrifice seem to be a misnomer for the depth or crux of the issues that the potlatch raises. There is no 'economy' about the potlatch, at least in so far as the common sense of economy means careful, cost-cutting measures. Potlatch hits the opposite of any common sense meaning of economy. Perhaps that shaking of the common sense of capitalist ideology explains the angst expressed over its practice in the earliest years of the twentieth century, when the government of Canada aimed to remove the practice from the indigenous communities of the north-west coast and banned its performance.

The ceremonial feast of the potlatch held the participants in a tight competition over who can give away the most. This means that the excesses of the potlatch extend into a kind of deep play (in the sense meant by Geertz, when he talks about the ways in which the person delves deeply into matters beyond the limits of rational economic practice). Potlatch is a test of personal prestige, and a way of making the hosts of the feast prestigious. Those who are giving away so much risk more than the loss of their wealth, they risk that they will fail to give enough and thereby lose respect.

This aspiration of potlatch, to evacuate wealth from all reserves, from the holds and storage rooms of a great house and clan, becomes the most frightening aspect of its practice because it leads to the kind of fantasy of power that Ruth Benedict described later as megalomania. In the case of the potlatch on the north-west coast, outside observers – government officials, settlers and even some anthropologists – believed that the competition endangered the well-being of the community and clans. Chiefs' power to impress the feasters at a potlatch, that is to give everything away, coincided with their ability to persuade others to give all of it away against the best interests of the material well-being of the community. The danger lay in the potlatch cycle accelerating and claiming the entire livelihood of the feasters. If the potlatch consumed the participants, if the cycles of giving devoured the prospects of participants for their own future, then it had swung badly out of proportion to its ends of establishing the power of the chief, his clan and their mutual trust and respect. It is in this way that Benedict came to see the potlatch as comparable to an era of megalomania among the elite of the community, a psychological disposition informing a habit of association to the detriment of the entire society.

Wolf (1999) tried to explain the excesses of human activity present in the potlatch. He argued that in north-west coast potlatch, people redistribute goods and burn ceremonial copper images because an idea about the way the world could be has taken hold of their imaginations, and made the actions seem reasonable. He argues that it is a feature of 'the gift' (both the act of making and that of receiving the gift) that a person might think through the significance of actions in most personal terms, and reconcile the apparently contradictory motivations to give with a utopian myth. Wolf shows us that people often claim to be economic rationalists by acting upon ideas that bring them harm.

How should anthropologists rectify Boas's ethnography of competitive exchange, made during the transformation of an entire society towards full participation in capitalist exchange, with Mauss's attention to the largesse of gift exchange? If in capitalist systems of value the gift becomes only a poor sign of itself, a shadowy phantasm of the life that values associations between people, then the gift as it is used among people beyond capitalist systems of wealth circulation is something different again.

The work of Boas and Mauss puts an enormous challenge in front of the capitalist economy by arguing that individuals do not act with economic rationality, and by arguing that analysis of political and economic life can begin in the examination of the intimacy of social relations where the peculiar matter of human consciousness can be addressed better than through looking at institutions, or structures. That challenge continues, especially to the recent forms of neo-liberal ideology in contemporary capitalism that entwines the person into limiting or constraining social structural commitments. A human person becomes *only* an individual with so much to risk and lose by going with the flow, thereby freeing him or herself to keep obligations.

Giving beyond reason?

Wolf (1999) argues that people give beyond reason in the north-west coast region in keeping with the response to the unreasonable effects of capitalist economic expansion into their social lives. This concurs with Gregory's interest in the flowering of gift exchange in the face of early intrusions of capitalist commodity transactions in Papua New Guinea (Gregory 1982, 1997). It is possible to consider potlatch as the efflorescence of gift exchange, in a kind of unusual activity that spreads as a shadow of the expansion of relationships shaped as commodity capital.

Wolf evaluates the potlatch of the north-west coast in this way. He assesses the importance of the ceremony for the indigenous community, pointing out their increasing dependence on the market economy as they seek wage-paying jobs or small business ventures. None of this would be worthy of comment, let alone ritual redress, if the community thrived under such circumstances. Instead, social relations fell into doubt among some people with firmer and longer-term relationships in the market society, and with more social resources to generate wealth. What should the wealthy do with wealth?

What can an anthropologist know about how others feel at the sight of excesses of ceremonial feasting? Wolf tells us that the colonial record shows something of this. The self-destructive feasting presented an interesting problem for the colonial government in British Columbia to solve. This government distrusted the intentions of large companies working to create large salmon fisheries off the coast and aiming to contract large acreages of land for logging. While clans held title on many of these, the companies said they did not. The provincial government aimed to keep those titles intact, dissuading the north-west coast Indians from selling to the southern-based companies and persuaded them to develop small-scale projects on the land so that their future well-being was conserved. As the advocates of small business development on the north-west coast, and as politicians with more than a modicum of distrust for big business, their eyes focused on the problem of clan well-being.

What can be learned from considering the colonial adminstrators' response? At the very least it could be an instance of how anthropologists should not respond to the events – that is, with fear and awe that exoticize what he or she fails to understand. Can the excesses of ceremonial display terrify some people while they enchant others? Bataille (1991) thinks so. He is writing at the time of the rise of fascism and finds the excesses of ceremony disturbing. Hutnyk (2003) suggests that Bataille might fear more than anything the possibility that profoundly human concerns can be lost to the ideals of the ceremony of nationalism. In such circumstances, the powerful displays of belief introduce a rigidity of action and a narrowing pathway of opportunities for changes in the course of that action. Ruth Benedict describes this kind of fascistic activity as megalomania, and warns that the political game of potlatch, gone out of control in the venue of nationalist politics, terrified even the sternest of competitors in the game.

Building on Boas's ethnography, Benedict argues that at periods in the history of a cultural group there may emerge a kind of cultural disposition that favours particular human traits. Benedict uses the example of the Kwakiutl potlatch as an example of the cultural basis of the psychology of megalomania. She draws provocative comparisons between the Kwakiutl obsessions with the display of wealth and the performance of ritual and the Nazi obsession with similar ritualized performance and display of power, ironically suggesting that, 'We have given scant justice to the reasonableness of cannibalism' (Benedict 1935: 44). Her comparison of each of the Kwakiutl and Nazi performances suggests that the display of power can also make power, and that failing to see it leaves participants at the feast vulnerable to its deployments in the hands of leaders.

The anthropologists Benedict and Hutnyk, different from Bataille the surrealist philosopher, might have shared their approaches had they met and conferred about it and had they been able to ask similar questions of the Kwakiutl. At the least they found that potlatch provided a mirror for examining excessive displays of power in Nazism, and a much-needed mirror too! Fascistic rituals of secular power were a West European political phenomenon of the twentieth century that overpowered its viewers with its own dazzling displays, suggesting the leadership-possessed charisma as a kind of intractable power. If fascistic ritual was a Gorgon monster that turned many thinking persons' hearts and minds to stone, then the anthropologist could use the mirror of the potlatch from the cold and rainy coasts of the Pacific Northwest to see its dangers and overcome its daze of signs. Perhaps more anthropological approaches suggest the need to ask different kinds of questions. When does excess create terror? When does excess generate possibilities of insight?

Consider how participants in other ceremonies talk about the possibility of a ceremony or a practice accelerating and going out of control, and thereby taking over the control of every action of their lives. In seeking to investigate this, during my own fieldwork I discussed the 'malanggan' complex in New Ireland with its hosts and participants. Malanggan is a funerary ritual, which is famous for its sculptures of strikingly complex beauty that are first displayed then destroyed as part of the ceremony. The word malanggan, which has no direct translation, describes both the sculpture and the feast prepared by mourners who come together to grieve the dead. The grieving at the ceremonial feast could continue indefinitely if the mourners decided to let it. Men, and even more so women, spoke about the dangers of past feasts, when the malanggan 'swung out of control'. In order to satiate the guests, the hosts used everything they had: pigs, magic, dance and food. Sometimes the women complained, women and men would retreat to the gardens in the midst of a malanggan feast in order to replenish the stacks of root vegetables used for feeding the guests. Young, mature and old crops would be uprooted until the feasters exhausted the garden crops. In times like these, women urged men to stop the festivities.

In a different example, the surrealist essayist and poet Bataille (1993) argues that the poetic imagination of the ancient Aztecs escalated out of control, ending in the act of ceremonial sacrifice of youths. Bataille's fabled account describes sacrifice as an event that gripped the imagination of the entire ancient Aztec civilization. In an evocative, fictive account, he depicts the imagined horrors of the Aztec sacrifice. He narrates those ceremonies fantastically, in order to show how wrong things can go. In a total society swinging out of control, because it was more in the control of a few priests, participants sacrificed war captives, slaves and their own young people to make the sun come back to give its warmth to the earth, and asked the stars to sing the names of the victims eternally. If the beauty of the stars surpasses everything, even injunctions against human sacrifice, then the participants in the ceremony should fear the excesses of powerful display. Bataille suggests something more than some latter day anthropologists who argued that the Aztecs sacrificed humans in order to keep the community working collectively in the seasonal corn harvest. Similar to Wolf, he argued that the Aztec ritual beliefs prevailed over the human costs as long as the symbolic economy stirred people to act to make an increasingly irrational world seem more reasonable.

Wolf and Bataille teach that it is a terrifying deceit of cultural knowledge that leads people to act inhumanely; and this is why anthropologists need to understand culture (and not just history) better than they do. The retelling of the account in fictionalized form allows Bataille to demand more of his reader; to consider deeply, without dismissing or putting down the book, what participants knew through the awe and fear that must be part of sacrifice. Taking this in, digesting the difficult image and the unpleasant experience with the human senses is necessary to an anthropological understanding of it. Knowledge of the event, of the ceremony, of the human acts can only be complete if it includes the irrationality of it all.

Can you give too much? Apparently you cannot; and necessarily, yes, you must. The excesses of giving cannot be explained in terms of how to rationalize the amount of expenditure, or of giving. Nor can the excesses of giving be explained in terms of covert self-satisfaction as when someone appears generous with small things while holding back the most valuable goods. Instead, the examples of the excessive generosity of feasting, of sacrifice to the gods, of giving all you can in the name of virtue, all share a concern with human existence. These gifts are made in the face of death, gifts made to acknowledge human mortality. It is not possible to give too much in the face of death, and it is absolutely necessary to give generously at the moment of recognition of that existential fact. A person works hard to keep relations and to meet obligations, but the fact remains that at the death of a friend, no exchange of gifts could rectify the loss. There is one certainty in all relationships: that they will end in separation of some kind.

Living after excessive giving

Elsewhere in the world across the Pacific, on the islands of New Ireland, people address the problem of what they have lost at the death of kin in a ritual in which they exchange food and shell wealth. The clan hosting the ritual will ask for support from the rest of the village, and request individual men and women to prepare by bringing taro and pigs to the feast. More spectacularly, the hosts invite a malanggan maker to assemble a team of artists. The team prepare for the ritual feast: they carve, weave and display sculptures for a brief viewing. After the short display the figures are destroyed. The malanggan moves people after they have seen it, after their departure from the feasting site. What they retain, in their mind's eye, is the image of the sculpture, so powerful that the German ethnographer of the turn of the last century wrote of how it came back to him in feverish dreams. No doubt it did, but Kraemer lacked the means to recreate the malanggan, a means that New Irelanders do have. In later years, a few who first saw it will aim to reconstitute the image that they saw. The malanggan glistens in the midday light, but its image imprints itself on the retina. A malanggan that carvers created for the tourist's eye does not capture the beauty of the ritual object. (This image is reproduced in Figure 11.1 on p. 201)

Ghosts, images of the dead, are not scary, but living with the obligations to them is. How people meet their obligations to others is a measure of their humanity, and it is possible to fail. In New Ireland, I have been told that mortuary custom is hard because it holds you in its grip. How that is so puzzled me, until I realized that there is no choice about opting out of customary work. Even those men and women whose religious conversion entailed 'giving up' custom eventually participated in it in later years. I recall one case in particular: a man whose years as a judge and whose conversion to the faith of the Seventh Day Adventists made him a very 'modern' man and unlikely to participate in traditional rituals. As he matured to middle age, he kept his obligations to the clans and community to host his parents' funeral with a malanggan feast. He attempted a hybrid feast, making an effort to blend his commitments to the ceremonial work with the Christian commitments to the funeral. Within days of the final event, the host was racing about the region, seeking proper ceremonial pigs to replace the chicken substitutes he had planned. At the last minute he consulted a weather maker to ensure a sunny day. The participants grumbled that the food was in short supply, not good, and the day rainy. Getting the aesthetic sensibility correct mattered in every way. They joked about the chickens when they should have been smacking their lips in appreciation of pork. The correct display of wealth in the funeral would have measured his success. Was this what malanggan feasting had come to be? It might have been better never to try to host the event because the man's failure to present the ceremonial wealth created ill-will towards him, whereas before his guests bore him none.

Learning to see the extraneous relations

How does an anthropologist learn to see the relations that would be easier to ignore? In his ethnography of Thailand mortuary ritual, Klima recounts a difficult fieldwork incident – one that he hoped to forget but later rethought and reconsidered as necessary to his understanding of the whole fieldwork situation. He examines how his purchase of a packet of cigarettes in a corner shop exploded into a violent confrontation between the shopkeeper and himself, when the shopkeeper gave back the incorrect amount of change from the purchase and sold him fake cigarettes instead of real ones. 'Under other circumstances on other days, it might have been possible to ignore it.' Klima explains that he felt frustrated by the exchange because he knew that the owner had participated in other events in the street the days before, in events that had caused the injury of a number of protesters against the meeting of the G7 countries to discuss trade. Was this the only reason for Klima's outrage? Could he really see himself as a victim of unfair trade while purchasing petty goods? Is anger the result of the ironic fact of being ripped off in a purchase by a local trader, while participating with him in an anti-capitalist demonstration? Is anger the result of irresolvable contradictions in the daily life of anthropologists with the extra burden of taking up an activist project as part of the period of fieldwork?

What does the display of anger succeed in creating in those relationships? What we do not know is what kinds of relationships Klima made for himself that day as a result of excessive displays of anger in the shop. Then too, what kind of relationships are made and unmade by excesses of human expression in the social protest that Klima described as an anti-capitalist demonstration? Is this effervescence of emotion and sensual knowledge constitutive of new reality or regenerative of old ones? The answers could only come with what Klima calls the courage to live with those aspects of the world that seem irrational.

A more complex event described by Klima has been the ceremonial work of setting up a gambling casino as part of the conclusion of his wife's father's funeral. The gambling edifice surprises him. At first the choice of ways to celebrate the work seems bizarre, so bizarre that the Western-born anthropologist admits that he cannot make sense of the importance of the ritual work. How could a time of grief and personal loss be addressed by such a frivolous activity?

As an ethnographer, he invites the reader to find the same answers as he does in their activity. It is a social activity in which people concentrate their attention on the enormity of life in these small bids for good luck. As the wheel of fortune turns, time after time, people place larger and larger bets. In the shadows of the funeral event they risk larger sums of material wealth than seems humanly wise. They participate in irrational behaviour, faced with the mundane fact of death and the irrational fact of its futility in human life. They have to risk that life counts for something, and that death means the loss of good friends and bodily pleasures of their company – sharing food at feasts, smelling the wind on the same day. This gambling is a form of deep play recorded by Geertz (1973), in which participants go well beyond the acceptable limits of rational economic choice because they stake more in the play as persons than in the gambling as economic actors. The funeral casino presents a case of how people recognize and address their fears of contingency and death within life, by participating in ritual with excruciating commitment to gambling it all away. Meeting obligations to ceremonial life is hard work because it puts celebrants face-to-face with each other and with the necessity of remaining human.

Of course mortuary ceremonies triumph the continuity of social relations in the face of loss and death. That is a rational response, which reasonable anthropologists can describe. But the experience of death is not rational and anthropological understanding does not grow from only reasonable experience of it. For all of an anthropologist's attention to the facts of social life and to the habits of transacting material goods with others in order to continue social life, one thing remains true. You will be at least physically separated from those whom you love. Recognizing this helps an anthropologist to make sense of the excesses of experience, the copious gifts of Trobriand fathers, the angry outburst at apparently unfair exchange, and the destruction of beautiful New Ireland sculpture in grief. Perhaps it is too easy to live an entire lifetime ignorant of the inevitable fact of the loss of the physical forms of relationship; that might be the case whether you choose to live in Manchester, Papua New Guinea or New York City. Perhaps that ignorance comes from simply denying the madness of mortality with the daily measure of small gifts made against infinity, as if death does not come in the end. Meditating upon that certainty of separation changes the anthropological argument, at least in so far as it makes all arguments about how to sustain human relationships a matter of the exchange of forms of gifts.

Conclusions: a meditation on giving beyond reason

Tying people into it even as it goes on, taking others along with it into the lives of others, the gift you take into your hands begs you to think of yet another person, maybe the one who gave it to you, or maybe another person you have not met. That is how the gift works. This is the hau of it, not bush spirits or spirits of the dead, but the spirits of living others that insist themselves upon you, the additional, unexpected share of the transaction that remains with you. Giving attention to excess – to figuring out what remains after a transaction appears complete – points to an unexplored anthropological concern for the spirit of the gift. The gift is not sacred and therefore kept back from risks of circulation. Instead, it is in the spirit of the gift to recognize that exchange creates moral outcomes by leaving behind traces of other people with you, after you thought the relationship ended. In the balance between the completed transaction between several people and the traces of that transaction lies the complexity of moral reasoning. Moral reasoning entails freeing the self – which is a complex act – to meet obligations.

Anthropology has much to give to a student of it. Fieldwork brings experience and knowledge about how to be a human being, and does so in ways that surprise the scholar who assumes that the familiar will continue to seem familiar anywhere. In addition to understanding what seems familiar, it is also necessary to consider how fieldwork 'failures', researchers' mistakes and misunderstandings are not barriers to anthropological knowledge. Instead, they are part of it. Perhaps, if anthropologists accept that gifts come to hand through unreasonable processes, then they can consider more fully the unusual, difficult parts of social life.

When it comes to writing it all down, the first problem is how to rid yourself of what you know, given that you have received too much. The second problem is how to live with the rest of it. That second problem is a little closer to what Mauss meant by the hau of the gift than either what Derrida meant by the difference that the gift makes, or quite what Bataille meant by the 'accursed share', as that portion of wealth that exceeds the needs of people to sustain themselves. How to live with the rest begs anthropologists to consider how the intersubjective nature of exchange stretches the terms of the gift beyond what is reasonable into considerations of the spectacular, and then again beyond the surreal. In the last chapter, I discuss how that extension of relationship is not exotic; instead, it is a matter of ethical concern.

Summary of chapter 9

How can anthropologists account for the total human experience if they systematically exclude from their fieldwork any material that seems excessive to the explanation, any evidence that seems unpleasant to consider, and the 'ugly' aspects of human experience. According to Bataille, a theory of society cannot exclude the irrational and the erotic from its explanations of how people live together. In this chapter I have examined examples of the aesthetics and ethics of Trobriand gardening such that the father's mapula gifts might be understood as expressions of affection as well as acts of reciprocal exchange. Further, I have examined the excessively generous acts of giving wealth away to be destroyed in potlatch feasts, considering what was made by giving too much and how people lived with giving too much. Critics of Bataille's celebration of the irrationality of excessive exchange, Wolf and Klima, point out that both colonial administrators and neo-colonial economic policy denigrate customary ceremonial exchange as irrational. In turn, these anthropologists expose that the belief that capitalist exchange for wealth accumulation is a pathway to individual freedom is founded in irrational belief in freedom outside social relations. While the studies also confirm Bataille's insight that capitalism is irrational in its inception, they raise a further concern too. Each of the case studies examines exchanges that take place at the time of death, and in the events of funerals and sacrifice. The problem that Bataille raises is: how can anthropologists understand death as a part of life when it is also an experience that exceeds rational explanations and exposes claims to know of powers and existence outside of social life? That people use ceremonial and everyday rituals to reproduce society in the face of death is a common anthropological understanding. Ghosts, spiritual presences and the material and immaterial legacies of the dead do not terrify people, but living with the obligations to acknowledge their presence is difficult when it requires that not all of social action is grounded in rational belief.

Part III

A PRESENT WITHOUT NOSTALGIA

10

VIRTUALLY REAL EXCHANGE

Does technology change the way in which exchange operates in social relationships? As people in the second half of the twentieth century came to terms with the possibilities of electronic communication, from music recordings to the internet café, some scholars suggested that the world had grown smaller and that intimacy remained possible across great distances creating what McLuhan (1964a) named a global village and later scholars theorized as 'ethnoscapes' (Appadurai 1996) or as the 'traffic in culture' (Marcus and Meyers 1995). The global village is 'virtually' a village. It requires that everyone in it bear an image of their intimate collaborative participation in constructing the village through technological mediums, but at a larger scale than before. This chapter examines the exchange of knowledge in virtual reality as a form of interaction that suspends disbelief in the possibility of face-to-face intimacy across great distances. Virtual reality interfaces those forms of sociality with technology and cultural media, as common as radio and television and as 'exotic' as cyberspace. In McLuhan's understanding of virtual reality people emphasize how their relations are meaningful, rather than what they mean, and so they convey meaning.

My Aim is True is the title of a music album from 1977 and comes from the song 'Alison'. This song concerns a man who recognizes that love breaks down the exchanges between the self and another because the lines between partners become blurred. There is something of the irrational about love; images and forms belonging to persons beyond the couple's direct experience inhabit the relationship as when one misnames a friend in a sentimental moment, or likens the gift of affection to earlier experiences of parental love. None the less, the lyrics by Elvis Costello acknowledge love's disappointment and illusions even in its mutual loyalty. In love neither ideal nor material aspects of affection can characterize or give evidence to its reality. If love is virtually real, then its truth is out there, over there, and inescapably present in the relationship.

I am writing about a popular culture song, making some comments about what might be commonly understood in mulling over the significance of it. During years of student life, it is common for people either to claim greater significance for songs, films or popular images, or conversely to deny their power to carry meaning as contrary to their seemingly over-determined significance in the popular art and music culture. That daily kind of reflection can be akin to thinking anthropologically, but what would an anthropologist interested in problems of the exchange of ideas or intellectual perspectives analyse in popular culture?

I use the example of this song because it introduces the problem of describing popular forms of sociality that create a sense of 'virtual reality'. Here, I consider the possibilities offered to anthropological thought by such recourses following new configurations of subject/object pairings. In virtual reality, it is hard to understand the world with the Cartesian philosophy that separates the sentient human subject from the intransigent objective world. Instead, in virtual reality the sceptical subject suspends disbelief and reconfigures its relationship to the object. For example, love and friendship are common experiences which might seem virtually real in the way in which other technologically assisted experiences seem real; the virtual reality of new forms of communication on internet and mobile telephones, the reality of social policy, the reality of development organizations. People experience virtual reality when placing their faith in thoughts and sentiments about the relationship. Common wisdom teaches that you perceive, rather than test another person's friendship before you risk demonstrating it with invitations to share your meal, your time and your home. The relationship is sustained as long as the other person participates in it in a friendly manner, which might be to say that it is simply 'virtually real'. Sceptical enquiry cannot confirm its truth, instead testing faith in a relationship creates doubts about it and effectively destroys the sense of affection and its sense of reality that makes it seem real. At the same time, it is common wisdom among any group of acquaintances that the conditions of virtually real gifts, such as gifts of friendship, depend upon accepting specific conditions. The belief in the reality of friendship depends upon sharing the belief that the camaraderie exists with at least one other person.

One can compare technologies of the self in creating virtual forms of social life such as friendship, with the experience of technologically assisted forms of virtual reality such as internet society, or the older forms such as television, film and music which connect through the imagination rather than through channels that open direct access to each other's chosen words and images. Whether in friendship or in cyberspace, people aim to make the connection true, even when the form might be false or the ideal might betray.

Technology as virtually real exchange

In this chapter, I want to examine the anthropology of virtual society by entering into a discussion of the exchange of ideas in a non-Cartesian space (see too Augé 1992). By non-Cartesian space I mean domains of experience in which the body does not appear as a material fact, separate from the mind, and by extension, the mind is not separate from the world as a material reality in any popular sense as essentially real, or in a materialist sense as a tool or resource for use by the sentient being. Virtually real exchange challenges anthropologists to enter into considerable investigation into the nature of anthropological technology and the nature of the society which uses them. Imitating exchange relations, I will alternate between discussions of virtual society, and the anthropological proposals for a new descriptive technology to comprehend it.

Anthropologists might meet the challenge to describe experiences that seem virtually real by choosing technologies of communication that evoke rather than record that reality. Wagner argued that through the uses of metaphor, which extend or carry meaning across to different contexts, people elicit understanding. Wagner (1986) distinguishes metaphor as the extension of meaning to new contexts of experience, from symbols as 'things' that represent the world. His position explores how meaning is made and distinguishes him from Geertz (1973) who argued that anthropologists must discover what actions and words represent, what symbols mean, and how people live meaningfully. Artistic expressions can guide anthropologists in this activity; however, the work of ethnographic description entails further reflection upon such evocations.

Here is an example, taking Wagner's guidance, because he admires popular culture. Consider the popular song named here, as a departure point for further consideration of how to conduct anthropology after acknowledging the failures of the Cartesian subject to comprehend the human condition. The lyrics describe a woman as seen by a man who loves her. The narrator catalogues the other suitors who adore her, marking the manifestations of those failed relationships. He recalls a memory of pretty fingers lying (lie-ing?) in the wedding cake as an image presaging the deceived marriage. Her display of a 'silly' valentine from another admirer belittles the unrequited love of the narrator. Acknowledging that purposeless and false loves can damage both lover and beloved, he begs someone to turn out the 'big light' because he 'can't stand to see her this way'. Fearful that love's various tawdry manifestations might betray his ideal, the narrator sustains his belief that, at its best, neither ideal nor material form confirms the sentiment. The song warns the listener that love's virtual reality can be pained and threatened both by the ideal of 'true love' as well as by the physical presence of the adored. Only love's aim is true because love is neither an ideal nor a material fact, but simply virtually real.

Such a departure for anthropological description is not at odds with everyday Euro-American commonsense and folk wisdom. There is a danger that virtual society might be an experience specific to the bourgeois consciousness. Indeed, Western folk wisdom tells us that romantic love opens a world of knowing in which the relations between the self and the other collapse, which is a fantasy held by the bourgeois individual in hopes against his ultimate alienation from others. Despite the efflorescence of self-help guides that advise on how to retain the self in love relationships (which is why they are called self-help books), most folk wisdom understands that the distinction between the self and other blurs in love. That basic idea makes possible two features of love.

First, consider how humans make unexpected or apparently irrational decisions in the name of love. This apparent vulnerability of persons in love also suggests the pathologies of the condition, and subsequently the general concern for the compromises made by the loving subject to the object of his or her affection. Conversely, consider how mature love transforms relationships with the mutual recognition that the successful relationship positively influences the quality of life of the person within it. This, paradoxically, acknowledges that love is a relationship that distinguishes persons, by making it necessary to acknowledge, even create, the loved one as distinct from the self. Perhaps love's successes elude people; perhaps those stories remain unsung.

Suppose I take the example of art-house cinema as a commentary on popular culture, as well as one of many different popular cultural forms. Goddard's *Eloge de l'Amour* (2000) is a eulogy mourning intimate human relationships and praising love's work in sustaining sociality, asking if being adult is truly possible without the possibility of loving. He asks if the failure of love, a failure of the spirit rather than of material reality, is the single fact of human alienation in a modern era. Goddard opens the film by inviting the viewer to recall that the theme of human relations consumed the attention of most ancient philosophers while modern theorists obsessed over theorizing the self, at great personal loss. Take for example a meditation from Plato's *Symposium* which searches for how ideal love might be known concretely within the human relationship. The *Symposium* defines love as the everlasting possession of the good and claims that the pursuit of love must be born in beauty, but not simply so. Even ideal love emerges from the basic fact of human relatedness. It is not thought to be a capacity of the individual so much as a virtue of those relationships that create human beings.

The song, and the film, the anthropological and philosophical text are each a different descriptive technology for exposing the elusive character of love. Neither popular nor clinical science measures love's profundity in human lives, and love cannot be diminished to chemistry, popular psychology or contemporary fascination with spirituality. Many questions can be asked. What relationships sustain love, how is it expressed, or how can its aim be true even when others fail to see it? Anthropologists risk creating analysis as a form of such virtual reality by trying to describe virtual reality; that is, each interpretation or translation recreates the virtual real, yet again.

Does anthropology need new descriptive technologies?

In the previous sections I have tacked (as does a sailing craft on wind) between evocation and analysis of the theme of popular culture renderings of love. It is a form of experience that can entrap the writer and researcher with metaphors that carry across the sense of the problem into the interpretation and analysis of the problem. Where the researcher is easily entrapped in a network of interpretations of a text – a web – one needs different technologies of communication and reflection. In an effort to identify guides to the study of virtual society, I have selected three anthropologists: Latour, Strathern, and Wagner. Each of them recalls the varied history of attempts to describe and change reality, even as they entertain the question of how to analyse virtually real gifts such as the exchange of ideas. In this section I will discuss the work of Latour (1988, 1999), Strathern (1999, 2000) and Wagner (1986, 2001) in relation to their instructions on how one might describe virtual society.

In virtual society, an anthropologist would err in the attempt to refer to reality in a material sense as a mute object or in any materialist sense as the transformative impact on a person of an object carried in the hand (Latour 1999: 174). Neither do they glibly refer to virtual reality (commonly understood as technologically assisted communication that apparently extends human capacities beyond the body of the subject) as a 'new' reality that compromises the immediate physical and corporal reality of direct, face-to-face speech. Instead, Latour evokes classical Greek philosophers' discussions of Daedalus' *techne* and reconsiders him as an engineer who uses science and technical skill to change the world in which he is entangled and lives. So inspired, Latour argues that technical skill creates reality as the symmetry of nature and society; he does not assume the verity of one over and above the other. A problem remains in regard to how to modify social theory to explain

> a continuity between nuclear power plants, missile-guidance systems, computer chip design, or subway automation and the ancient mix of society, symbols and matter that ethnographers and archaeologists have studied for generations in the cultures of New Guinea, Old England or sixteenth century Burgundy.
>
> (Latour 1999: 195)

In *Pandora's Hope*, Latour elaborates his earlier argument for continuities across modern and ancient society as made in *We Have Never Been Modern* (1988). The reader learns that technical skill in the modern era deepens the intimacy between the ideal and the material by repeatedly cross-cutting their separation as if finely making a long chain to weave them together. In supposedly primitive society mobilizing chains of relations can imbue any object with the history of transactions producing it.

Wagner and Strathern seem less certain that the separation of material from ideal defines the modern era, and subsequently that the remarriage of material with ideal form defines contemporaneous relations. More so, as scholars with experience in seemingly non-modern society, they are less assured that technical skill of moderns ever worked differently from the skills of others, and even less convinced about differentiating between modes of description of reality in modern and primitive society, as has been Latour's aim. Instead, Strathern, drawing on Battaglia's ideas about displacement (1999), urges readers to consider 'why we think technology requires special techniques of habitation and why, in effect we distance it from us' (2001: 2). Drawing upon commonalities between Euro-American and New Irelander habits of 'separating themselves from what they see enveloping them', Strathern poses her doubts about 'the opposition between nature and the application of knowledge that Euro-Americans call technology' (2001: 3). Wagner argues that both Melanesian world views and holographic reality can impact positively the techniques and the practice of anthropology at home and abroad: 'What an absolute holographic reality might be is simply the right question' (Wagner 2001: xix).

Although Latour raises clearly the possibility of a new science after the critique of Descartes by proposing that research into hybrid forms of nature and society should lead scholarship into forms of association needed by the collective, his work does not realize the goal of creating a post-Cartesian anthropological thought. Instead, it is the work of Strathern and Wagner that succeeds in going beyond the limits of the sentient Cartesian subject's knowledge of an objective world. Most generally, their work helps anthropologists to understand those experiences of sociality that seem virtually real; that is, such meaningful experiences in which absent persons can be known through substituted images and forms and even composed of other persons.

Indirectly, by describing virtually real exchanges and interchanges, these anthropologists have raised a critique of postmodern thought. Postmodern criticism has challenged the discipline's ability to describe an objective world. In this, they differ from other anthropologists who have recorded this critique, without replying to it with alternatives (see Marcus and Fischer 1986, Rabinow 1996). It is widely agreed in anthropology now that descriptive accounts can be accused of failing because they leave incomplete coverage or inaccurate representations of experience. More eloquent analyses of the crisis of representation endorsed poststructuralist insights that perhaps had been best elaborated in *The Order of Things* (Foucault 1972). Foucault had correctly recognized that efforts to represent experience severed the representation of life, labour and language from the meaningful contexts of their practice. This ironic fact of knowledge made scientific thought impossible. As a stunning critique of even the interpretative social sciences, he showed that failure lies with the scientific limits placed upon descriptive practice. That is, it is impossible to meaningfully understand any lived experience through describing it, whether thickly or symbolically. In the worst-case scenario, attempts at accurate description kill off the meaning won in experience. Unfortunately the postmodern caveat that symbolic representation saps life of meaning had few rejoinders. These authors offer a response and a course of action.

Some critics of virtual reality believe that technology is somehow distinct from society, rather than a part of it. How have we forgotten that tool making, technology and general artisan skill facilitate and define human society? The creation of the funereal sculptures which I described in chapter 9 shows that expert uses of technology, especially artisan skill, permeate fundamental social experiences. Without skilled carvers to create beautiful sculptures that keep the attention of the mourners on the nature of their loss, participants in the ceremony could not experience grieving as fully as they do. The beauty of the form is etched upon the imagination of the viewer, such that the image rather than the material form remains as the reality of the experience of mourning and grief. Here, I follow Strathern's descriptive definition of malanggan as an example of virtual reality, 'Present bodies may at once substitute for absent bodies (New Ireland exegesis) on the carving as a body for the deceased, and (exegesis mine) may be presented as composed of other bodies, as this (malanggan) head is composed of birds and fish' (Strathern 2001). Strathern's essay discusses the ways in which technology can be animated. The effect is a series of resonating forms of social experience that cannot be simply classified as material or ideal.

How can anthropologists understand the experience of viewing the sculpture at the mortuary feast without falsely assuming it is a thing to be described? Such questions pose afresh Gregory Bateson's search for an anthropology that begins with empathy, and his efforts to expose its effects in social relationships. In a modern world, would that be a more radical point of departure, scepticism or empathy (Bateson 1972, 1987a, b and c)? Empathy entails escaping Cartesian objectivity that simply finds examples of the general rule in particular experience. The most persistent intellectual habit of Cartesian scepticism recreates a distinction between subject and object, repeatedly valorizing the subjectivity of the scholar as the knowing researcher of the world. A few anthropologists have risked putting the human relationship as love or empathy in the centre of their scholarly work so that they could see it. David Schneider did not discuss love as a means for understanding, but as an object that took the form of a core symbol in American families. In his book *American Kinship* (1975) Schneider reminded readers that the study of kinship must comprehend the intricacies of love. He argued that acknowledging the significance of love to kin relations presents the possibility of critiquing both the primary role of 'blood' as the substance that links people and the powerful place of the law as it governs relations. Schneider writes, 'Relatives are friends who are with you through thick and thin, whether you like it or not and whether they do the job properly or not' (1975: 54). That relatives are loved complicates the claim that American kin feel intimacy through the assumption that they are of the same blood, but Schneider acknowledges that relatives might disappoint you frequently, but that they rarely abandon you. Simultaneously, he argues that a better understanding of love presents the chance to critique the failings of legalistic approaches to human relationships. In American kinship, marriage is a legal relationship, emulating emotional bonds. The law makes affined kin out of those relations allegedly made by love and affection. Schneider's discussion of the exchanges of both affectionate and erotic love, as well as his discussion of the transactions of friendship, can disturb a reader so much that they might be tempted to dismiss the analysis or put the book down. Schneider acknowledges that writing about experiences so close to home misleads the reader into thinking that his book simply reports on the banal or that he writes about family life without discretion (1975). None the less, from Schneider's perspective, a study of kinship that fails to acknowledge the significance of love – whether it is taken as real, virtual or a category of experience to be interrogated by psychoanalytic anthropology – might also risk misunderstanding human relationships as they are lived.

Bateson's studies of communication and ritual life deployed intelligent uses of empathy in description. Wagner, following Bateson, argues that anthropology needs new mediums of expression following the failure of Cartesian reasoning to comprehend the complexity of social relations. If poststructuralism initiated the crisis of representation as a Kuhnian revolution in normal science, then Wagner responds in the terms of a revolutionary science in his proposal for a holographic anthropology. Wagner's proposal for a holographic anthropology thus distances itself from normal anthropology, just as Gregory Bateson championed anthropological science as 'metalogue' years after the contemplations of Whitehead and Russell on the nature of reality (Bateson 1958: 280; 1972). Holographic anthropology embraces the law of fractals in chaos theory to aid truthful description, thereby modelling reality. In chaos theory, models are not representations or descriptions in the common sense. They are the traces of attempts to apprehend reality's complexities that contain an internal record of shifts of vision or corrections of scale as a measure is taken of reality. Holographic anthropology is a self-scaling medium. If this is hard to understand, consider the common Euro-American experience of love, whereby empathy, one of love's mediums of expression, can create love by expressing love – empathy brings about changes in both the person who gives and the person who receives love. In such deployments of empathy, love becomes a self-scaling medium adjusting its expression to the changing nature of the love relationship, whereas empathy cannot be separated from love, and to call it a technology would require conscious difficult distinction of the experience of love from the demonstrations of empathy.

Alternatively, the work of self-scaling mediums in holographic anthropology might parallel the work of 'metalogue', as Bateson meant it. Metalogue carries the sense of communication at the same time that it carries its meaning, finding sense in a perpetual shifting of the question in response to the answer. In metalogue, as in holographic anthropology, the truth is out there, over there, and inescapably present in the relationships that make the model of reality, because reality always moves ahead of the means of modelling it.

If anthropologists were enabled to think well about virtual reality, they would do better to forget the essential categories of body and mind, of inside and outside, of consanguine and affine. Instead, anthropologists can approach the description of virtual reality as if it were a network of exchanges, such as Latour, Strathern and Wagner have theorized it. By using the example of love and the empathetic approach I explore the idea that virtual reality is a modern construct different from non-modern ideas about the nature of reality.

Technocracy of virtually real exchange

The anthropologist Riles (2000) offers a different kind of case study. She looks at how Pacific societies, such as the Walbiri of Australia, use artworks to underscore how they communicate and create social relations. The image, then, exists both as a form that represents a place and as a pathway for travel through that place (see Munn 1973, Glowczewski 1983). Riles explores, then in a manner similar to Munn, how a network of aid organizations operates internationally as a model for and of social life. Walbiri make patterns on the sand, iconographic images that operate to model social relationships. Drawing on Munn's example of Walbiri art, she aims to explain that icons – such as artefacts and policy documents – do not represent society; but rather, the models effectively make it.

Riles discusses the work of the non-government organizations (NGOs) that deliver support to the underdeveloped nation of Fiji, a nation whose colonial past I discussed in chapter 6, in an account of the exchanges that made indebtedness. Riles's account helpfully demonstrates that the anthropological attention to virtual reality need not universalize human emotions; it does, however, find a common capacity in human beings to make aesthetic judgements about beauty and virtue in human relationships. Her case study follows.

The public culture world of bureaucrats, documents, NGOs and networks takes on a life of its own with the confusion of social action, its documents and its general effects in the same way as empathy animates popular culture. Riles is a legal anthropologist who successfully modelled the complex network of aid organizations operating in the South Pacific, as a network. Although this similarity between what she describes and her model of it sounds superfluous rather than informative, she shows ethnographically that it is not. Far from being redundant, the efforts by Riles to describe networked interaction help her to analyse the most unnerving aspect of their operation: namely, the effect that they have on social life in the region. Anthropological researchers working in the vicinity of any network of aid organizations can note that effect. The organizations' policies start to be self-replicating across different field locations, so that problems such as the empowerment of women begin to be addressed in the same way everywhere. This is not because the causes of women's disempowerment are the same everywhere, but because the organizations use the same strategies for exposing women's empowerment as a problem.

Before I discuss Riles's analysis of Fiji's place in the network of aid organizations working with men and women there, it helps the reader to recall a few details about the country. Fiji became an independent Pacific Islands nation after a century of British administration as a colony of the empire and a territory of the Commonwealth. The history of labour trade and plantation work supported the growth of a large South Asian population in Fiji, where nearly 50 per cent of the total population in 1980 claimed that heritage. South Asians in Fiji became most politically active there in the period after the achievement on the Asian sub-continent of Indian independence in 1947 and through the years of political development leading to Fijian independence. The south Asian constituency of the Fijian Labour Party outnumbers any other, and these Indo-Fijians could be said to define the party itself (although it is not an Indo-Fijian political party by prescription). In addition to this, an entrenched commitment to the continuation of native or indigenous Fijian rights to land complicates the ethnic division in the Fijian state, which prevents the purchase of land by non-indigenous Fijians. Such conditions challenge most definitions of democracy and Fiji was ousted from the British Commonwealth in 1987 for undemocratic actions leading to the staging of a coup against a democratically elected government. How can the work of NGOs as a vanguard of civil society proceed? Does the enormously complex policy work undertaken to ascertain civil society in Fiji defeat the most implicitly democratic ideals of NGOs, and challenge thereby the legitimacy of their efforts?

Fiji is an excellent example of the advantages of using a network model for understanding the exchange of ideas that NGOs use because the complexities of the situation threaten to overpower the researcher with its machinations. Riles describes the public culture of the network not as a representation, but as an entity that embraces the ethnographer and tailors her work to its own rule. As a white woman, with legal expertise, working with third world women in a network of NGOs, she is both shunted into some roles and enveloped in others. The life of the network takes over the research itself. In the earliest sense, Riles's interest falls upon the exchange and circulation of documents: files, folders and papers that people use in the course of their participation in the network of aid organizations.

Virtual society captures aspects of global relations that otherwise escape us. The expanding network of connections between people cannot be represented ethnographically as layers upon layers of descriptive meaningful stories (as in thick description). Neither can the network of links be contextualized in some greater worldwide political economic system such that it becomes meaningful with reference to that. An analysis of a global network of NGOs and international organizations draws upon disparate sources of knowledge, and might be more akin to outlining how kula partners make trade links, or to how artists find patrons, amass materials, organize their work schedules and complete creations. The analysis of virtual society requires an aesthetic sensibility for how people create relationships with each other. Communication and exchange each are mediums for making relationships. In that context, Riles insightfully shows us that 'the network is a set of institutions, knowledge practices and artefacts that generally generate the effects of their own reality by reflecting on themselves' (2000: 3). This sense of self-similarity, the network described as a 'network', is simply the virtual reality of social life in such situations that seemingly expand beyond the forms of normal social life.

Riles makes use of an example invented by the women of Fiji. They create a document for the Beijing meeting of the Women's Congress in 1995 in the style of a Fijian mat. The mat, which is a trade item within Fiji, is woven of bamboo and holds a series of statements on its surface, which delegates can present to other delegates in the effort to place their positions on the table. Mats are traded ceremonially in Fiji between women at funeral feasts, between women in the work place and at churches, and between senior male bureaucrats whose work might take them into the long history of exchange of NGO paperwork. The women refigure men's most 'inventive' uses of the ceremonial mat for international negotiation, whereby men make an artefact of the village into an artefact in the global network. However, in this case the women do not trade mats, but they use the mat as an artefact of the network itself. As Riles artfully shows us, the mat is interlaced natural fibre, an image of a network in its crossover and extensions of conventional forms. Its virtual reality is the NGO network; the network's virtual reality is the ceremonial mat.

Surely wit and good humour moves Riles to show us that the stacks of mats that Fijian women place on low tables at the times for ceremonial feast compare sentimentally to the stacks of documents that they keep for meetings, carry to meetings and arrange in piles at meetings. Whereas women arrange mats on tables in meaningful patterns (one layer over another), the significance of the pattern remains invisible because a woman must remember the layer of mats in order to know the patterns (much like the simple card game of rummy, where remembering the preview cards in the deck which lie in the pile on the table centre enables the person to make patterns of cards known as runs, pairs and sets). Getting the documents right, as Riles shows us, entails getting the patterns of speech correct, not their meaning. In virtual reality, 'getting the wording right' means making parsimonious and elegant forms of expression on the document so that it looks good. Aesthetics and efficacy combine in one form, and to understand the social effect of the form requires one to understand how the beauty of that form pleased the delegates preparing their representation to the conference.

For anthropology, not technocracy

Strathern generalizes from Riles's work to elaborate her theory of the relation, a programme of analysis that she has been developing over recent years (Strathern 1991). As in the example above, some anthropologists have argued that complexity of virtual exchanges lies simply in the problematic of description (Marcus and Clifford 1986, Rabinow 1996, Strathern 1991; cf. Strathern 1999). I agree that description is both a common and professional activity and that the complexity of social life is a matter of human fabrication, as designs are made upon designs in the effort to comprehend their own attempts to understand each other. Like Wagner and Latour, Marilyn Strathern recognizes the complexity of sociality and the need for a method to address that complexity. Like Wagner, she advocates the ethnographic practice of anthropology: 'If at the end of the twentieth century, one were to invent a method of enquiry by which to grasp the complexity of social life, one might wish to invent something like the social anthropologist's ethnographic practice' (1999: 1). This compares judgmentally with Latour's call for a new discipline (rather than the old one of anthropology) that honours the symmetry of nature and society, not the domination of nature by the social. Pottage (2001), in reviewing Strathern's and Latour's ethnography, points out that Latour fails to find the ethnographic edge to escape what Latour has called the 'modern settlement' (Latour 1999: 310). Pottage shows this by contrast with Strathern's project. Of Strathern's work Pottage writes:

> The ambition is to generate an analogical counterpart to the cultural domain of Euro-America, a perspective from which the presuppositions and contexts of that domain can be made visible. This is the key to the difference between Strathern's analogy and Latour's model of symmetry: whereas the latter folds the thematic difference (the peculiar contents of other cultures) into the self-explanations of one mode of social action, the ethnographic analogy emphasizes thematic difference in order to generate alternative domains of social action, neither of which may be entirely real, but each of which affords a context or perspective from which to explore the presuppositions of its counterpart.
>
> (Pottage 2001: 113)

Pottage's review of Strathern's and Latour's work helped me to see that the advantage of Strathern's argument over Latour's lies in her ability to rescue research from a modernist project that would seek simplicity in the complex. Latour's network theory expands infinitely as he, like other modernist researchers, describes a modern world; Strathern holds up ontological knowledge for the reader to see, making the contingencies of her claims evident in the course of building her argument. Hence, Strathern's theory of complexity lies in her ethnographic practice, combining both description and analysis.

Strathern's enthusiasm for ethnography as a destabilizing activity emerges from the insights of her earliest fieldwork in Papua New Guinea – she insisted that women's subjectivity was not obviously compromised or alienated in ceremonial bride-wealth exchanges (1987, 1988). Strathern did not err by assuming this was a commodity exchange; her ethnographic insight emerged as she examined the *transactions* in ceremonial exchanges rather than focusing on the entities – pigs, pearlshells and women (1972). By re-shifting anthropological focus from object to transaction, Strathern drew attention to the combination of relationships and objects, demonstrating that they are inseparable when people generate meaning in ceremonial exchange. For example, by challenging the distinction between subject and object she argued that the complexities of bride-wealth exchanges exposed better understandings of the differences between men and women. Gender was neither a biological nor a sociological fact as much as it was a means of marking differences between points of view among Highland New Guineans (1988).

Strathern doubts the authenticity of any description that assumes that an eloquent and parsimonious account of the universal principles underlying the world might be revealed in analysis of a particular case. For example, participants in ceremonial matrimonial exchange assume that objects and persons are not isolates before the exchange but are made by the event itself. Unlike Lévi-Strauss's structuralism, Strathern (1985) does not use ethnography to describe how nature and culture are reinvented in the event of ceremonial exchange. Instead, she describes how ceremonial exchange makes specific forms of relationship into objects to be held, as a pig becomes the substantivization of the history of relations mobilized towards the amassing of bride wealth. In ceremonial exchange, this history is self-evident to all involved in the ceremony and the transactions leading to it. The knowledge practices of ceremonial exchange can be extended to virtual society.

Strathern exposes the claims to knowledge that an anthropologist might make as part of a process of the 'substantivization of social relations' (her original subtitle for *Property, Substance and Effect*). The danger, as she reminds readers, lies in the chance that the fact might be mistaken for knowledge, or that the object might be abstracted from the social relations that produced it, as if a germinal entity can be isolated from the nurturing partner. There is a risk that an insight would be taken from relations in which it might be meaningful rather than described within the social relations that brought it into the researcher's view. She describes this relation as the *merographic*, a habit of thought common to relations made through commodity exchanges whereby a person sees his or her attributes in another person or thing. Examples of the merographic are seeing creative potential in nature or confusing love with finding oneself reflected in the eyes of another. Merographic processes constitute social forms as if they were isolates, when they are not.

Strathern's personal effects from anthropological fieldwork include a trove of images – an intellectual wealth of memories and insights that can be handled and contemplated for their worth to disciplinary practice. She recalls one such image caught in her peripheral vision; the image is now a memory from her first fieldwork. Two men, carrying a display of pearlshells – the ceremonial wealth of the Melpa – appear over the shoulder of a hill only to hurry away again along a sloping path. The year was 1964, but Strathern writes of recalling this image in late 1999. Just as anthropologists continue to return to visit the people of their field sites, it is equally true that the people they knew and know from those places continue to come to them in the course of their daily living and work – in memories and with emotional force in daily life. This discussion is far from being an aside about the play of memory; Strathern begins with the recognition that such anthropological knowledge effects changes in the course of social science, even when only briefly and/or indirectly catching the attention of the scholar. In Strathern's study, an experience returns to the anthropologist. Memory niggles at the conscience; unresolved ethical dilemmas from fieldwork experiences can haunt the imagination. With all of the contemporary effort to establish an ethical programme for anthropological research, and with all of the contemporary effort to search out the grounds for responsible reporting, discerning how to create a discipline that is true to the ethnographic experience remains a worthy undertaking.

Melanesian research provided, and continues to provide in *Property, Substance and Effect* (Strathern 1999), an opportunity to think about larger questions in social theory; it also suggests critiques of social policy (Strathern 2000). Strathern named the technocracy of virtual society audit culture. Scholars in audit culture calculate social life, fracturing human experiences into discrete economic units. A critical approach is needed if anthropologists are to describe the contemporary process by which the world fractures at an accelerating pace into subjects and objects without reducing anthropological analysis to the process of audit. If anything, a holistic perspective such as the one shared by those people anywhere who practice ceremonial gift exchange, enhances anthropological understandings of the fracturing of the world through the privatization of wealth, as the audit of property claims. From my understanding, I see in Strathern's position similarities with Wagner's claim for a holographic worldview that helps anthropologists to see that an event images itself (Wagner 1992, 2001). The increasing range and numbers of claims on property made by people everywhere – from land claims by traditional owners in Papua New Guinea to claims on genetic resources by legal, biological and affective parents in the United States and Europe – testify to their assumption of the separation between the objective world and the human subject. They assume the fact of alienation, which is hard to see and hard to know, from an experience of alienation itself. To comprehend that condition, scholars require an ethnographic approach that begins with the connectedness between people. Departing from Strathern (1999), I find that the measure of the separation of subjects and objects – the measure of the disengagement from human relationships – can begin with a better understanding of the condition of the relation itself.

Virtual society is an effect of technologies of visualization, description and exchange (broadly understood), like other forms of social life. These technologies are social like other forms of life. As a term, virtual society captures the sense of involvement in forms of life that are neither material nor immaterial: empathy, love, popular culture, bureaucratic life, and discursive formations such as the effects of government. These life forms can only be described by evocation; that is, by learning to see them.

Some anthropologists argue that research in virtual society requires new technologies of description simply to expose or make explicit the web of connections through which people live. Technologies of description trace the effect of visualizing relations that would otherwise remain misunderstood as self-same versions of each other. A famous image evocated by technologies of description is fractal imagery, the efflorescent forms of life that emerge in the effort of measurement of the rate of change of difference – as in the effort to trace images on paper as the after-effects of mistakes made in trying to describe, copy or isolate the realist depiction of any entity.

Technologies of exchange trace the pathway of the extensions of the self outside the more conventionally held perceptions of the individual as self-contained. Love is one example of Euro-American common knowledge of the immaterial extension of the self into the life of another person, such that the imagination of love into relations has real effects upon them, as when expressions of love can generate love in return. In that example (different from the hau as the spirit of the gift) people exchange glances, tokens of affection, or they can share sentiments and a history of personal experience. Another example would be the aesthetic appreciation of virtue, as when a person expresses him or herself in deeds that others recognize or 'see' as good works and virtuous acts of that individual, or when a group, such as an organization for women's empowerment, shows that it is 'good' by its ability to create a documentary record of its intentions to change the life ways of women. That is a question for another chapter that aims to understand virtue, whether (or not) it monitors relations in virtual reality or in other forms of society. In the final chapter, I discuss ethics in the discipline of anthropology.

Summary of chapter 10

The global village is a term used to describe the worldwide society made by information technology since the second half of the twentieth century. How can the global village be analysed anthropologically by examining the exchange practices that are common to the small village of the earliest part of the century, which the first part of this book examined? How does the analysis of gift exchange as a total social fact succeed in exposing how people live in what is now termed virtual society? First, we looked at a paradox in the example of a love song. On the one hand virtual society is defined as a Cartesian space because it first appears as a technologically constituted reality mediated by modes of transmission, which make face-to-face communication unnecessary for affective expression and social connections. On the other hand, virtual society is a non-Cartesian space in which people make claims on each other through empathetic and sentimental modes of expression evoked through that technology. The paradox exposes a new need for anthropologists to surpass postmodern approaches to the study of society, especially those in which the analysis ends with reflexive criticism of limits of textual descriptions. I have discussed three different proposals for new descriptive technologies to describe virtual society by Latour, Wagner and Strathern respectively. Finally, I have examined a case study from Fiji in which one non-governmental organization aimed to influence the global community of policy makers by shaping the terms of a debate about what it means to be human in the virtual society of human rights policy. New questions might include the following. How does a technocracy of knowledge practices manage some visions of what it means to be human to the exclusion of other ones (perhaps shown in the process of creating audit documents)? And how does the exchange of words, documents, images and policies create new opportunities to define a space of social connection in which people might create different ways of living? The chapter ends by reviewing some of the departure points for an anthropology that is not simply a technocracy.

11

INTERESTS IN CULTURAL PROPERTY

Until this point I have not discussed the legal aspects of the gift, although at different points throughout this book I have suggested the importance of understanding the jural implications of exchanging gifts. If gift exchange becomes a concern of the legal mechanisms of globalization, as it does for example in the Fair Trade movement, then international law is being assessed against the possibility of the loss of ethical interests. I made the suggestion in the first chapter that the analysis of gift exchange could be brought into contemporary debates about globalization because it made legible the ethical aspects of most interchanges by demanding the assessment of the total human condition. In chapter 3 I discussed the gift exchange between a Trobriand father and his child's mother's brother, an exchange that implies that he recognizes the jural authority of the child's senior clansman. Previous chapters showed the various ways in which gift exchange embraces the domains of the political, economic, social, virtual and spiritual, emphasizing the gift as a total social fact that comprises and condenses all of social life. What then can be circumscribed as the legal domains of gift exchange if it precipitates the outcomes of both international law and family jural authorities? This question can be answered best by anthropological research. I intended that the total effect of that sequence of chapters would make it clearer how anthropological analysis of gift exchange would be a valuable critical tool against the pro-globalization movement's notion that humans are primarily economic beings. In part, this chapter aims to place a series of question marks over the use of the concept of economic man in globalization debates, and considers other avenues.

Let's make a general claim that would be hard to dispute from wherever a person stands in the pro- and anti-globalization debate. Globalization is a worldwide revolution in how to live, if not simply how to be in the world. The emergence of the Fair Trade movement suggests the need to reappraise principles of association among humans; not only as new forms of association (to monitor economic work), but also as new forms of legal relations (see for example, Monbiot 2003). Although not part of that movement, the United Nations advocated increased awareness and scrutiny of the claims to develop the cultural knowledge of indigenous people – from plant specimens to ritual performances. Here is the contradiction: indigenous knowledge should be available, and paradoxically the claim that its diversity should be protected. At the heart of that debate is a series of assumptions about the role of international law in protecting cultural heritage, often assumed to be a gift handed down from the elder generations (see Blake 2001). In this chapter I will examine the ways in which a focus on gift exchange explains how people make conscious choices about how to regulate and legalize human relations as a concern for how they might live together globally, including the making of legal provisions to protect culture as property.

How do contemporary debates seemingly make almost all claims on personal relations into matters of private ownership of property, against assumptions about commonly held property? The answer lies in understanding the negotiation. Property debates raise key legal matters immediately because property is a legal construct, and not a thing. (Nothing about objects inherently makes them property.) Property is a kind of claim that is made upon another person that extends to the material that is his or her wealth. Anthropologists can think better about this, by thinking through theories of gift exchange. More importantly for anthropology, debates about property expose central ontological matters, concerns that must be addressed if the discipline of anthropological argument is to have any sagacity for people who try to make their lives viable and reasonable in a global world. Property debates are not new. It is a problem with which the people of the world have lived for nearly three hundred years.

A comparison of the seventeenth and the twenty-first centuries: common wealth and property debates

In the rest of this chapter, I wish to explore the possibility that the contemporary concern that cultural property be justly distributed and claimed through legal mechanisms that respect cultural difference is an extension of Enlightenment debates. The twenty-first and seventeenth century compare in fascinating ways on matters of what is common about cultural property. That issue entails asking first, what the concept of the commons entails in the current period by comparison with what we know about property debates of the earlier one, and further, reflecting upon the common grounds of existence as an ontological problem that arises when many people feel concerned with a crisis of how to be in the world (Crook 2004).

I think that contemporary debates about cultural property compare intriguingly with seventeenth-century property debates among intellectuals and politicians following the enclosures of common land. In the earliest period, the times of the enclosures of common land as private property, people became deeply concerned with the loss of the commons to individual interests. I wrote about this in chapter 2, where I argued that Rousseau used the ideal of the Noble Savage to create a philosophy of political relations. To what extent do the current debates about property compare with the earliest property revolutions of the early Enlightenment period?

The social historian of the seventeenth century, Hill (1972), argued that the revolution won for individuals the means and legal right to make claims on private property, largely by providing for their protection in democratic parliament. According to Hill's account of the revolution in the social imagination that brought about parliamentary democracy, as different from the medieval past, individuals learned that they could now make legal claim on the material world as private wealth. Hill's thesis is intriguing because it sets the framework of ontological problems to be considered for politics in the late twentieth century. Working with the privilege of hindsight about the previous 300 years, Hill and others asked what should be the course of contemporary social revolutions of the last half of the twentieth century. The question was: how did the problem of how to be in the world (as a concern of ontology) become the precise matter of how to manage private property (as the subject of politics), and more specifically, how to express an individual share of interest in the common wealth of the world (as a discourse on rights)?

The time came in the early 1990s for the recognition that the new commons did exist. In the 1992 meeting of the UN Convention on Biodiversity, a new analysis emerged which posited that the world's biological diversity constituted a common resource of the globe. This created difficulties for indigenous peoples whose specialist knowledge of biological resources facilitated the identification of the resources and the specific uses in which the biological entity could be identified as useful. It seemed that indigenous peoples held responsibility for its custodianship, but were not clear owners of the rights to exploitation, transmission and dispersal. Despite the concerns of indigenous peoples for a say in the uses and preservation of their knowledge of cultural and natural resources, new international conventions claimed their knowledge of first biological diversity, then cultural diversity as the common resources of the planet.

Recently, Blake (2001) sets forward the claim that culture is the new commons. Although he does not cite the property debates of the seventeenth century, this provocation to argument comes within the terms of Hill's claims that there exists a tension between private interests in property and the common wealth. Whereas Hill believed that the political and social revolution to establish common property would yet come, Blake argues that the debates around cultural property will establish the legal provisions for common wealth in the world. The idea that culture is a common wealth is so powerful that the UN Declaration on Cultural Diversity (2001) acts to designate and negotiate this distinction between the integrity of culture in diverse settings, and the recognition of the common interest in the preservation of culture as a diversely inflected and expressed form. A somewhat ironic position emerged for different people across the globe, especially indigenous communities. Each distinct heritage of peoples could be protected only if those peoples admitted that their cultural heritage could be held in common with other cultures across the world.

If culture is the new commons, then the regulation of the grounds of common claims on ownership must be clarified. Anthropologists have much to add to this debate about the contemporary dilemma. Not surprisingly, some of the most useful arguments to be made are those that draw on the ways in which earlier theorists imagined gift exchange as a form of legal arrangement or negotiation. In the first instance, Parry's 1985 Malinowski Lecture (published in 1986) offered an inventive re-reading of gift exchange that called for deeper understanding of South Asian ethnography in order to fill in the gaps of Mauss's arguments about the legal significance of gift exchange. His triad of concerns with Malinowski's kula, Mauss's gift-exchange, and the South Asian gift establishes an important concern, that the rule of culture in establishing different forms of gift exchange pushes anthropologists to clarify what it means to be a legal person. That culture should be a 'rule' is a problem for further consideration, which I will address in the last part of this chapter. The definition of property makes a number of assumptions about 'interest' as an ontological concept, losing interest and protecting interests in particular govern legal provisions for cultural property.

Differentiating legal ontologies: the problem of interest in Malinowski and Mauss

Parry's insightful essay (1986) urges anthropologists to differentiate between Malinowski and Mauss on their respective ontological assumptions. I will summarize his essay, and push his analysis towards an understanding of legal implications of ontologies of exchange. Malinowski, as early as his studies of the kula, assumed that the person was moved by physical and libidinal interests to make social life work out for his or her own interests. Parry points out that by the time he wrote *Crime and Custom in Savage Society* (1926), Malinowski had routinized his thought more thoroughly. According to Malinowski, self-interest underpinned social life, as contrary or perverse as that may sound to the nature of living in social relationships.

We learn that Malinowski's ideas are as old as Hobbes, who began to write about the concept of interest as it was related to human desires when he wrote *Leviathan*; following on, Parry continues helpfully along these lines. Self-interested parties can make the social contract in face-to-face interactions. He shows us a resonance between Hobbes and Manderville's *Fable of the Bees*, which teaches, 'Public Benefit derives from Private Vice'. Parry summarizes Malinowski's position, 'Society is created by, and its cohesion results from, an endless sequence of exchanges in which all pursue their own advantage (however conceived)' (1986: 455). Malinowski offers a vision of a kula world, and the world of exchange more generally as a regime of self-interest. He reduces his project to the work of self-interested individuals and personal ontology becomes the grinding stone of legal devices based in gift exchange.

By contrast to Malinowski's individualist's version of law in society, Mauss's work is to create an essay, an argument about gift exchange as a device for making the social contract. The case of the hau described by the Maori as the spirit of the gift provides a good illustration of the problems in coming to terms with the relationships here. In my earlier discussions in chapter 3, I emphasized that the gift worked to extend aspects of the person's self into others' selves. The hau works between humans by making 'the absence of any disjunction between persons and things' (Parry 1986: 457). In Mauss, as Parry shows, the spirit of the gift creates the social contract (and does not stand alternative to or dependent upon the social contract as in Sahlins's arguments.) The hau is akin to a third party to exchange partners, albeit an invisible partner. For Parry, the possibility of making a generalization of gift exchange to the whole of society was not a habit of either French or Maori thought, but also elaboration of South Asian knowledge of the gift. In all these cases, understanding gift exchange requires that the anthropologist acknowledge that the social exists as a kind of third party to the transactions.

The finest discussion of the south Asian gift comes from the description of the Jati system. In this system, a series of offerings across castes ensures a person's moral claims for continuing residence within a particular region. But the outcome of these gifts does not confirm or protect the interests of the individual; instead it confirms the hierarchical society. It is also the case that men of different castes align their hierarchical relationships with each other through honouring their obligations to make devotional offerings. The social form, in this case the caste system, becomes visible through giving gifts throughout the system.

The questions of how to compare different types of gift exchange against this general form appears clearly in Parry's lecture and helped later scholars to focus their work to greater understanding of the nexus of gift exchange as a legal and political construction. His paper sets forward a rationale for better understanding of the terms of comparison of gift exchange and that has required deep questioning of how similar acts can be measured across cultures. All in all, Parry's Malinowski Lecture inspired subsequent anthropology to find deeper understanding of Mauss's meanings of gift exchange for anthropological work in cross-cultural encounters.

Parry is correct to take us to the problem of ontology in his considerations of gift exchange as a question of how to be in the world. That it should be a question of law and legal provision should not surprise us because it is in law that this matter finds clearest expression in Western democratic philosophies. Although much has been written on the cultural habits that influence moral rationales for action, it is in legal debates about property that culture receives explicit attention. The grounds for ownership require clear thought about the work of culture in determining claims on residence, or the custodianship, disposal and use of material culture. In the next pages, I will look at how ontological concerns are differently expressed in debates about cultural property, depending upon the disparate legacies of Malinowski's self-interest or of Mauss's social spirit.

Global interests in tournaments of value

One of the leading advocates of Malinowski's theory of gift exchange as self-interested competition has been Appadurai, who made a profound impact on efforts to bring into studies of globalization a more sophisticated appreciation of gift exchange (Appadurai 1986, 1996). Malinowski sets out a discussion about gift exchange in the Trobriand islands that has been appropriated, both directly and indirectly, by many other theorists working after him. If we take Malinowski's claims directly, then cultural property debates in global relations are about 'tournaments of value' (to borrow the term from Appadurai 1986). Appadurai seeks to use theories of gift exchange to think better about globalization; however, an analysis of the differences between Mauss and Malinowski such as that by Parry would help him to see that the terms of Malinowski's debates do not enable the fuller sense of the discussion. Tournaments of value is a difficult term, an agonistic one which leaves the reader with the sense that gift exchange is reduced to a strategic struggle over claims on common resources. At risk in such struggles is the loss of opportunity to express private interests in the uses of the common wealth.

Appadurai finds the concept of self-interested kula exchange most useful for his own thoughts on globalization, and makes excellent use of Malinowski's model of the self-interested kula trader without pursuing the important differences between Mauss and Malinowski on the legal and economic aspects of making gifts. He takes from the architecture of Malinowski's ethnography a series of theoretical claims about the struggles over the determination of value. Broadly speaking, value is determined in negotiation as the traders invest themselves in the negotiation so as to extract both social and moral claims on each other as kula traders.

Before I discuss Appadurai's concerns with the moral parameters of global exchange, I will describe how Malinowski exposed notions of self-interest (even the habits of non-capitalist entrepreneurialism) in his ethnography. One of the more puzzling descriptions of kula (which Appadurai does not cite) suggesting that it might be construed as competitive tournament of value, comes from Reo Fortune's book *Sorcerors of Dobu* (1963 [1934]).

For example, consider how Gell makes the story of the exchange of kula wealth into a mockery of rule and the gravity of prestige relations. He recalls Malinowski's observation that the kula wealth should be sent into circulation, as if several people had claims on it at once and it is safest moving around, rather than resting in one place. In the kula cycle, members enter and continue to play on speculation, rather than on certainty. Conjecture and speculation, rather than promises and certitude, keep people in the game of kula.

The negotiations of the monitor lizard fascinated Gell, who argued that Reo

Fortune, even more than Malinowski, had been able to show us that the kula traders were strategic and canny individuals, aiming to maximize the number of trading relations they held in order to enhance their renown. He quotes Kisian, a famous Dobuan kula trader of his day, who explained the work of decoys and deceptions in making the trade work.

> Suppose I Kisian of Tewara, go [north] to the Trobriands and secure an armshell called Monitor Lizard. Then I go [south] to Saranoroa and in four different places secure four different shell necklaces, promising each man who gives me a shell necklace, Monitor Lizard in return. Later I, Kisian do not have to be very specific in my promise. It will be conveyed by implication and assumption for the most part. Later, when four men appear in my home at Tewara each expecting Monitor Lizard, only one will get it. The other three are not defrauded permanently, however. They are furious, it is true, and their exchange is blocked for a year. Next year, when I Kisian go again to the Trobriands I shall represent that I have four necklaces at home waiting for those who will give me four armshells. I obtain more armshells than I did previously, and pay my debts a year late . . . I have become a great man by enlarging my exchanges at the expense of blocking [the exchanges of others] for a year. I cannot afford to block their exchanges for too long, or my exchanges will never be trusted by anyone again. I am honest in the final issue.
>
> (Fortune 1932: 215, in Gell 1986: 280)

I review Gell's (and Fortune's) example here because it helps to clarify the most interesting aspect of gift exchange as a moral relationship. Notably, the moral claims of the trader on other traders emerge through the course of the transaction. In Malinowski's model, ethical choices remain the purview of the individual, and the moral order exists only to confine self-interested action against abuses of others' interests. In this case, Kisian the Dobu trader on the kula ring ensures the fair play of trade, by compensating for the failure to deliver the monitor lizard to the individuals promised it. From the viewpoint of self-interest, the trader's success lies in his ability to keep active trading relationships with the same men whom he secretly intended to disappoint. The men's disappointments, had they not been appeased, might otherwise have cut Kisian off from future trade with them.

In such a model, in which individual self-interest prevails, the grounds of moral reasoning lie in retrospection (rather than prospective deliberation). That means that the participants refer to their memory of how transactions were made in order to adjudicate the fairness of the exchange of wealth. In such circumstances, the elaboration of custom as a moral and legal code of behaviour in ceremonial exchange is replete with injunctions for how to respect and honour such personal behaviour that supports the achievement of the wider social good. In this case, Kisian compensates the men who failed to acquire the monitor lizard and admonishes them for their own failures. If they could have been forthcoming with more of their own gifts to senior kula traders and made earlier gifts, then they would have received the monitor lizard valuable. Kisian's prestige turns on his ability to deceive his trading partners and make his victims happy for it.

The exchange of the monitor lizard valuable is a good example of how a 'tournament of value' works with deceitful and covert action. It perpetuates specific assumptions about the universality of moral, social and economic values of self-interested giving of kula goods that are created in the event of the exchange. Appadurai's model of 'tournaments of value' as a form of cross-cultural exchange in globalization adopts Malinowski's model uncritically, although Appadurai is clearer than Malinowksi that cross-cultural exchanges are played out in the matrix of differential power relations. In addition to his dutiful following of Malinowski, Appadurai's debts to Bourdieu's practice theory of exchange (Bourdieu 1977) are obvious. However, Appadurai does not use Bourdieu's idea of misrecognition in estimating the nature of false consciousness when deceits and trickery apparently affect the outcome of kula trade. Instead, he examines power differentials as a precondition of exchange, and as its determinative framework for the outcomes of the transaction. People reason about the transaction in order to vindicate or elaborate the terms through which the traders made their deal. Much of the moral discussion of gift exchange triumphs the final result of creating social hierarchy, and only in some cases critiques the outcome. The anthropologist's task, according to Appadurai, is to give an account of the moral struggles across cultures, which are often fought in cultural terms. Appadurai's aim has been to better understand the moral dilemmas of globalizing economic processes through the theory of gift exchange.

It is common to find that other anthropologists have used the opposition between personal interest and common wealth to explore the generalized dimensions of a theory of gift exchange. The distinction is an old one, belonging to the last 300 years of reasoning about political theory beginning with the concept of what Hobbes called the Leviathan, a form of collective existence which is greater than the sum of all of the individual interests that support its continuing existence. Hobbes had used the word Leviathan (a biblical monster that had swallowed a shipwrecked man and kept that individual within its belly) to describe that experience of being a part of a world bigger than an individual's immediate experience. All humans lived in society, but not all humans knew it in totality through their personal experience over a lifetime. Since Hobbes's day, anthropologists have reasoned about political life, especially the moral injunctions that legal thought sustains, by addressing the constraints on the relationship between the individual and the collective.

A number of different theorists of political life made this axis of decision-making (between the individual and the collective) into the cornerstone of their theory. Although in the next section of this chapter I will turn to the ways in which recent anthropologists leave behind this assumption, I want to review the different ways in which they have used it to discuss the political and legal dimensions of the uses of collective and private claims in cultural property. Not all of the anthropologists I discuss should be referred to as Hobbesian; many are committed wholly to Rousseau's project. The two approaches to the social contract divide simply on the disagreement about human nature as altruistic or nasty. I think that human social relationships are fundamentally neither one nor the other because that is to privilege nature outside society, whereas it is better to examine arguments over what is human nature as a modality for the discussion of ideas about the fixity of human relationships (for example, see Strathern 1981a and b). I take the problem here to be how anthropologists repeatedly use the concept of a social contract between individuals and the collective, whether they share assumptions by Hobbes or Rousseau, to make the work of political life appear self-evident.

To make clearer the conceptual problem of assuming that the self-interested individual can be the fundamental or ontological ground in tournaments of value, I would like to use a general example, one which Parry elucidates plainly through his discussion of Sahlins's theory of gift exchange as a part to the domestic mode of production. Sahlins tells us that gift exchange emerges under duress, when in household economies the membership of the household perceives that there is a lack or shortage of wealth among them. This proposal has such a powerfully reasonable feel to it that other anthropologists have extended to other situations Sahins's observations that gift exchange arises under strain and duress in the domestic mode of production. Although not all anthropologists cite Sahlins's approach as a basic orienting paradigm, they do share his concern to show that the framework of historical contingencies creates the need for altruistic behaviour from disparate participants in the collective interests of the group; for example in the attempts to create a more humane lifestyle in concentration camps (Narotzky 1998), in the effort by indigenous groups to assert commensurate interests in displays of artefacts in museum collections (Clifford 1997), and in attempts to explore the terms by which people's livelihood can be remade in disaster areas (Kirsch 2004). All of these anthropologists document the success of collective interests against people's perception that they have lost the cultural values which helped to sustain their lives before the contemporary period. I think that these efforts compare similarly with Appadurai's notion that tournaments of value can be fought between people who do not feel that they manage or control the terms of their shared lives, while undertaking transnational migrations away from places where they hold a sense of belonging.

Parry's argument against Sahlins's concept of gift exchange in the domestic mode of production applies very well to these works. Parry points out that Sahlins confuses 'the work of history with the work of human nature' as shown by reading carefully through Malinowski's research on the free gift.

Similarly, Parry shows that Sahlins mistakes the altruistic gift for what Malinowski called the free gift. According to Sahlins, the altruistic gift is made as compensation for suffering, as recognition of the common humanity of giver and receiver in the face of existential adversity, material constraints and social duress. Sahlins assumes that historical contingencies catch human beings by surprise (see the account in Sahlins 1985 of the early Hawaiian encounter with British explorers). Through adjusting their relationships to amend the damages of unexpected disasters, they find the best of their common humanity by helping each other to survive. Sahlins would argue that humans share a common history of disappointment and oppression; gift exchange is a reasonable moral response to the tragedy of history.

Malinowski meant the free gift to be only that. He did not perceive the Trobriands to be caught up in a struggle against the oppressive flow of world history. Instead, the mapula gift made by a father to his brother-in-law recognizes that they share a relationship to the child. The father bears nurturing affection for the child, and his own interests in being a good father can only be realized if the child reciprocates the affection and nurture with ceremonial gifts at the time of the father's death to build or elucidate the renown of the father's virtue. The child is no less than the reason for the father's continuing relationship to his wife's brother; as such, the child is a reminder that humans do not have to make lives together in affectionate relationships but they choose to do so anyway. Love is a free gift; humans need the practice of gift exchange only to be able to express it.

Losing interests in cultural property

The confusion between definitions of the total social fact of gift exchange, and the free gift, can interfere with progress towards an account of gift exchange for the development of protective measures for indigenous claims in cultural property. Sahlins's approach to the 'free gift' as altruism shows anthropologists how they can mistake a noble response to historical adversity with the facts of human nature. Sahlins would remind us that historical contingencies could be forgotten at the risk of an improper analysis of the anthropological account. The better approach is to examine the free gift as a story of how we think we need it; that would be a more thorough-going analysis of the grounds upon which humans make or recognize themselves as thoroughly social beings.

So the question at the centre of the problems of understanding the legal dimensions of gift exchange remains an ontological one, at least in so far as legal provisions of the gift must express the distinctive concerns of human collective existence. Two anthropologists writing about cultural property laws have perceived this very well. Brown (2001), for one, makes very clear that much is at risk in the discussion of cultural property. He argues that the transformation of culture into a thing to be held, used and disposed of to others hands opportunities for people from diverse cultural backgrounds to retain control over the ethical choices, choices that are informed by implicit cultural life, that they have in their lives. Brown correctly summarizes the existing limits in the debates over cultural property. He clarifies that culture cannot be copyrighted because it is a fluid entity, vulnerable to the processes of change that those who hold it set in motion and enlivened to their ethical vision for its future work.

Coombe (1998) by contrast comes closer to identifying the ontological dilemma presented by negotiations over cultural property. She recognizes that cultural life is not as easily or simply compromised and lost as Brown suggests. Instead, she makes a case for the analysis of cultural life of intellectual property (here she defines intellectual and cultural property as broadly similar), that is, the products of the human imagination. She discusses the cultural life of such intangible forms of property, which are understood as the products of the individual or collective mind. For example, she examines the uses of indigenous myth by Canadian novelists, who sought to enhance public understanding of the traditions of 'First Nations People' by using themes from ancient indigenous stories in contemporary art forms. The ensuing public debate tore open loosely held assumptions that culture circumscribed discrete and localized ways of life. The negotiations over what constituted a multicultural literature or a multicultural literary tradition advanced a new, shared assumption among readers, artists and authors in the 'creative community', the world of expertise in creative production. The public and legal debate no longer aimed to recover the legal provisions to protect a lost or disappearing indigenous past as the preserve of white insights into other ways of living. Instead, the public debate identified that the new legal concern lay in the designation of commensurate modalities of participation for indigenous communities, with the disparate cultural and linguistic traditions – both English and French – and with ethnic migrant groups in the Canadian nation. That debate continues over the ontological grounds of pluralist legal and political vision. It is limited by a model that would see debate and negotiation as a tournament of value, modelled on the disparate values expressed by self-interested individuals or the singular interests of the corporate group – including cultural industry companies and the indigenous councillors who must act as if the clans, bands or tribes could proceed as individuals.

There is much to do on a global scale. Dutfield and Posey (1996) produced a handbook of case studies, written to inform the reader of the landmark decisions made in each debate. In this book, they advocate a possibility for indigenous communities; they think about how to identify cultural resources and guard rights to their exploitation based on the claims they hold by heritage of such cultural wealth as ritual, arts, ethno-botany, and traditional healing. I have seen the people of Zia village on the north coast of Papua New Guinea work towards an inventory of resources that they could name among them collectively. They negotiated a sharing agreement, in order to free them to expose knowledge that, previous to their management of a cultural trust, had been selective to the clan, to the men's society or to individuals. They aimed to contain the entirety of their cultural resources within the community, and authorized a group of senior men and women to act as trustees of that knowledge.

Keeping interested in cultural property

I have discussed the extent to which anthropologists have played out the distinction between theories of exchange that focus on utility for individual gain, and those that focus on exploitation of the commons. Neither of these two theories of political economy has much play within an anthropology that takes as its axiom that life should be examined only as it is lived in the round. Much good work of recent years builds on Mauss's earlier insight into the total social fact of gift exchange, because these anthropologists begin with the centrality of the concept of obligation. Obligation matters, but not because it is a spiritual principle or a felt psychological state. Rather, obligation matters because it can be described sociologically; that is, it introduces the social context back into the analysis of many ceremonial events that anthropologists recorded in those societies undergoing rapid transitions to capitalism.

The anthropologist Gregory made the most important use of these insights about the character of gift exchange within his study of the ways in which ceremonial exchange is elaborated and escalates in situations that capitalist market practices also escalate (Gregory 1982, 1997). His question arose from the observation in the new nation of Papua New Guinea, when in the national capital of Port Moresby he observed that the uses of gift exchange in Melanesia actually increased to the point that many people were participating in even more market exchanges than before independence. Gregory points out that on the north-west coast of Canada, after independence, the Kwakiutl joined in more ceremonies of potlatch. Wolf and others record how both the frequency and the size of potlatch ceremonies escalated, concomitant with both the pervasive market relations and the national legislation promoted to stop it, as authored and administered by the Department of Indian Affairs of the Canadian government (Halliday 1935; Codere 1950; Drucker 1967; Wolf 1999). Potlatch ceremonies spread as more people than ever before tried to protect and extend their work of making personal status in a system of prestige, which was found perversely in the overt and public rejection of wealth.

Anthropologists working in Mauss's shadow know that they must be vigilant about marking analytical differences between the social relations through which people make gifts and the substance of the gifts in order to accomplish the aim of understanding social relations in cultural heritage. In any account of ceremonial exchange – whether the exchange of women and bride wealth, or the exchange of cultural artefacts or objects of ritual wealth over the generations – the slippages of attention to the object from the social relationships disarm the anthropologist. The anthropological work of examining the social relations remains wholly necessary to understanding cultural heritage and the global effort to protect its diversity and at the same time to make it available to a maximum number of people.

In Bastar, central India, Gell (1986) and Gregory (1997) worked in tandem. Each anthropologist's understanding of cultural property there differs from first premises. Each chooses the analytical category of the social relations differently; this also affects their respective understandings of other dimensions of market and gift life.

Bastar presents interesting problems to the anthropologist because it is home to tribal communities, allegedly falling at the bottom of, if not outside, the different forms of caste relations that are sustained throughout the country. In Bastar, tourists collect tribal artefacts because these curiosities give them imaginary access to ancient India. Of course, the tribal artefacts are not authentic in themselves, but the dealers promise the authenticity of provenance. Makers of 'tourist artefacts' are of the Ghassyia caste, allegedly makers with long histories of skilled craftsmanship who turned out the iron figure for the benefit of other castes who would use them ceremoniously.

Gell finds a paradox in the activity of artefact making. These figures have no obvious value to the Muria, and they do not seek to use them or to collect them as emblematic of their own ethnicity. The iron figurines are almost meaningless to the Muria castes because they have not yet made the imaginative leap to understanding that cultural life can be performed in order to live it, that its symbolic value is as great as (or greater than) its ontological values.

Gregory takes Gell to task for making the assumption that imaginative leaps can and do occur. If people do come to the decision that they can imaginatively become Muria, rather than just live Muria lifestyles, then a fuller understanding of the social context helps. Gregory holds Gell accountable for the explanation of the ways in which lost-wax iron figurines come into the hands of modern Muria, without an account of the complex ways in which the younger generation receives that information in the first instance. At least, some account of the role of government law in defining the Ghassyia as the worker's caste of the makers is needed. Gregory tells us that the official government line is that Ghassyia are the poorer members of the caste system whose work in artefact making includes the bronze figurines. This is not the case, and instead Gregory insists that the problem is not how to locate people in the caste system, but how to use the caste system in order to locate people. It might help to understand that process of social differentiation as a system of values, rather than as a system of barter over goods. The caste of artefact maker cannot be more straightforward than Gell describes it, yet caste itself never works to locate people with such conformity. Gregory argues that the Ghassyia might be living within a dual system.

In the best of this work that takes forward Mauss's insights into the social nature of exchange of gifts, several anthropologists addressed the cultural property debates in order to expose the best legal precepts for the exchange of material forms of cultural life. There is nothing self-evident about the way in which people come to exchange material as cultural property. For example, Demian explains that before people can exchange property they must see it; before they can give it away, they visualize it as discrete from the landscape in which they dwell. She echoes Malinowski's basic observation from the history of Trobriand research, as he notes the diver's ability to 'see' a shell necklace in the form of the giant sea clam that he recovers from the ocean floor. What they see as a potential pearlshell necklace entails them visualizing the totality of work and exchange relations that would put it into circulation on the kula ring as an item of wealth. Compare Malinwoski's insight into the visualization of pearlshell valuables in giant sea clams, with that of his student, Powdermaker, who wrote two decades later about New Irelanders' worries that European visitors to the museum displays of their malanggan sculptures would fail to recognize the immense work that had been given to their construction. Demian (2004), Malinowski (1927), and Powdermaker (1933) each make a similar point: that the work of exchanging cultural property first entails visualizing it as an object of value, and seeing it as separate from its context. In the work of all three authors, people can see the valued object only at the point at which the social relationships disappear from view. It would seem that before a person can exchange cultural property, he or she must first let slip from the field of vision most of the hands through which the object has passed. Oddly, forgetting where the object comes from aids in the work of valuing it for future transactions.

I would like to end by reference to the idea of owning creativity. In his essay on the pretexts for cultural property, Leach (2004) aptly discussed the problem of creativity as an aspect of social relationships. Leach reminds us that creativity lies simply within social relationships, neither within the intellect as inspiration nor in the 'genes' as if a naturally given talent. It is the combination of different relationships that makes possible the work of keeping alive a social life; and that would be a social life in which people retain interest. The problem remains: how can anthropologists assist in the formation of legal provisions that recognize the fundamentally social basis of cultural property? One way in which this is possible is to consider the social collaboration of different people (and clans) as the creative effect of the perceived felt-needs of protection for indigenous cultural property. In the final chapter, I will discuss how that collaboration would be as much an ethical, as it is a legal, creation. Here, I will discuss the complexities of a particular case in protecting social-cultural relations through the use of cultural property: that of the public display of malanggan.

In central New Ireland, Papua New Guinea, provincial bureaucrats argued that one of the best ways of preserving or protecting culture is to use it. In the interest of cultural protection, they embarked on a series of installations of public artwork. The most notable was the creation of many carved posts to hold aloft the roof of the departure hall at the new airport terminal, in the provincial capital of Kavieng (Figure 11.1). The posts are made of aquila wood,

Figure 11.1 Malanggan carvings on the departure hall posts of Kavieng International Airport, New Ireland, Papua New Guinea. Karen Sykes (2000).

commonly understood to bear ceremonial importance because it is used for house posts of the men's house, or in the gateways to the enclosures surrounding burial grounds adjacent to the men's house. These wooden posts, when properly dried before carving, will turn as hard as iron and weather the elements for many decades. In the men's houses of yesteryear, only those men invited to enter the enclosure could look upon the carved images; but contemporary men's houses rarely use artfully carved posts. Each post at the airport terminal is emblazoned with images used in malanggan carvings, collected from the area throughout the nineteenth and twentieth centuries and now stored in European museums. Many of the images have been used in more contemporary malanggan ceremonies, when the displayed carving had been thrown into the sea or burnt over the fire. In this context, the carvings might be more familiar to the eye of European tourists visiting the region than to many New Irelanders who would not view malanggan images under everyday circumstances of the late twentieth century. The provincial government seemingly sought to protect malanggan as a cultural property by celebrating it, that is by putting it on public display and thereby making it possible for New Ireland residents to see in the departure hall the kinds of images that Europeans had seen in museums for a long time.

Two kinds of problems emerged. The first lies in the irony that everyone in New Ireland can see the malanggan images, which in the past only select persons viewed at special ritual occasions. The hidden images were now made public in order to protect them. The first problem could have been solved if the proper care had been taken with how to reveal to wider public view the images on the posts. In this, as in other cases of ritual use, proper care meant negotiating the wide and complex network of social relationships necessary to complete any single malanggan carving. The second problem is related to the first. It lies in the misunderstanding of the role of the 'malanggan carver'. The government sought to employ master carvers, as individual artists. Unfortunately, they erred because the malanggan carver is 'several people', working together in a formation more like the entire musical ensemble. As a result the carvers could not explain to the satisfaction of their bureaucratic employers how the work on each post had been apportioned among the men working on each. Further, the government could not allocate the time and resources necessary to negotiate the complex network of people to finish the carving, when the time required for the completion of the carved posts outran the schedule.

The government did not protect malanggan carving in New Ireland as fully as it might have done. If the bureaucrats had wanted to protect cultural property, they needed to negotiate fully the social network in which the malanggan can be publicized, or simply 'revealed' to the public eye; which they did not. Malanggan carvers understand that they hold multiple claims on each other, and that to withdraw one claim jeopardizes the artwork, as well as the people who helped to make it. They are not 'shareholders' in the carving, with proportional investments in the final artwork. Neither do they believe that they participate in creating an artwork of public and common property because no individual carver believes that he comes as representative of his language group, or clan, to constitute a social totality. Instead, each person participates in the carving of the post so that it becomes the property, 'in effect' of his clan's interests in sharing in the work and social life of creating cultural property. By similar argument, the carving is neither simply common property nor cultural wealth held in common. The malanggan is collectively 'owned', when revealed and seen properly after the negotiation of the network of social relationships that facilitate its completion and display. The correct and complete negotiation of that network of social relationships allows people to look at, or to view, the malanggan with intelligence rather than ignorance. Contrary to the claim of the artist, Damien Hirst, who argues that when people view art they kill its meaning and take the life from it by taking it out of life, the New Irelanders would argue that to reveal and gaze properly at malanggan art is to make it come to life in the imagination of everyone who is free to see it. The catch for this in New Ireland – and it is the same catch by which bureaucrats might succeed in protecting malanggan art by making it public – is simply this: a person should not look without protection at the improperly revealed malanggan. The protection of cultural property entails living with an apparent contradiction; that is, if you know who you are in relation to the rest of the people who dreamed, carved, painted, enchanted and displayed it, then you are free to gaze at it. When someone looks intelligently at cultural property in New Ireland, they preserve it as a form of social and cultural life.

Summary of chapter 11

If culture is the new commons, then does anthropology have the means to assess it? First I have looked at the debates ensuing from the UN Declaration on Cultural Diversity to expose the dilemmas faced by those writing legal devices for the protection of culture. How should one protect a form of association that is seated in human relationships rather than in the individual or in artefacts exchanged between individuals? After looking at the concept of the commons in the seventeenth-century property debates, this chapter has examined the problem of the extent to which culture is shared. Malinowski's research and Mauss's can each be discussed for what it exposes about their different assumptions about the ontological grounds of cultural knowledge. Malinowski preferred to locate the significance of cultural knowledge in individual needs and their negotiation in shared society, whereas Mauss preferred to locate the significance of cultural knowledge in human relationships, as the motive to keep obligations. While Appadurai used Malinowski's model of exchange to delineate global exchanges as tournaments of value, both Brown and Coombe raise objections to this. Brown asks to what extent people can participate in a negotiated exchange of cultural values, for example in a process of copyrighting culture, without first alienating culture from themselves. Coombe objects by pointing out that intellectual property has a cultural life, and that debates about it are embedded in other debates about how to live. As new departures for the discussion of cultural property as the new commons, several researchers suggest that cultural property is first and foremost a problem of visualizing culture as an entity, as a form or a thing to be separated from social relationships. Other researchers suggest that cultural property cannot be discussed as a communal form without risking it to corporate models of ownership, as when clans are erroneously encouraged to register lands on the model of corporations. Instead, cultural property can be analysed within a network of social relations such that all claims on it can be addressed respective to the needs of the different participants.

12

GIVING ANTHROPOLOGY A/WAY

Some researchers aim to give anthropology away, in the sense of making ethnography freely available. In the best sense, giving anthropology away means making a gift of it, an act of making a connection to readers. In giving anthropology 'a way' into the debates of other scholars, anthropologists make their research results vulnerable to the scrutiny of others; and by implication they make vulnerable those who assisted in the research, the informants. Each time anthropologists 'give anthropology away' they make the value of anthropology vulnerable to challenges: against their authority to speak and write what they know, against their claims for how they know it and for the routines of their disciplinary practice. In the best sense of intellectual exchange, giving anthropology a way opens the pathways for debate. Anthropologists communicate their research and thereby make a way for the research to be used by others. They become vulnerable by sharing ideas, just as the people with whom an anthropologist lives become vulnerable by inviting him or her to stay with them and risking that they will be treated fairly. An anthropology that builds on ethical practice exchanges in the vulnerability of humans from fieldwork to publication.

That vulnerability should not be a problem because it is necessary to let research reports and ethnography remain open to reconsideration. Vulnerability is a problem in the circumstances in which an anthropologist's report also endangers informants, students and colleagues, by creating a pathway of knowledge that links anthropological commentary and argument to specific people. Ethical anthropology transacts in the vulnerability of informants and researchers, in the first and the last instance, and cannot ignore or forget this condition of research. Because it is not possible for either fieldworker or hosts to remain invulnerable to human relationships in fieldwork, the better approach is to acknowledge vulnerability as a condition of each other's humanity. The anthropologist can acknowledge the vulnerable informants by being alert to their own vulnerability. That is a capacity that can be enhanced by disciplinary study and debate about ethics. I will look at anthropological ethics as it is valued in the discipline, by noting how codes and guidelines protect research subjects and by considering how the interpersonal exchange of vulnerabilities precipitates moral reasoning.

Codes and guidelines

In chapter 10, I described what Strathern (2000) has called 'audit culture', or the bureaucratic regulation of social action (beyond the ken of individual bureaucrats). Peter Pels (1999, 2000) argues that audit culture enters anthropology in the form of codes for ethical conduct. Anthropologists meet disciplinary obligations to respect codes, guidelines, and human subject's boards, ethics committees, in order to learn about ethical conduct and prevent unethical practice. Drawing on the classical philosophy of Aristotle and the heavily debated example of Malinowski's fieldwork (a case that I discussed in chapter 3), Pels correctly argues that to know the goal of ethical research is not the same as to know the ethical practice of research. I argue that, although these different mechanisms have made anthropologists better aware of their responsibilities to each other and to the people they come to know in the course of their fieldwork that using these devices to guide conduct can lead the anthropologist to forget that they trade in vulnerability as a matter of research practice itself. It is impossible to understand human behaviour without acknowledging common vulnerability.

The codification of conduct into ethical practice makes it possible for anthropologists to monitor each other's responsibilities, and in so doing they show each other that they are professionally responsible. Contemporary codes of ethics for professional anthropologists begin with the assumption that knowledge is information won through fieldwork, and that the fieldwork encounter entails negotiation and exchange between anthropologist and informants. Ethics codes assume that anthropological knowledge cannot be 'bought' without compromising both truth and ethical relations with informants. The codes do assume that knowledge can be given freely, and that it can be given in exchange for fair compensation in value for the informants' time, and perhaps their expertise. The code exists, in the way a rulebook does, in order to ensure that anthropologists conduct these exchanges fairly.

There is a second sense of knowledge as understanding that is assumed within disciplinary and professional codes of practice. Anthropologists can ask too well, just what kind of understanding comes without vulnerability. This question paraphrases Geertz's defence of Malinowski's fieldwork methods, and more generally, his defence of the interpretive method in fieldwork (Geertz 1988). The definition of knowledge as understanding comes from the fieldwork experience and acknowledges that the ethnographic account is made between anthropologists and informants in a negotiation of their joint understandings. Ethical interchange in this case opens up anthropological research as a pathway towards understanding, a pathway that is made through a sequence of translations from field to study. I will look at each of these meanings for ethical practice in the light of the vulnerability of informants and researchers: first, as a gift within codes of practice and second, as a pathway for exchange within guidelines for conduct.

Codes of practice and guidelines for professional conduct are not new. In the Anglophone world, the American Anthropological Association (AAA) adopted a code of ethics which Pels (2000) names Principles of Professional Responsibility (PPR). The PPR aimed to create an explicit hierarchy of obligations for anthropologists to meet, differentiating the different communities of people to whom they hold debts: the informants in research communities, students, the home and host governments, and collegial and professional groups. The PPR uses the hierarchy of responsibilities to protect the more vulnerable member of any negotiation, transaction or dispute by making it clear that the more powerful or higher status person is less vulnerable and more responsible to the lower status person on the hierarchy of groups and discrete professional milieus.

This code of practice assumes that knowledge empowers anthropologists and that what they do and say with that knowledge can endanger each group of people differently. The code aims to designate the differential vulnerability of each group from the others. An absolute hierarchy of vulnerable groups was created; informants were more vulnerable than host governments, students more vulnerable than colleagues, but fieldwork rarely presented conditions of absolute moral certainty. Commonly, an anthropologist finds him or herself confused about how to act in relation to any of these groups, without compromising his or her relationship with the others of the group. The Code of Ethics ensconces a hierarchy of vulnerability; it does not proclaim a hierarchy of different kinds of values or obligations. By giving attention to vulnerability, the code acknowledges that anthropological knowledge grows out of social relationships, many of which admit to the mutual vulnerability of researcher and informant. This sophisticated approach to the code of ethics of the AAA demands clear thinking about both vulnerability and responsibility. It allows for anthropologists to repeatedly remind each other that ethnography depends upon being totally human in the company of others, who are fully persons as well. It is responsible to acknowledge and project vulnerabilities.

By comparison with the AAA, the Association for Social Anthropology (ASA) adopted a statement on Guidelines for Good Practice in 1986. The guidelines are meant to enable and guide reflection on the nature of anthropological practice; they are guidelines, and do not regulate or judge the fieldwork and ethnography of colleagues. The guidelines instruct and remind anthropologists of their responsibilities. In many ways the guidelines of the ASA reflect a more personalized approach, in so far as they focus on the individual choices that a single researcher makes in fieldwork and hence on their duty to the informant, to their colleagues and to their host and home countries. Unlike the AAA codes, the guidelines do not distinguish one milieu from another in a hierarchy of vulnerability; but they detail distinct responsibilities held by anthropologists to informants, to host and home governments and to colleagues. There is no hierarchy of orders because vulnerability is measured differently in each situation, whereas professional responsibilities to informants, peers and hosts can be distinguished clearly as a guideline of professional practice.

Principles of professional research: the Yanomamo case

More recently, American anthropologists struggled to understand the implications of encoding ethics in terms of the differentiated vulnerability of research, student and professional communities. They entered an intense conversation about the nature of ethical practice, with the intention to revise their code of ethics. In an iconic debate over the work of the anthropologist Chagnon who worked in the 1950s in the Venezuelan Amazon, American anthropologists aimed to create a public statement on their ethical practice that would reflect disciplined approaches for future research by its members. There is much to consider in the debate about what ethical conduct is and how anthropologists can recognize and monitor it. How should anthropologists open pathways of moral reasoning in intellectual exchange with their informants?

Chagnon was criticized by an investigative journalist (Tierney 2000) for his fieldwork ethics in the midst of an influenza epidemic in which many villagers of the Yanomami died. His peers (AAA 2002) raised more questions about this tragedy forty years later, querying what Chagnon did to protect indigenous people, whom many perceive to be vulnerable members of the Amazonian communities. Some asked questions about the decisions he made that took him to the Amazon in the early 1960s, about the sources of funding for his project, about his choice to give medical treatment to informants, and about his personal conduct in the field. Many of the answers to these questions show that Chagnon acted in a paternalistic way when he chose to act on partial knowledge of the nature of the epidemic. Because of the nature of medical treatment plans for epidemics, some felt that he risked the health of the villagers by surmising that he could act in their best interests on his privileged but limited personal knowledge of Western medicine. (Usually anthropologists have some personal knowledge of medical care based upon their experience of medicines used in developed countries, but not professional knowledge of medical drugs and treatment.)

In defence, Chagnon's supporters argued that he was making reasonable decisions in the field in the effort to protect informants from further illness. He was not mortally vulnerable to infection, but his informants were and he aimed to rectify that balance. By most accounts, Chagnon's record of behaviour could be defended within the PPR, as drafted by the AAA. He acknowledged his superior responsibility given the personal advantages he enjoyed as an educated man from the developed Western world. However, was research vulnerability quantifiable, that is, only a matter of measuring who was more and who less vulnerable?

How does remaining vulnerable in fieldwork become instrumental to the transactions entailed in its conduct? Chagnon's example does not show this vulnerability; neither does the anthropologist acknowledge his vulnerability to others, nor does he recognize fully the vulnerability of the Yanomami people to his research. If Chagnon never relinquishes his paternal role in the field, if he never gives up his 'god's eye' to the situation, then his research makes other people appear as archetypes of the Western imagination. Under such circumstances research becomes a fable and people who can act as informants become nothing other than exotic people, who cannot meet anthropologists face-to-face and exchange life-stories and the work of daily living in fieldwork.

The guidelines for professional conduct and the Yanomami

Chagnon's ethical practice intrigued professional anthropologists for many months, and is worth a brief introduction for what it tells about the ethics of representation. In chapter 2 I described Chagnon's research with the Yanomami as an effort to establish the argument that political forms evolve as people respond to human acts of violence by trying to contain and restrict it with legal and institutional mechanisms. In his effort to understand the human nature that informed Amazonian Indian behaviour, he had undertaken to describe environmental and historical causes for the events unfolding at the time of Lévi-Strauss's visit in his effort to discredit structuralist's arguments and to re-establish the Yanomami case as one upon which to build the argument for the theory of political evolution. The involvements of Chagnon with the Yanomami become iconic of the wider problem: what are the ethics of representing people who do or do not conform to ideals of the Noble Savage?

Although Chagnon published his research findings widely, I do not offer a full study of how he depicted the Yanomami people here. Instead, I will look only at how he worked with the film maker Asch to present their social life, in a film entitled *The Ax Fight*. Chagnon tried to provide more authority for his research into the nature of non-state violence by using the visual evidence provided on film. There is nothing simple or straightforward about such a plan. The film is comprised by the sequence of events, presented and re-presented three different times. Each presentation offers a different edit of the first rush of film, to demonstrate that the final product was true to the initial filming and also that the work of editing (like the work of writing) could highlight or bring forward the social structures that lay behind the surface. The final edit is followed by the construction of a kinship diagram (to the eyes of the viewer, this is a somewhat strange moment in the filming). They make the effort to represent, several times, the process by which the very same event could be viewed and reviewed for new information. Grimshaw 2001 tells us that later reassessments (Moore 1994, Winston 1995) show that the evidence in the film itself could undermine the empirical claims of Chagnon that warfare in the Amazon region constituted an intermediary stage of political evolution, from which the state emerged with the purpose of using legitimate forms of violence to end the condition of warfare.

Chagnon had worked hard with the film maker Tim Asch to create a compelling portrayal of an event in which violent fighting erupted in the Amazon. Asch worked with conventions of ethnographic film making that did not assume that 'natural shots' were the only authentic record. Asch followed traditions of ethnographic film begun in the 1920s by Flaherty, which assumed that the fieldworker should endeavour to keep the camera's eye innocent from human prejudice about the scene in front of them. Flaherty used film to expose the patterns of everyday life, by building up the evidence layer upon layer until the picture or image emerged clearly. Following Flaherty's form of film making, Asch filmed numerous versions of the same actions, thereby exposing to the eye of the anthropologist the ideal or archetypical image contained within apparently disparate and unconnected human acts.

Subsequent historians of the ethnographic film discussed how Flaherty and Asch worked to expose the ideal forms of behaviour, illuminating these with effective reviews and additions to make the image clear (Banks and Morphy 1997). For the creation of *The Ax Fight*, which appeared to be a realistic shot of the events that developed naturally in front of them, the film makers worked to create opportunities to record effective images of the violent conflict on the screen and images of the build-up to that conclusive conflict. In the course of their work Chagnon had made gifts of axes to Yanomami men, and subsequently these weapons appear in the fight. The film focused on the build-up of antagonism by filming the different events leading to the conclusive conflict.

Remember the context of Chagnon's research and filming. His effort to illustrate in film that warfare was a natural condition challenged the converse claim that peaceable activity is the work of human beings in social relations. By creating a stage in film for the presentation of the evidence of violent conflict, he eliminated the occasions of more peaceful human activity. Intriguingly, this attention to one facet of human experience set him at odds with Flaherty's aims for documentary film, which were to record the visual manifestations of deep patterns informing everyday life (not only dramatic events such as the conflict Chagnon and Asch filmed in *The Ax Fight*).

Asch expressed doubts about the editing and presentation of the film, as well as the work of creating the scene of filming. In later years, he reflected upon the experience and argued for explicit reflection upon the processes by which a film maker records human behaviour. Asch's reflection contributed to a richer discussion of the work of ethnographic film than had existed in the techniques of film making before the Second World War, enlivening discussion to include the role of various ways of enabling artistic presentations of visual 'evidence' in either documentary film or ethnographic cinema. Anthropologists began to explore earnestly the visual technologies, in the broadest sense, that mediated best the ethnographic science with the art of ethnography. How do anthropologists contribute to the 'scene' to be documented on film? This question took the film-making approach in new directions towards cinema. But my concern here is how the exchanges and interchanges of fieldwork open an ethical pathway to anthropological understanding.

Chagnon had filled a conceptual space that Trouillot named 'the savage slot', the conceptual space imagined by anthropologists as the counter example, the alternative to, life within the state. He gave up opportunities for developing his best personal relationships with the Yanomami, to support the fashioning of a picture of the lives of men and women whose lives on film are about their lives as 'natural savages'. In this sense, he gave away any chance of success at ethical practice within anthropology.

There remains an alternative to representing the Yanomami as the archetypical noble savage in transition to political evolution. In the next section I will discuss the exchanges that a fieldworker makes in order to record their experience and thoughts. Experience might be exchanged for field notes, and field notes for ethnography, as an anthropologist negotiates the way of his or her research into a wider community of readers. Each exchange negotiates a moral relationship. I will discuss transaction in fieldwork and intellectual exchanges sustaining ethnographic writing as it opens pathways of ethical reasoning. I assume that humans make themselves vulnerable in fieldwork exchanges, and I thereby recognize that vulnerability makes anthropological knowledge possible. Research with human subjects remains interesting, enlightening, and important as long as humans acknowledge each other's humanity. Face to face, this entails acknowledging the vulnerability of each human to his or her social relationships. Eyes see and mouths speak, and thereby assist humans in the exchange of knowledge. These vulnerable orifices, the open eye and the speaking mouth, are as much the eye that receives the world, and the mouth that devours it with surprised utterance, or spoken request that reduces felt experience to words. These bodily openings to the world are the savage slots that all humans share, as anthropologists and as research subject.

Fieldwork and the ethics of recording experience

Can ethical practice create a pathway for moral reasoning, rather than a moral code for behaviour? I take a case from my own work. In the early months of my fieldwork I learned to make small feasts for guests who would help me with my research. The elderly women who were my guests are pictured in Figure 12.1 (overleaf). I cooked large pots of chicken stew and I invited a group of elderly women in order to conduct an all night party, a group interview about their common experience of an initiation into a selective women's society, through which they acquired the name Ladaven to indicate their prestige. I was curious about the links between initiation into selective societies in the rituals of the past, and the leap or initiation into secondary education in the present. I knew that each woman joined the society in a different ritual at a different time over the past fifty years, yet at my invitation on this occasion they joined together to talk about the past events. It amused them, but not unpleasantly so. The evening passed easily and with much laughter.

I had hoped to recreate the conviviality of the original feasts with this small event, or party as they called it. Good food, a warm fire and good conversation created the ambience for successful conversation in many different places for

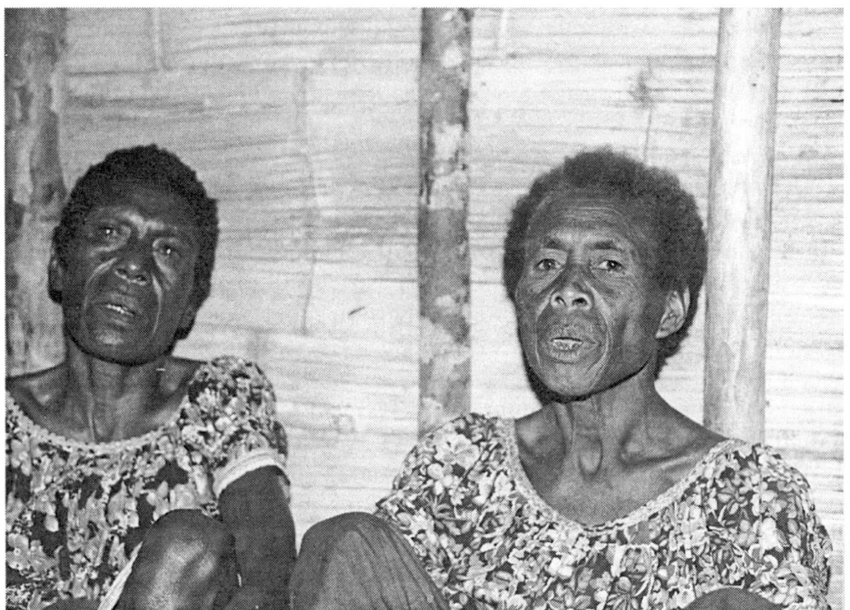

many people, and it seemed reasonable to hope for the same social effects after giving a feast in the village. We laughed about the songs that they sang into my tape recorder. They said their voices were no longer as sweet and true as they had been when they were adolescents. I did not aim to create a semblance of a ritual event, but wanted to create the conditions of conviviality and thereby make it possible to recall with alacrity the details of the early years, despite the distant memory or the time passed between the present and their first participation in the rituals. They punctuated the songs with riotous laughter, a stanza of a ritual tune interrupted with uproars and collapse. They heard their own aged voices singing the words and melodies most meaningful to the adolescent girl. They could not sing poetic evocations of the nature of men's desire for beautiful young women's bodies without realizing that they created a ridiculous scene; they had ancient withered skin and their voices cracked on high notes of a melody carrying lyrics about young love. They told me that the event was comically obscene, and that it was fun to make jokes about the past. This initially confused and saddened me because I had hoped to honour their past. Worse, in their attempts to reassure me that they found the time together happy, I learned that had men been present or nearby (none were) then the women would have been ashamed of their situation. That night the women turned my work into frivolity, a frivolity they shared by revelling in the ludicrous. They knew that they were elderly women, but they sang as if they were pubescent girls.

At this party I recorded material restricted from common use, but I have never exploited that knowledge in publications, although they agreed to release

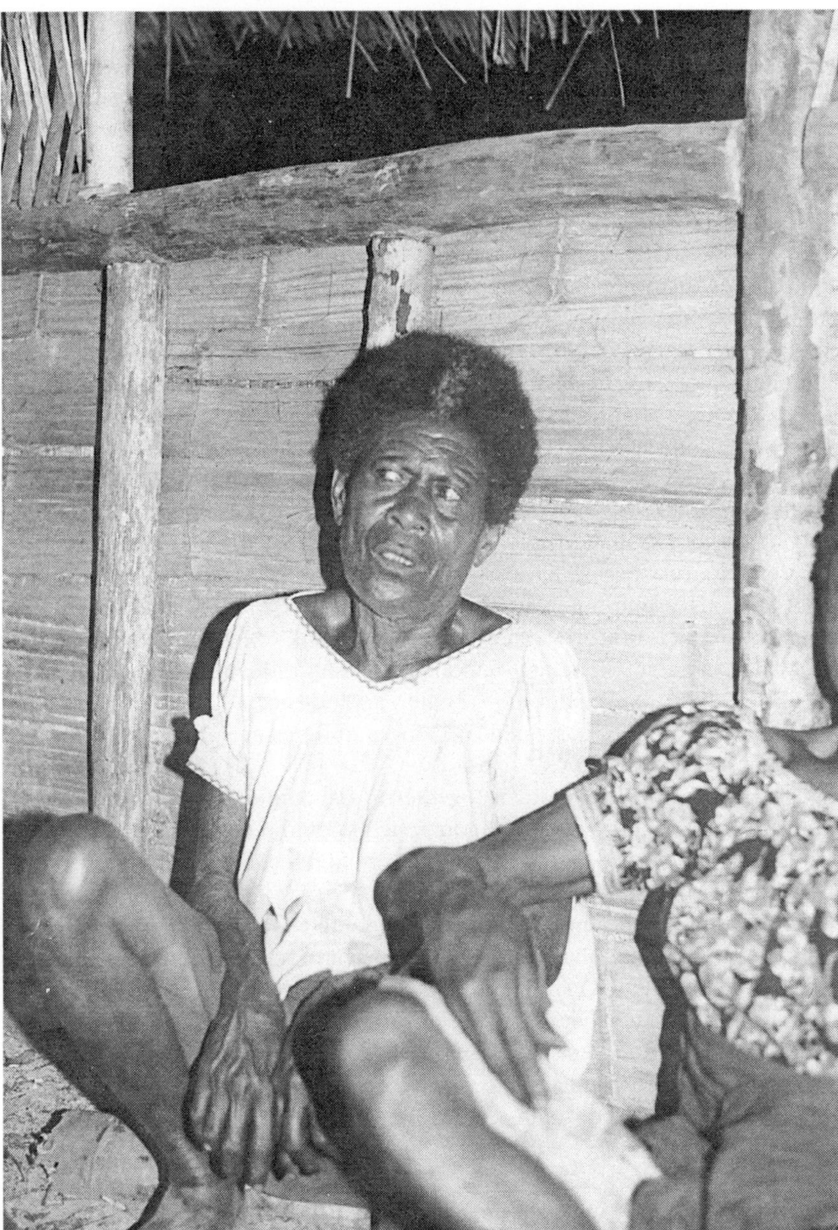

Figure 12.1 (above and left) Former Ladaven initiates from Central New Ireland, Papua New Guinea. Karen Sykes (1991).

it to appear in my 'book'. The event recalled and the songs sung once were open to a selective group of people, and normally not publicly available in ways that a book might permit. I did not want to risk misusing their trust in me by assuming that they understood the public nature of publishing.

The most interesting difference between my record of their experience and their uses of the presentation lies in how the ritual is meaningful more than what it means. At that event they exposed my naiveté about feminine erotics. They discovered my ignorance and they decided I was unteachable; my elderly companions tried to make me appear and behave as a younger woman should, but with no luck. My elderly friends worried that I could fail as a woman (what kind of man would want to marry a woman who did not understand femininity, especially a Melanesian style of femininity?). Women's femininity is learned indirectly among women, the erotic required an imaginative leap. Women educate each other in femininity through parody and burlesque. It is humorous.

The songs that the women sang have greater public dissemination if they are sung at school graduation ceremonies, but such reconstructed ritual events of the contemporary period have less potency. Women's power and edginess that night made the event more than theatre. The event of ritual performance differs from the event of a theatrical presentation of ritual, which differs from its burlesque. Giving a ritual status to another is a very different matter than either giving a dramatic presentation of ritual to an audience, or giving comic insight into the ritual for a scholar educated to its different meanings through published sources.

That evening we broke down together in the confluence of our respective educations, how I, as a naïve ethnographer, started research and how elderly women learned for the first time that they could remember their initiation into a secret women's society. First their laughter, then my inescapable sleep eclipsed all my attempts at note taking. The maddening transcripts of that evening's work lie between that place and me. I can listen to my recordings in which the laughter is punctuated with phrases and words, uttered in answer to some question I had asked. The point was not to record accurately all the details of their earlier youthful experience and the secret knowledge that they learned. The goal was to learn in this experience of the ways in which a person transforms him or herself through relationships with others. Learning about personal transformation cannot be a failure, nor can it be a success. It is merely the elicitation of the necessity of our relationship, elder women who had lived there forever and a younger immigrant woman. My attempts to record them turned my work into a parody of anthropology and their experience into frivolity. An ethical anthropology, but done in the dramatic mode of comedy, and with a few laughs? Or not?

An anthropologist getting started at fieldwork, like a kula trader getting started in ceremonial exchange, sets a chain of other transactions into play. When I had finished my evenings of interviews with elderly women about their youthful initiations at the time of the malanggan mortuary ceremony, a new debate opened. The small settlement where I lived in a small house asked me how they could best help me to write. Writing, in central New Ireland parlance, is known as malanngan. The word malanggan is used to describe the practice of mortuary feasting, and the specific work of carving a sculpture of wood or weaving one of hand-made rope. It is intriguing to consider what it means to draw equivalences between writing and malanggan because according to New Irelanders' wisdom, the work of malanggan ends meaningful communication. Making a malanggan ends all conversation, discussion and talk about the life of the deceased. This transformation of the social person from the world of speech to that of silence could be called the death of communication. Different from the New Irelanders, I took the work of recording and of writing to be the technologies that make up social relationship. I write and inscribe; I interpret and translate what can be claimed as shared understandings of experience.

Every day at noon an elderly man sat with me over cups of sugared tea. He came to talk when I stopped writing on the typewriter. All morning he had sat and listened to the machine strike keys on the paper; he liked to hear it 'pira ap', to make a clattering noise like a bad truck engine. He asked me a very good question that bothers me still. How did all my experiences there get inside those little black marks on the page? Indeed. What did I have to forget just to write it all down?

Fieldnotes are the product of moral technologies; that is, writing is not a neutral technology. Writing creates moral relations (either in text or by elicitation) by making these relations clear in practice and by inscribing some of them on the page. A debate grew in the hamlet in which I lived. Was writing my 'work'? Was the fieldworker who did not find her wealth in the gardens really a grown woman? If I wrote down their stories, then what would that record of them mean to them? If writing is malanggan, then what does that imply? Malanggan makers needed to be hosted, but who would host me as a writer/malanggan creator? If I sculpted experience into notes on a page that they called malanggan, then should I receive gifts of food and shells in exchange for the artistic creation that I gave them?

My experience is not uncommon. In his book, *The Invention of Culture* (1975) Wagner recalls the existential angst in the years of his first fieldwork. His hosts, the Daribi, wondered about the work of the 'storimasta', as they called the anthropologist who wrote down the stories they told him. The 'storimasta' wrote stories. Was this the work of a grown-up? Was Wagner, who lived among them, a grown man? Who really has claims on such knowledge, and what does it rely upon in order to be understood sufficiently for a final account? These questions about the making of fieldnotes take me in turn to the problems of ethnographic writing, and the politics of translation across cultures, of translating the distant places into face-to-face relationships.

Pathways for ethical exchange

Some anthropologists doubted the role of scientific reason in the ethical practice of anthropology and advocated an assessment of the uses of rhetoric, style and genre. Marcus and Cushman (1981), Marcus and Clifford (1986), Clifford (1988, 1997) and Marcus and Fischer (1986) initiated an assessment of narrative style and genre of writing in ethnography in order to examine how anthropologists created the authority and credibility of their ethnographic descriptions. These anthropologists tried to think about anthropological narratives because ethnography begins with writing about experience. Many anthropologists refer to this legacy of reflection upon the way in which anthropologists write it down as 'the literary turn' in anthropology. Many literary anthropologists' books explored poetic devices for the end of being able to communicate more evocative portrayals of the beliefs that other people hold, and the ways in which they act towards each other. They acknowledge that ethnography can be aesthetically beautiful or can comprise challenging accounts which engage the reader in order to illuminate the life of people who are not easily known. These efforts in anthropological writing do not claim to be 'science' and often raise doubts about the certainty of what an anthropologist can know while conveying some insights, as does good literature.

Many anthropologists experimenting with different forms of anthropological writing also hold the aims of a more broadly construed scientific project. Marcus drew on the work of the philosopher of history, White (1981), who appealed to the philosopher Vico, to show that by using a range of aesthetic styles anthropologists aimed to create realistic portrayals of the people and places they knew. Marcus welcomed Vico's aims to create a new history, and a new historical critique of the arts. As Marcus observed in his efforts to map this terrain for anthropology, early and later anthropologists accomplished the realist aims of early ethnography by using a number of different rhetorical devices to convey their authority to write about a particular place. Some anthropologists simply used a literary device of establishing an authorial voice that conveyed to the reader the sense of 'being there', that is of actually having been in another place far away from the chair of the reader.

Marcus raised a second interesting question about terms of ethnographic writing; he asked how the anthropologist introduced the sense of time to the ethnography. In some cases the ethnography seemed to have been written about events that had happened in the past, providing the reader with a sense that the world being described had stopped in the ethnography. This style of writing supported ethnographers' assumption that they described a life style under threat by modern times, or even the claim that they described a whole society of complete, enduring, unchanging structures and institutions. Marcus's creative critical observations about ethnographic writing became part of a wide-ranging debate among anthropologists about the different value of scientific and literary approaches to the discipline.

A considerably wider-reaching critique of the uses of the concept of time by Johannes Fabian (1983) drew on Foucault's philosophical and historical critique of social sciences. Fabian's book analysed the various ways in which anthropologists represented their research community as different from their home society. The anthropologist's habit of finding the research community to be very different from his or her home society implicated anthropologists in an ideological framework, even where they aimed to avoid it. For Fabian, as for Foucault (1972), descriptive writing is a political act and anthropologists should reflect on the circumstances in which they write. For Fabian, as for Foucault, analysing experience different from the writer's own draws anthropologists into a necessarily critical exercise. But what kind of criticism did anthropologists make in ethnography? Fabian explored the ways anthropologists used the sense of passing time in their ethnography so as to describe the 'other' as different from them. Often the other's habits reflected aspects of life from the anthropologist's society's past, customs and traditions left behind with modern life. Fabian argued that anthropologists should critique the ways in which they used the 'other' to legitimate their own version of human history as a natural progression towards a more enlightened society.

A third response came from Clifford Geertz (1988). He reflected upon the history of anthropological scholarship and pointed out that this might be accomplished through conventions of writing that communicated a sense that the researcher had been 'eye-witness' to the events described. In equally complex efforts, like those of Ruth Benedict whose work I have mentioned in the introduction (see p. 7), the sense of 'being there' could be communicated with more 'whimsical' illustrations of what the observations on another society's ceremonies meant for understanding the peculiarities of our own habit. These concerns with 'being there' and 'eye witnessing' in ethnography underline that anthropology can extend a radical and profound critique of what it means to be human. Geertz's anthropology as a critique of ontology elaborates distinctly different ideas about how people think they exist socially, or should 'be', in the world. Geertz has been criticized wrongly for fetishizing culture as text. He does not make texts his object of study, but he does privilege meaning of social processes. He believes that meaningful communication is the goal of every social act. (His assumptions are hard to displace because how can we assume that some social action is not meaningful?) An anthropologist who assumes it is his or her work to translate others' social acts into fieldnotes and eventually into ethnography also assumes that ontological critique is the justification for fieldwork. Geertz's interpretive approach to anthropology returns anthropologists to the field, yet again.

At first, as a student of anthropology, I welcomed Fabian's and Marcus's assessments of the intellectual history of the discipline and their call for a new anthropology that was self-consciously critical about its work. I think that they contributed to the contemporary work of the discipline by recalling that anthropology is basically a critical project because anthropologists often doubt any claim to the certainty of knowledge. Later, I took seriously the injunction that as an ethnographer I must be able to take responsibility for describing the social life of another community in the way I did, even when I lacked the deep knowledge of community history that those who live there forever can assume in their daily work.

Ethics of translation: the mistakes of modern people

The crisis of representation is one of the most powerful critiques of anthropological science. Fabian, Geertz and Marcus have recorded this critique, without replying to it with alternatives (see Marcus and Fischer 1986, Rabinow 1996). The crisis of representation arose as postmodern thought challenged the discipline's ability to describe an objective world. The more eloquent analyses of this crisis endorsed poststructuralist insights that perhaps were best elaborated in *The Order of Things* (Foucault 1972). Foucault correctly recognized that efforts to represent experience severed the representation of life, labour and language from the meaningful contexts of their practice. This ironic fact of knowledge made scientific thought impossible. As a stunning critique of even the interpretative social sciences since Descartes, Foucault showed that failure lies with the scientific limits placed upon descriptive practice. That is, it is impossible to understand meaningfully any lived experience through describing it, whether thickly or symbolically. In the worst-case scenario, attempts at accurate description kill off the meaning won in experience. Unfortunately, the postmodern caveat that claims that symbolic representation saps life of meaning has had few rejoinders. In chapter 10, Latour, Strathern and Wagner, in approaches to the description of virtual society, offer a response and a course of action in their respective discussions of the ethics of translation. Here, I will discuss each in turn, referring to Geertz's concern with translation as a foil to their claims.

It seems that the intellectual habits distinguishing people in modern society after the Enlightenment hobble rather than enable researchers. As I discussed earlier, anthropology needs better mediums of description in order to escape the current crisis of representation that has been associated with postmodernity. Latour details the concept of network as a narrational field, recalling for me an earlier anthropological approach to ethnography that Clifford Geertz (1973) called thick description. Geertz's work, like Latour's, has been wrongly targeted in the science wars of the past decade as simply anti-realist. Both scholars have worked to clarify the intellectual techniques that social scientists use to explore and interpret the real world to create the impression of a real world that can be discovered. For both Latour and Geertz, translation remains the principal intellectual activity. In Geertz's thick description, anthropological science's legitimacy depends upon the acknowledgement that all humans share the work of translating experience in communicable thought into speech and language. All humans, anthropologists included, interpret culture and, in the process, invent it. As I have shown, Roy Wagner (1986, 2001) focuses on *how* things mean, thereby differing from Geertz whose anthropological record infinitely explains away human experiences, even those made in the act of interpretation.

For Latour, translation is also the work of purification; it abstracts a description from the social relations of shared experience, thereby leaving that description untainted by multivalent meanings of the concept as it is used. Instead of making translations, Latour argues, scholars must attend to the mutual processes of purification and translation as just that – as processes. Scholars should comprehend the experiential world in the swerve of its translation and know the translated world in the sway of its enactment. Network theory promises to hold the creative act within the grasp of the intellect – especially an intellect that comprehends the world in action. Translation remains the common ground between Geertz's and Latour's science of society.

Cross-cultural translation, according to Geertz, is the fact of social life that makes moral reasoning possible. In his essay 'Found in translation' (in Geertz 1983), Geertz shows that an anthropologist must first tolerate difference in order to understand cultural phenomena when describing the habits of one society for members of another, and then later convey to others his or her understandings of local knowledge. Geertz maintains moral reasoning as the preserve of the sceptical Cartesian subject because the anthropologist, not the informant, weaves ethnographic meaning from his informants' accounts. As such, Geertz does not surpass or escape realism because the anthropologist remains the interpreter of the real world throughout the process of creating thick description. Geertz's mistake lies in his acceptance of the sceptical subject as the reasoning anthropologist whose knowledge falls between 'experience near to the native's point of view' and 'experience distant' from that perspective in the world of academic writing (Geertz 1983: 57). For Latour, translation makes moral reasoning necessary. Latour understands the translation of experience not as the narrative of thick description but as the long thread of connection elaborately deepening intimacies between material and ideal reality, at the very point of the severe abstraction of the representation. An anthropologist who follows that long chain from one end to the other links the translation to reality. Latour then discovers the world as networks that are hybrids of culture and nature rather than translations of nature by culture. On the surface, this appears to be a critique of scientific rationalism, but it is not. Latour leaves readers with such insights as 'An experiment is an event' and 'we speak truthfully because the world itself is articulated, not the other way around' (1999: 296), recalling Geertz's own evocations of thick description's particular truths. I think that Geertz would concur with Latour; in his essay 'The cerebral savage' Geertz (1973) offers similar critiques of scientific rationalism. But neither Geertz nor Latour forgoes the Cartesian distinction between mind and body that makes scientific scepticism possible.

Through highlighting critical comparison, Strathern's ethnographic practice shifts the work of moral reasoning on to the shoulders of her reader. The unsettling of received wisdom, as described earlier, acts as an impetus to assessing the implications of ethnography for how to live. In carrying out their research, people create knowledge of the world and, in so doing, change the world in which they act. How should a reader of Strathern's ethnography then swing that knowledge into action in the world? Ironically, to act might require doubting the role of the sceptical Cartesian subject. Akin to the impetus of Strathern's ethnographic practice, Wagner's holographic theory of the subject makes clear that times come when moral reasoning risks becoming an apology for conventional social life and its efforts are suitably shifted to unsettling those habits inventively. Wagner first developed this theme in *The Invention of Culture* and elaborates it for *The Anthropology of the Subject*.

Anthropologists could return to conventions of Cartesian science after the postmodern turn. In doing so, they might even rectify the scientific method with the history of its effects, as Latour's account suggests. But to do that would be to risk so much of everything that surrounds humans and gives them cause to wonder about the condition of life. Faith, hope and love are some of the forgotten preconditions of knowing about something; they are ways of knowing that confound any social science whose practitioners assume that only the sentient, sceptical subject could know the world. These preconditions of knowledge are as necessary to critical thought as tolerance is to understanding difference.

Exchanging vulnerability

So far, I have been arguing for an ethics of fieldwork that acknowledges its pathways of exchange, especially those that acknowledge different vulnerabilities of fieldworker and informant. In the first pages of this chapter, I introduced the idea that fieldworkers should acknowledge their own and the informants' vulnerability in making ethical decisions along the way. Here, I want to discuss the exchange of vulnerability in fieldwork, both as its ethical and as its genuine route to anthropological understanding.

Fieldwork is a daunting undertaking, but it would be a mistake to try to triumph over it. Fieldwork can begin slowly, and understanding of social life improves gradually with thickening knowledge of the processes of daily life playing out. This slow learning in fieldwork depends largely on active adult participation and observation, and less on child-like inculcation into the habits of the place. This entailed living with a kind of double bind: on the one hand, rejecting adolescent-style relationships to adults and, on the other hand, acknowledging that I held imperfect understandings of how adults act. This is partly why my discussion of initiation with the elderly women became a ludicrous activity.

I experienced a breakthrough in my work when I acknowledged that if I thought about how to claim responsibility for what I did not know (rather than what I did), then other people could help me to understand better what is happening. Sometimes I can claim responsibility for my lack of ethnographic understanding, if I remain sceptical in the field, checking his or her misassumptions and assumptions about all that is happening. In different situations, I can confront and acknowledge all that I do not know if I concede to vulnerability in fieldwork, admitting that my ignorance of particular ways of the place seems ludicrous to my hosts. Whether that mutual recognition of ignorance is fair-minded, or even-handed by standards set by the profession does not matter. There is no way of getting fieldwork right according to the code; that is similar to having a destination without knowing how to get there.

Perhaps it is time to rethink this 'savage slot' that is part of fieldwork experience. Trouillot (1992) used the term 'savage slot' to warn against mistaking material grounds of anthropological knowledge for the ideal construct. He reminds us that it is not possible to continuously discover new 'things' to describe as if perpetually discovering another kind of Noble Savage, whether that might be the 'condition of poverty' or the 'culture of violence'. Recording and analysing experience is the work of eyes and mouth, as much as it is the work of the hands that draw, write and push the button of the recorder. The 'savage slot' is marked upon each human. The eyes and the mouth mark vulnerability; they open us to the world beyond ourselves, and admit the world to us as thinking, perceiving humans.

Perhaps, acknowledging vulnerability in anthropological exchanges is the beginning of ethics. This mode of knowing, this mode of making relationships in order to understand how people live in the world, uses the 'savage slot' as much as the recording technologies. You can recall that you are vulnerable because you try to understand with the gaping holes of your face, with its eyes and its mouth. You can speak with your mouth, and you can write with a pen or on a keyboard. The sentences communicate thoughts clearly because you have a language. Trying to describe an immediate experience in words pushes it away from you, as if it were beyond your knowledge (which of course it cannot be). The body to use and learn cannot be separated from the discipline of seeing and saying things clearly and well. It is a discipline of vision and gaze and of language and lips. This discipline to find a way between the ideal and the material, and between the noble and the savage, keeps anthropology faithful to its perambulations between giving and receiving.

REFERENCES AND SUGGESTED READINGS

CHAPTER 1

Allen, N. (2001) *Categories and Classifications: Maussian Reflections on the Social*, Oxford: Berghahn.

Benedict, R. (1935) *Patterns of Culture*, London: Routledge and Kegan Paul.

Benedict, R. (1963) 'The uses of cannibalism', in M. Mead (ed.) *An Anthropologist at Work*, New York: Avon Books: 44–8.

Benedict, R. (1974 [1946]) *The Chrysanthemum and the Sword*, New York: Meridian Books.

Durkheim, E. (1922) *The Elementary Forms of Religious Life*, London: The Free Press.

Fournier, M. (1994) *Marcel Mauss*, Paris: Fayard.

Gane, M. (1992) *The Radical Sociology of Durkheim and Mauss*, London: Routledge.

Godelier, M. (1999) 'The Legacy of Mauss', in *The Enigma of the Gift*, Oxford: Polity Press: 10–107.

Gofman, A. (1998) 'The total social fact: a vague but suggestive concept', in W. James and N. Allen (eds) *Marcel Mauss: A Centenary*. Oxford: Berghahn: 63–71.

Gregory, C. (1982) *Gifts and Commodities*, London: Academic Books.

Gregory, C. (1997) 'Towards a radical humanist anthropology', in *Savage Money*, Cambridge, MA and London: Harwood Academic Publishers: 297–311.

James, W. and N. Allen (eds) (1998) *Marcel Mauss: A Centenary*, Oxford: Berghahn.

Karsenti, B. (1998) 'The Maussian shift', in in W. James and N. Allen (eds) *Marcel Mauss: A Centenary*. Oxford: Berghahn: 71–82.

Mauss, M. (1983 [1930]) 'An intellectual self-portrait', trans. S. Bailey and J. Llobera, in P. Besnard (ed.), *The Sociological Domain*, Cambridge: Cambridge University Press: 139–56.

Mauss, M. (1990 [1925]) *The Gift: The Form and Reason of Exchange in Primitive and Archaic Societies*, trans. W. D. Halls, London and New York: Routledge.

Montaigne, M. de (1987 [1575]) 'Of cannibals', in *Montaigne: The Complete Essays*, trans. M. Screech, Harmondsworth: Penguin: 228–41.

Montaigne, M. de (1987 [1575]) 'Of custom', in *Montaigne: The Complete Essays*, trans. M. Screech, Harmondsworth: Penguin: 331–36.

Rivers, W. H. R. (1914) *Kinship and Social Organization*, London: Constable and Co.

Strathern, M. (1994) *The Relation*, London: Prickly Pear Press.

Strathern, M. (2003) 'Living science', plenary address, Association of Social Anthropologists, Manchester, 14 July.

Strathern, M. (2004) 'A community of critics? Thoughts on new knowledge', Huxley Memorial Lecture, Royal Anthropological Institute, London, 8 December.

CHAPTER 2

Asad, T. (1973) *Anthropology and the Colonial Encounter*, London: Ithaca Press.

Chagnon, N. (1977) *Yanomamo: The Fierce People*, New York: Holt Reinhardt and Winston.

Clastres, P. (1987) *Society against the State*, trans. R. Hurley, New York and Cambridge, MA: Zone Books and MIT Press.

D'Andrade, R. (1995) 'Moral models in anthropology', *Current Anthropology* 36 (3): 399–408.

Diamond, S. (1977) *In Search of the Primitive*, London: Transaction Books.

Durkheim, E. and Mauss, M. (1963 [1903]) *Primitive Classification*, trans. and intro. Rodney Needham, London: Routledge and Kegan Paul.

Elligson, T. (2001) *The Myth of the Noble Savage*, Berkeley: University of California Press.

Gledhill, J. (1994) *Power and its Disguises*, Oxford: Pluto Press.

Grimshaw, A. (2001) *The Ethnographer's Eye*, Cambridge: Cambridge University Press.

Herle, A. and S. Rouse (1998) *Cambridge and the Torres Straits*, Cambridge: Cambridge University Press..

Kuklick, H. (1991) *The Savage Within*, Cambridge: Cambridge University Press.

Kuklick, H. (1996) 'Islands in the Pacific: Darwinian biogeography and British social anthropology', *American Ethnologist* 23 (3): 611–38.

Kuper, A. (1992) *The Invention of the Primitive*, London and New York: Routledge.

Lévi-Strauss, C. (1960) 'On manipulated sociological models', *Anthropologica, Bijdragen tot de Taal – Land-en-Volkenkunde* 116 (1): 45–54.

Lévi-Strauss, C. (1963) *The Savage Mind*, Chicago: University of Chicago Press.

Lévi-Strauss, C. (1967 [1949]) 'Dual organizations', in *Elementary Structures of Kinship*, Boston, MA: Beacon Press: 69–84.

Lévi-Strauss, C. (1973 [1955]) *Tristes Tropiques*, trans. J. and D. Weightman, New York: Antheum.

Obeyesekere, G. (1992) *The Apotheosis of Captain Cook*, Princeton, NJ: Princeton University Press.

Rousseau, J.-J. (1968 [1743]) *The Social Contract*, Harmondsworth: Penguin.

Rousseau, J.-J. (1974 [1764]) *Émile*, Harmondsworth: Penguin.

Rousseau, J.-J. (1984 [1758]) *A Discourse on Inequality*, Harmondsworth: Penguin.

Ruby, J. (1995) 'Out of sync: the cinema of Tim Asch', *Visual Anthropology Review* 11 (1): 19–36.

Sahlins, M. (1958) *Social Stratification in Polynesia*, Seattle: University of Washington Press.

Sahlins, M. (1963) 'Rich man poor man big man chief', *Comparative Studies in Society and History* 5: 285–303.

Sahlins, M. (1972) *Stone Age Economics*, New York: Aldine Press.

Sahlins, M. (1976) *Culture and Practical Reason*, Chicago: University of Chicago Press.

Sahlins, M. (1981) *Historical Metaphors and Mythical Realities*, Chicago: University of Chicago Press.

Sahlins, M. (1985) *Islands of History*, Chicago: University of Chicago Press.

Scheper-Hughes, N. (1995) 'The primacy of the ethical: propositions for a militant anthropology', *Current Anthropology* 36 (3): 409–39.

Spencer, J. (1997) 'Postcolonialism and the political imagination', *Journal of the Royal Anthropological Institute* 3 (1): 1–20.

Stocking, G. (1987) *Victorian Anthropology*, Madison: University of Wisconsin Press.

Stocking, G. (1988) *Functionalism Historicized*, Madison: University of Wisconsin Press.

Stocking, G. (1996) Volkgeist *as Method and Ethic: Essays of Boasian Ethnography and the German Anthropological Tradition*, Madison: University of Wisconsin Press.

Thomas, N. (1984) *Out of Time: History and Evolutionism in Anthropological Discourse*, Ann Arbor: University of Michigan Press.

Trouillot, M.-R. (1992) 'The savage slot', in *Recapturing Anthropology*, Santa Fe, NM: School of American Research: 17–45.

Wolf, E. (1986) 'Introduction', in *Europe and the People without History*, Berkeley: University of California Press: 3–23.

CHAPTER 3

Boas, F. (1897) *The Social Organization and the Secret Societies of the Kwakiutl Indians (based on personal observations and on notes made by Mr George Hunt)*, Washington, DC: US Government Printers.

Boas, F. (1966) *Kwakiutl Ethnography*, Chicago: University of Chicago Press.

Boas, F. and G. Hunt (1913–14) *Ethnology of the Kwakiutl*, 35th Annual Report of the American Bureau of Ethnology, Washington 1921 (2 vols).

Clifford, J. (1988) 'On ethnographic self-fashioning: Conrad and Malinowski', *Predicament of Culture*, Berkeley: University of California Press: 92–113.

Firth, R. (1957) 'Introduction: Malinowski as scientist and man', in Raymond Firth (ed.) *Man and Culture: An Evaluation of the Work of Bronislaw Malinowski*, London: Routledge and Kegan Paul.

Geertz, C. (1983) 'From the natives' point of view', in *Local Knowledge*, New York: Basic Books: 55–70.

Geertz, C. (1988) 'Malinowski's children: I – witnessing', in *Works and Lives*, Stanford, CA: Stanford University Press: 73–102.

Gell, A. (1992) *The Anthropology of Time*, Oxford: Berg.

Gellner, E. (1988) 'Zeno of Crakow', in J. Mucha, Ellen E. Gellner, and G. Kubica (1992) *The Polish Roots of an Anthropological Tradition*, Cambridge: Cambridge University Press: 164–94.

Hutnyk, J. (1998) 'Clifford's ethnographica', *Critique of Anthropology* 18 (4): 339–78.

Kuper, A. (1973) *Anthropology and the Anthropologists: The Modern British School*, London: Routledge.

Malinowski, B. (1916) 'Baloma: spirits of the dead in the Trobriand Islands', *Journal of the Royal Anthropological Institute*, 46: 354–430.

Malinowski, B. (1920) 'Kula: the circulating exchange of valuables in the archipelagoes of eastern New Guinea', *Man* 20: 97–105.

Malinowski, B. (1926) *Crime and Custom in Savage Society*, London: Kegan Paul.

Malinowski, B. (1927) *The Father in Primitive Psychology*, London: Kegan Paul.

Malinowski, B. (1929) *The Sexual Life of Savages*, London: Routledge.

Malinowski, B. (1935 [1922]) 'The aim and scope of this method', in *Argonauts of the Western Pacific*, New York: Dutton: 1–25.

Malinowski, B. (1944) *A Scientific Theory of Culture*, Chapel Hill, NC: University of North Carolina Press.

Malinowski, B. (1954 [1926]) 'Myth as primitive psychology', in *Magic Science and Religion*, introduction by R. Redfield, New York: Anchor Books: 1–128.

Malinowski, B. (1967) *A Diary in the Strict Sense of the Term*, New York: Harcourt Brace and World.

Mucha, J., Ellen E. Gellner and G. Kubica (1992) *The Polish Roots of an Anthropological Tradition*, Cambridge: Cambridge University Press.

Stocking, G. (1988) *Functionalism Historicized*, Madison: University of Wisconsin Press.

Strathern, M. (1981) 'Culture in a netbag: the manufacture of a subdiscipline in anthropology', *Man* n.s. 16: 665–88.

Tambiah, S. (1992) *Magic, Science, Religion and the Scope of Rationality*, Cambridge: Cambridge University Press.

Vincent, J. (1992) 'Engaging historicism', in *Recapturing Anthropology*, Santa Fe, NM: School of American Research: 45–58.

Weiner, A. (1977) *Women of Value, Men of Renown*, Austin: University of Texas Press.

Weiner, A. (1990) *The Trobrianders*, New York: Holt Reinhardt and Winston.

CHAPTER 4

Benedict, R. (1935) *Patterns of Culture*, London: Routledge and Kegan Paul.

Best, E. (1977 [1909]) *Forest Lore of the Maori*, Wellington: E. C. Keating, Government Printer.

Boas, F. (1897) *The Social Organization and the Secret Societies of the Kwakiutl Indians (based on personal observations and on notes made by Mr George Hunt)*, Washington, DC: US Government Printers.

Boas, F. (1966) *Kwakiutl Ethnography*, Chicago: University of Chicago Press.

Codere, H. (1950) *Fighting with Property: A Study of Kwakiutl Feasting and Warfare 1792 to 1930*, New York: J. J. Augustin.

Drucker, P. (1967) *To Make my Name Good*, Los Angeles: University of California Press.

Firth, R. (1929) *Primitive Economics of New Zealand Maori*, London: Routledge.

Gane, M. (1992) *The Radical Sociology of Durkheim and Mauss*, London: Routledge.

Godelier, M. (1999) 'The legacy of Mauss', in *The Enigma of the Gift*, Oxford: Polity Press: 10–107.

Goldman, L. (1975) *The Mouth of Heaven: An Introduction to Kwakiutl Religious Thought*, London and New York: Wiley.

Halliday, W. (1935) *Potlatch and Totem: Recollections of an Indian Agent*, London and Toronto: Dent.

Hubert, H. and M. Mauss (1964 [1898]) *Sacrifice*, trans. W. Halls, foreword by E. Evans Pritchard, Chicago:University of Chicago Press.

James, W. and N. Allen (eds) (1998) *Marcel Mauss: A Centenary*, Oxford: Berghahn.

Lévi-Strauss, C. (1976) *An Introduction to the Work of Marcel Mauss*, trans. Felicity Baker, London: Routledge and Kegan Paul.

Malinowski, B. (1926) *Crime and Custom in Savage Society*, London: Kegan Paul.

Malinowski, B. (1935 [1922]) *Argonauts of the Western Pacific*, New York: Dutton.

Mauss, M. (1983 [1930]) 'An intellectual self-portrait', trans. S. Bailey and J. Llobera, in P. Besnard (ed.), *The Sociological Domain*, Cambridge: Cambridge University Press: 139–56.

Mauss, M. (1990 [1925]) *The Gift: The Form and Reason of Exchange in Primitive and Archaic Societies*, trans. W. D. Halls, London and New York: Routledge.
Mosko, M. (2000) 'Inalienable ethnography: keeping while giving and the Trobriand case', *Journal of the Royal Anthropological Institute* 6 (3): 377–96.
Orwell, G. (Eric Blair) (1989 [1933]) *Down and Out in Paris and London*, Harmondsworth: Penguin (in association with Secker and Warburg).
Parry, J. (1986) 'The gift, the Indian gift and the "Indian gift"', *Man* n.s. 21 (3): 453–73.
Sahlins, M. (1972) 'The spirit of the gift', in *Stone Age Economics*, New York: Aldine: 149–84.
Strathern, M. (1988) *The Gender of the Gift: Problems with Women and Problems with Society in Melanesia*, Berkeley, CA: University of California Press.
Strathern, M. (1994) *The Relation*, London: Prickly Pear Press.
Walens, S. (1981) *Feasting with Cannibals: An Essay on Kwakiotl Cosmology*, Princeton, NJ: Princeton University Press.
Weiner, A. (1992) *Inalienable Possessions*, Berkeley: University of California Press.
Wolf, E. (1986) *Europe and the People without History*, Berkeley: University of California Press.
Wolf, E. (1999) *Envisioning Power*, Los Angeles: University of California Press.

CHAPTER 5

Augé, M. (1995 [1992]) *Non-Places: Introduction to an Anthropology of Supermodernity*, London: Verso.
Clifford, J. (1988) *The Predicament of Culture*, Berkeley: University of California Press.
Durkheim, E. and Mauss, M. (1963 [1903]) *Primitive Classification*, trans. and intro. Rodney Needham, London: Routledge and Kegan Paul.
Gell, A. (1992a) 'Leach', in *The Anthropology of Time*, Oxford: Berg: 30–6.
Gell, A. (1992b) 'Lévi Strauss', in *The Anthropology of Time*, Oxford: Berg: 23–79.
Godelier, M. (1986) *The Making of Great Men*, Cambridge: Cambridge University Press.
Godelier, M. and M. Strathern (eds) (1991) *Big Men and Great Men*, Cambridge: Cambridge University Press.
Leacock, E. (1953) 'Introduction', in F. Engels, *The Family, Private Property and the State*, New York: International Publishers: 7–67.
Lévi-Strauss, C. (1943) 'The social use of kinship terms among Brazilian Indians', *American Anthropologist* 45 (2): 398–409.
Lévi-Strauss, C. (1967a [1949]) 'Cycles of reciprocity', in *Elementary Structures of Kinship*, Boston, MA: Beacon Press: 438–58.
Lévi-Strauss, C. (1967b [1949]) 'Nature and culture', and 'The problem of incest', in *Elementary Structures of Kinship*, Boston, MA: Beacon Press: 1–25.
Lévi-Strauss, C. (1967c [1949]) 'The principle of reciprocity', in *Elementary Structures of Kinship*, Boston, MA: Beacon Press: 52–68.
Lévi-Strauss, C. (1963) *The Savage Mind*, Chicago: University of Chicago Press.
Lévi-Strauss, C. (1973) 'Men, women and chiefs', in *Tristes Tropiques*, London: Cape: chapter 29.
Ortner, S. (1974) 'Is female to male as nature is to culture?', in M. Rosaldo and L. Lamphere (eds) *Woman Culture Society*, Palo Alto, CA: Stanford University Press: 67–88.
Rubin, G. (1975) 'The traffic in women: notes on the political economy of sex', in

R. Reiter (ed.) *Toward an Anthropology of Women*, New York: Monthly Review Press: 157–210.

Schneider, D. (1970) *A Critique of the Study of Kinship*, Chicago: University of Chicago Press.

Strathern, M. (1980) 'No nature, no culture: the Hagen case', in C. MacCormack and M. Strathern (eds) *Nature Culture Gender*, Cambridge: Cambridge University Press: 174–222.

Strathern, M. (1981a) 'Domesticity and the denigration of women', in Denise O'Brien and Sharon Tiffany (eds) *Rethinking Women's Roles: Perspectives from the Pacific*, Berkeley: University of California Press: 13–31.

Strathern, M. (1981b) 'Self interest and the social good: some implications of Hagen gender imagery', in S. Ortner and H. Whitehead (eds) *Sexual Meanings: The Cultural Construction of Gender and Sexuality*, Cambridge: Cambridge University Press: 359–409.

Strathern, M. (1984) 'Subject or object? Women and the circulation of valuables in Highlands New Guinea', in R. Hirschon (ed.) *Women and Property, Women as Property*, London: Croom Helm:159–75.

Strathern, M. (1985a) 'John Locke's servant and the Hausboi from Hagen: thoughts on domestic labour', *Critical Philosophy* 2: 21–48.

Strathern, M. (1985b) 'Kinship and economy: constitutive orders of a provisional kind', *American Ethnologist* 12: 191–209.

Strathern, M. (1988a) 'A place in the feminist debate', in *The Gender of the Gift*, Berkeley, CA: University of California Press: 22–42.

Strathern, M. (1988b) 'Producing difference: connections and disconnections in two New Guinea Highland kinship systems', in J. Collier and Sylvia Yanigsako (eds) *Gender and Kinship: Essays towards a Unified Analysis*, Palo Alto, CA: Stanford University Press: 271–300.

Strathern, M. (1988c) *The Gender of the Gift: Problems with Women and Problems with Society in Melanesia*, Berkeley, CA: University of California Press.

CHAPTER 6

Dilley, R. (1999) 'Introduction', in Roy Dilley (ed.) *The Problem of Context*, Oxford: Berghahn: 1–46.

Duffy, C. (1987) *Selling Manhattan*, London: Anvil.

Graeber, D. (2001) *Towards an Anthropological Theory of Value: The False Coin of our Dreams*, New York: Palgrave.

Kaplan, M. (1995) *Neither Cargo nor Cult*, Chapel Hill, NC: Duke University Press.

Kaplan M. and J. Kelly (1994) 'Rethinking resistance: dialogics of disaffection in colonial Fiji', *American Ethnologist* 21 (1): 123–51.

Kelly, J. (1988) *From Holi to Diwali Man* (ns) 23 (1): 40–55.

Kelly, J. (1991) *A Politics of Virtue: Hinduism, Sexuality and Counter-colonial Discourse in Fiji*, Chicago: Chicago University Press.

Kelly, J. (1997) 'Gaze and grasp: plantations, desires, indentured Indians and colonial law in Fiji', in L. Manderson and M. Jolly (eds) *Sites of Desire, Economies of Pleasure: Sexualities in Asia and the Pacific*, Chicago: University of Chicago Press: 72–98.

Kelly, J. and M. Kaplan (2001) *Represented Communities: Fiji and World Decolonisation*, Chicago: University of Chicago Press.

Lal, Brij (1985a) 'Kunti's cry: indentured women on Fiji plantation', *Indian Economic and Social History Review* 22: 55–71.

Lal, Brij (1985b) 'Veil of dishonour: sexual jealousy and suicide on Fiji plantations', *Journal of Pacific History* 20: 135–55.

Leacock, E. (1954) *The Montagnais 'Hunting Territory' and the Fur Trade*, American Anthropological Association, Memoir no. 78.

Leacock, E. and M. Etienne (1980) *Women and Colonization: An Anthropological Perspective*, New York: Praeger.

Morgan, L. H. (1878) *Ancient Society; or Researches into the Line of Human Progress from Savagery, through Barbarism to Civilization*, Chicago: C. H. Kerr.

Prakash, G. (1988) *Bonded Histories: Genealogies of Labor Servitude in Colonial India*, Cambridge: Cambridge University Press.

Sahlins, M. (1962) *Moala*, Seattle: University of Washington Press.

Sahlins, M. (1985) *Islands of History*, Chicago: University of Chicago Press.

Sahlins, M. (1992) 'The economics of develop-man in the Pacific', *Res* 21: 13–25.

Sahlins, M. (1994) 'Cery Cery Fukabede', *American Ethnologist* 20 (4): 848–67.

Sahlins, M. (1995) *How 'Natives' Think: About Captain Cook, For Example*, Chicago, Chicago University Press.

Said, E. (1977) *Orientalism*, London: Verso.

Thomas, N. (1992a) 'The permutations of debt', in *Entangled Objects*, Cambridge, MA: Harvard University Press: 35–82.

Thomas, N. (1992b) 'Substantivization and anthropological discourse: the transformation of practices in institutions in neo-traditional Pacific societies', in J. Carrier and A. Carrier (eds) *History and Tradition in Melanesian Anthropology*, Berkeley: University of California Press: 64–85.

Thomas, N. (1992c) 'The inversion of tradition', *American Ethnologist* 19: 213–32.

Thomas, N. (1994) 'Beggars can be choosers', *American Ethnologist* 20 (4): 868–76.

Thwaites, Reuben G. (ed.) (1896–1901) *The Jesuit Relations and Allied Documents: Travels and Explorations of the Jesuit Missionaries in New France*, 73 vols., Cleveland, OH: Burrows Brothers.

Trigger, B. (1969) *The Huron: Farmers of the North*, Case Studies in Cultural Anthropology, Toronto: Holt Reinhardt Winston.

Wallace, A. (1970) *The Death and Rebirth of the Seneca*, New York: Knopf.

CHAPTER 7

Bourdieu, P. (1977) *Outline of a Theory of Practice*, Cambridge: Cambridge University Press.

Bourdieu, P. (1979) *Algeria 1960, The Disenchantment of the World, The Sense of Honour, The Kabyle House or the World Reversed: Essays*, Cambridge: Cambridge University Press.

Bourdieu, P. (1990a) 'Matrimonial land strategies', in *The Logic of Practice*, Palo Alto, CA: Stanford University Press: 147–61.

Bourdieu, P. (1990b) 'Matrimonial strategies and social reproduction', in *The Logic of Practice*, Palo Alto, CA: Stanford University Press: 187–99.

Bourdieu, P. (1990c) 'Structures, habitus, practice', in *The Logic of Practice*, Palo Alto, CA: Stanford University Press: 52–65.

Bourdieu, P. (1990d) 'The work of time', in *The Logic of Practice*, Palo Alto, CA: Stanford University Press: 98–112.

Bourdieu, P. (2004) *Esquisse pour une auto-analyse*, Collection Cours et Travaux, Paris: Raisons d'Agir Editions.

Geertz, C. (1968) *Islam Observed: Religious Development in Morocco and Indonesia*, Chicago: University of Chicago Press.

Geertz, C. (1973) 'Thick description', in *The Interpretation of Culture*, New York: Basic Books: 1–23.

Geertz, C., H. Geertz and L. Rosen (eds) (1979) *Meaning and Order in Moroccan Society: Three Essays in Cultural Interpretation*, Cambridge: Cambridge University Press.

Geertz, H. (1979) 'Family relations', in C. Geertz, H. Geertz and L. Rosen (eds) *Meaning and Order in Moroccan Society: Three Essays in Cultural Interpretation*, Cambridge: Cambridge University Press: 315–91.

Gellner, E. (1973) *Arabs and Berbers: From Tribe to Nation in North Africa*, London: Duckworth.

Gellner, E. (1981) *Muslim Society*, Cambridge: Cambridge University Press.

Godelier, M. (1986) *The Making of Great Men*, Cambridge: Cambridge University Press.

Godelier, M. and M. Strathern (eds) (1991) *Big Men and Great Men*, Cambridge: Cambridge University Press.

Jenkins, R. (1992) *Bourdieu*, Key Thinkers in Sociology Series, London: Open University Press.

Leach, E. (1954) *Political Systems of Highland Burma*, London: G. Bell and London School of Economics.

Mead, M. and R. Métraux (1979) *A Way of Seeing*, New York: McCall.

Messick, B. (1993) *The Calligraphic State*, Berkeley: University of California Press.

Reed-Danahay, D. (2004) *Locating Bourdieu*, Bloomington: University of Indiana Press.

Rosen, L. (2002) *The Culture of Islam*, Chicago: University of Chicago Press.

Strathern, M. (1988) *The Gender of the Gift: Problems with Women and Problems with Society in Melanesia*, Berkeley, CA: University of California Press.

CHAPTER 8

Banks, Mrs G. L. (1876) *The Manchester Man*, London: Hurst and Blackett.

Battaglia, D. (1990) *On the Bones of the Serpent: Person, Memory and Mortality in Sarbarl Island Society*, Chicago: University of Chicago Press.

Battaglia, D. (1995) *Rhetorics of Self-Making*, Berkeley: University of California Press.

Carruthers, M., S. Collins and S. Lukes (1985) *The Category of the Person*, Cambridge: Cambridge University Press.

Derrida, J. (1992) 'Counterfeit money I: poetics of tobacco (Baudelaire, painter of modern life)', in *Given Time 1 Counterfeit Money*, Chicago: University of Chicago Press: 71–107.

Derrida, J. (1995) *Specters of Marx*, New York and London: Routledge.

Dumont, L. (1970) *Homo Hierarchicus*, trans. M. Sainsbury, Chicago: University of Chicago Press.

Dumont, L. (1986 [1983]) *Essays on Individualism: Modern Ideology in Anthropological Perspective*, Chicago: University of Chicago Press.

Engels, F. (1892 [1853]) *The Social Conditions of the Working Classes of England in 1844*, London: Swan Sonnenschein and Co.

Grimshaw, A. (2001) *The Ethnographer's Eye*, Cambridge: Cambridge University Press.

Hutcheon, L. (1989) *The Politics of Postmodernism*, London and New York: Routledge.

Macpherson, C. (1963) *The Political Theory of Possessive Individualism*, Cambridge: Cambridge University Press.

Marx, K. (1978 [1857–8]) 'Externalization of historic relations of production – production and distribution in general – property', in *The Marx–Engels Reader*, ed. Robert Tucker, New York: Norton: 223–6.

Marx, K. (1978 [1857–8]) 'Independent individuals eighteenth century ideas', in *The Marx–Engels Reader*, ed. Robert Tucker, New York: Norton: 222–3.

Marx, K. (1978 [1867]) 'Commodity fetishism and the secret thereof', in *The Marx–Engels Reader*, ed. Robert Tucker, New York: Norton: 319–29.

Orwell, G. (Eric Blair) (1989 [1933]) *Down and Out in Paris and London*, Harmondsworth: Penguin (in association with Secker and Warburg).

Orwell, G. (Eric Blair) (1989 [1937]) *The Road to Wigan Pier*, Harmondsworth: Penguin.

Yeatman, A. (1994) *Postmodern Revisionings of the Political*, London and New York: Routledge.

CHAPTER 9

Bataille, G. (1991) 'The gift of rivalry: potlatch', in *The Accursed Share 1*, London: Zone Books: 63–77.

Bataille, G. (1993) 'The prohibition of incest', in *The Accursed Share 2&3*, vol. 2, London: Zone Books: 27–58.

Bataille, G. (1994) *Visions of Excess: Selected Writings, 1927–1939*, edited and with an introduction by Allan Stoekl, trans. Allan Stoekl with C. Lovitt and D. Leslie, Jr, Minneapolis: University of Minnesota Press.

Benedict, R. (1935) *Patterns of Culture*, London: Routledge and Kegan Paul.

Boas, F. (1897) *The Social Organization and the Secret Societies of the Kwakiutl Indians (based on personal observations and on notes made by Mr George Hunt)*, Washington, DC: US Government Printers.

Boas, F. (1966) *Kwakiutl Ethnography*, Chicago: University of Chicago Press.

Codere, H. (1950) *Fighting with Property: A Study of Kwakiutl Feasting and Warfare 1792 to 1930*, New York: J. J. Augustin.

Drucker, P. (1967) *To Make my Name Good*, Los Angeles: University of California Press.

Geertz, C. (1973) 'Deep play: notes on the Balinese cockfight', in *The Interpretation of Cultures*, New York: Basic Books.

Godelier, M. (1999) *The Enigma of the Gift*, Oxford: Polity Press.

Goldman, L. (1975) *The Mouth of Heaven: An Introduction to Kwakiutl Religious Thought*, London and New York: Wiley.

Gregory, C. (1982) *Gifts and Commodities*, London: Academic Books.

Gregory, C. (1997) *Savage Money*, Cambridge, MA and London: Harwood Academic Publishers.

Halliday, W. (1935) *Potlatch and Totem: Recollections of an Indian Agent*, London and Toronto: Dent.

Hutnyk, J. (2003) 'Bataille's wars: surrealism, Marxism, fascism', *Critique of Anthropology*, 23 (3): 264–88.

Jones, E. (1925) 'Mother-right and the sexual ignorance of savages', *International Journal of Psychoanalysis* 6: 109–30.

Kan, S. (1986) 'The 19th century Tlingit potlatch: a new perspective 2', *American Ethnologist* 13: 191–212.

Klima, A. (2002) *The Funeral Casino: Meditation, Massacre, and Exchange with the Dead in Thailand*, Princeton, NJ: Princeton University Press.

Kraemer, A. (1925) *Die Málanggane von Tombára*, Munich: Georg Müller.

Kuchler, S. (2001) *Malanggan*, Oxford: Berg.

Malinowski, B. (2001 [1935]) *Coral Gardens and Their Magic*, Vols 1 and 2, London: Routledge.

Parsons, A. (1964) 'Is the Oedipal complex universal: the Jones–Malinowski debate revisited and a south Italian nuclear complex', *The Psychoanalytic Study of Society* 3: 278–328.

Schneider, D. and K. Gough (1964) *Matrilineal Kinship*, Chicago: University of Chicago Press.

Spiro, M. (1982) *Oedipus in the Trobriands*, Chicago: University of Chicago Press.

Veblen, T. (1967 [1899]) *A Theory of the Leisure Class*, Harmondsworth: Penguin.

Walens, S. (1981) *Feasting with Cannibals: An Essay on Kwakiotl Cosmology*, Princeton, NJ: Princeton University Press.

Weiner, A. (1985) 'Oedipus and ancestors', *American Ethnologist* 12: 758–62.

Weiner, A. (1992) *Inalienable Possessions*, Berkeley: University of California Press.

Wolf, E. (1999) *Envisioning Power*, Los Angeles: University of California Press.

Young, M. (ed.) (1979) *The Ethnography of Malinowski*, London: Routledge and Kegan Paul.

Young, M. (ed.) (2004) *Malinowski: Odyssey of an Anthropologist*, London and New York: Routledge.

CHAPTER 10

Appadurai, A. (1986) *The Social Life of Things: Commodities in Cultural Perspective*, Cambridge: Cambridge University Press.

Appadurai, A. (1996) *Modernity at Large: Cultural Dimensions of Globalization*, Minneapolis: University of Minnesota Press.

Augé, M. (1995 [1992]) *Non-Places: Introduction to an Anthropology of Supermodernity*, London: Verso.

Bateson, G. (1958 [1936]) *Naven*, Palo Alto, CA: Stanford University Press.

Bateson, G. (1972) *Mind and Nature: A Necessary Unity*, London: Fontana.

Bateson, G. (1987a) 'Cybernetic explanation', in *Steps to an Ecology of Mind*, New York: Ballantine: 399–410.

Bateson, G. (1987b) 'Style, grace and information in primitive art', in *Steps to an Ecology of Mind*, New York: Ballantine: 153–6.

Bateson, G. (1987c) 'Form, substance and difference', in *Steps to an Ecology of Mind*, New York: Ballantine: 448–66.

Battaglia, D. (1990) *On the Bones of the Serpent: Person, Memory and Mortality in Sarbarl Island Society*, Chicago: University of Chicago Press.

Battaglia, D. (1994) 'Retaining reality: some practical problems with objects as property', *Man* 29: 631–44.

Battaglia, D. (1995) *Rhetorics of Self-Making*, Berkeley: University of California Press.

Baudrillard, J. (1981 [1972]) *For a Critique of the Political Economy of the Sign*, trans. Chas. Levin, St Louis: Telos.

Benjamin, W. (1973 [1955]) 'The work of art in the age of mechanical reproduction', in *Illuminations*, New York: Shocken: 217–53.

Foucault, M. (1972) *The Order of Things*, New York: Vintage.

Geertz, C. (1973) *The Interpretation of Cultures,* New York: Basic Books.

Gell, A. (1992) 'The technology of enchantment and the enchantments of technology', in J. Coote and A. Shelton (eds) *Anthropology, Art and Aesthetics*, Oxford: Clarendon Press: 40–66.

Glowczewski, B. (1983) 'Death, women, and "value production": the circulation of hair strings among the Walpiri of the Central Australian Desert', *Ethnology* 22 (3): 225–39.

Latour, B. (1988) *We Have Never Been Modern*, Chicago: University of Chicago Press.

Latour, B. (1999) *Pandora's Hope: Essays on the Reality of Science Studies.* Cambridge, MA: Harvard University Press.

McLuhan, M. (1959) *The Mechanical Bride: Folklore of Industrial Man*, London: Routledge and Kegan Paul.

McLuhan, M. (1964a) *Understanding Media*, London: Routledge and Kegan Paul.

McLuhan, M. (1964b) *The Medium is the Message*, Boston, MA: MIT Press.

Marcus, G. and J. Clifford (1986) *Writing Culture*, Berkeley: University of California Press.

Marcus, G. and M. Fischer (1986) *Anthropology as Cultural Critique*, Chicago: University of Chicago Press.

Marcus, G. and F. Meyers (1995) *The Traffic in Culture*, Berkeley: University of California Press.

Munn, N. (1973) *Walbiri Iconography. Graphic Representation and Cultural Symbolism in a Central Australian Society*, Ithaca, NY, and London: Cornell University Press.

Plato (1983) *Symposium* and *Phaedrus*, trans. B. Jowett, New York: Dover Publications.

Pottage, A. (2001) 'Persons and things: an ethnographic analogy', *Economy and Society* 30 (1): 112–38.

Rabinow, P. (1996) *Essays in the Anthropology of Reason*, Princeton, NJ: Princeton University Press.

Riles, A. (2000) *The Network Inside Out*, Ann Arbor: University of Michigan Press.

Schneider, D. (1975) *American Kinship,* Chicago: University of Chicago Press.

Strathern, M. (1972) *Women in Between*, London: Academic Books.

Strathern, M. (1985) 'Kinship and economy: constitutive orders of a provisional kind', *American Ethnologist* 12: 191–209.

Strathern, M. (ed.) (1987) *Dealing with Inequality*, Berkeley: University of California Press.

Strathern, M. (1988) *The Gender of the Gift: Problems with Women and Problems with Society in Melanesia*, Berkeley, CA: University of California Press.

Strathern, M. (1991) *Partial Connections*, Savage, MD: Rowman and Littlefield.

Strathern, M. (ed.) (1999) *Property, Substance and Effect*, London: Athlone.

Strathern, M. (2000) *Audit Cultures: Anthropological Studies in Accountability, Ethics and the Academy*, London: Routledge.

Strathern, M. (2001) 'The patent and the Malanggan', *Theory, Culture and Society*,18 (4): 1–23.

Wagner, R. (1986) *Symbols that Stand for Themselves*, Chicago: University of Chicago Press.

Wagner, R. (1991) 'The fractal person', in M. Godelier and M. Strathern (eds) *Big Men and Great Men*, Cambridge: Cambridge University Press: 159–74.

Wagner, R. (1995) 'If you have the advertisement, you don't need the product', in D. Battaglia (ed.) *Rhetorics of Self-Making*, Berkeley: University of California Press: 59–76.

Wagner, R. (2001) *The Anthropology of the Subject*, Berkeley: University of California Press.

CHAPTER 11

Appadurai, A. (1986) *The Social Life of Things: Commodities in Cultural Perspective*, Cambridge: Cambridge University Press.

Appadurai, A. (1996) *Modernity at Large: Cultural Dimensions of Globalization*, Minneapolis: University of Minnesota Press.

Blake, J. (2001) *Developing a New Standard-setting Instrument for the Safeguarding of Intangible Cultural Heritage*, Paris: UNESCO.

Bourdieu, P. (1977) *Outline of a Theory of Practice*, Cambridge: Cambridge University Press.

Brown, M. (2001) 'Can culture be copyrighted?', *Current Anthropology* 19 (2): 193–222.

Brush, S. (1992) 'Indigenous knowledge of biological resources and intellectual property rights: the role of anthropology', *American Anthropologist* 95 (3): 653–86.

Clifford, J. (1988) *The Predicament of Culture*, Cambridge, MA: Harvard University Press.

Clifford, J. (1997) *Routes*, Cambridge, MA: Harvard University Press.

Codere, H. (1950) *Fighting with Property: A Study of Kwakiutl Feasting and Warfare 1792 to 1930*, New York: J. J. Augustin.

Coombe, R. (1998) *The Cultural Life of Intellectual Property*, Durham, NC: Duke University Press.

Crook, T. (2004) 'Transactions in perpetual motion', in E. Hirsch and M. Strathern (eds) *Transactions and Creations: Property Debates and the Stimulus of Melanesia*, Oxford: Berghahn: 110–31.

Demian, M. (2004) 'Seeing, knowing, owning: property claims as revelatory acts', in E. Hirsch and M. Strathern (eds) *Transactions and Creations: Property Debates and the Stimulus of Melanesia,* Oxford: Berghahn: 60–82.

Descola, P., P. Harvey, M. Strathern and E. Viveiros de Castro (1999) 'Exploitable knowledge belongs to the creators of it: a debate', *Social Anthropology* 6 (1): 109–26.

Drucker, P. (1967) *To Make my Name Good*, Los Angeles: University of California Press.

Dutfield, M. and D. Posey (1996) *Beyond Intellectual Property: Toward Traditional Resource Rights for Indigenous Peoples and Local Communities*, Ottawa: International Development Research Centre.

Fortune, R. (1963 [1934]) *Sorcerors of Dobu*, London: Routledge and Kegan Paul.

Gell, A. (1986) 'Newcomers to the world of goods: consumption among the Muria Gonds', in A. Appadurai (ed.), *The Social Life of Things: Commodities in Cultural Perspective*, Cambridge: Cambridge University Press.

Gregory, C. (1982) *Gifts and Commodities*, London: Academic Books.

Gregory, C. (1997) *Savage Money*, Cambridge, MA and London: Harwood Academic Publishers.

Halliday, W. (1935) *Potlatch and Totem: Recollections of an Indian Agent*, London and Toronto: Dent.

Harrison, S. (1992) 'Ritual as intellectual property in Melanesia', *Man* 27: 225–44.
Hill, C. (1972) *The World Turned Upside Down*, Harmondsworth: Penguin.
Hirsch, E. (2001) 'New boundaries of influence in Highlands Papua: culture, mining and ritual conversions', *Oceania* 71: 298–311.
Hirsch, E. (2004) 'Boundaries of creation: the work of credibility in science and ceremony', in E. Hirsch and M. Strathern (eds) *Transactions and Creations: Property Debates and the Stimulus of Melanesia*, Oxford: Berghahn: 176–92.
Hobbes, T. (1968 [1655]) *Leviathan*, introduction by C. B. Macpherson, Harmondsworth: Penguin.
Kirsch, S. (2004) 'Property limits: debates on the body, nature and culture', in E. Hirsch and M. Strathern (eds) *Transactions and Creations: Property Debates and the Stimulus of Melanesia*, Oxford: Berghahn: 21–39.
Leach, J. (2000) 'Situated connections: rights and intellectual resources in a Rai Coast society', *Social Anthropology* 8 (2): 163–79.
Leach, J. (2004) 'Modes of creativity', in E. Hirsch and M. Strathern (eds) *Transactions and Creations: Property Debates and the Stimulus of Melanesia*, Oxford: Berghahn: 151–75.
Malinowski, B. (1926) *Crime and Custom in Savage Society*, London: Kegan Paul.
Malinowski, B. (1927) *The Father in Primitive Psychology*, London: Kegan Paul.
Monbiot, G. (2003) *The Age of Consent: A Manifesto for a New World Order*, London: Flamingo.
Narotzky, S. (1998) *New Directions in Economic Anthropology*, London and Chicago: Pluto Press.
Parry, J. (1986) 'The gift, the Indian gift and the "Indian gift"', *Man* n.s. 21 (3): 453–73.
Posey, D. (1996) *Traditional Resource Rights: International Instruments for Protection and Compensation for Indigenous Peoples and Local Communities*, Cambridge and Gland, Switzerland: IUCN – the World Conservation Union.
Powdermaker, H. (1933) *Life in Lesu*, London: Williams and Norgate.
Sahlins, M. (1985) *Islands of History*, Chicago: University of Chicago Press.
Strathern, M. (1981a) 'Domesticity and the denigration of women', in Denise O'Brien and Sharon Tiffany (eds) *Rethinking Women's Roles: Perspectives from the Pacific*, Berkeley: University of California Press: 13–31.
Strathern, M. (1981b) 'Self interest and the social good: some implications of Hagen gender imagery', in S. Ortner and H. Whitehead (eds) *Sexual Meanings: The Cultural Construction of Gender and Sexuality*, Cambridge: Cambridge University Press: 359–409.
Strathern, M. (1996) 'Potential property: intellectual rights and property in persons', *Social Anthropology* 4 (1): 17–32.
Strathern, M. (2001) 'The patent and the Malanggan', *Theory, Culture and Society*,18 (4): 1–23.
Weiner, J. (1998) 'Culture in a sealed envelope: The concealment of Australian Aboriginal heritage and tradition in the Hindmarsh Island Bridge affair', *Journal of the Royal Anthropological Institute* 5: 193–210.
Wolf, E. (1999) *Envisioning Power*, Los Angeles: University of California Press.

CHAPTER 12

AAA (2002) *Eldorado Task Force Papers*, submitted to the Executive Board of the American Anthropological Association as a final report, 18 May.

Asch, T. (1975) *The Ax Fight*, Philadelphia: Pennsylvania State University Press.

Breton, S. (2004) 'Interview du réalisateur Stéphane Breton par Stéphane Breton', www.arte-tv.com/fr/connaissance-decouverte/le-monde-des-Papous.

Banks, M. and H. Morphy (1997) *Rethinking Visual Anthropology*, New Haven, CT: Yale University Press.

Chagnon, N. (1977) *Yanomamo: The Fierce People*, New York: Holt Reinhardt and Winston.

Clifford, J. (1988) *The Predicament of Culture*, Cambridge, MA: Harvard University Press.

Clifford, J. (1997) *Routes*, Cambridge, MA: Harvard University Press.

Fabian, J. (1983) *Time and the Other: How Anthropology Makes its Object*, New York: Columbia University Press.

Fleuhr-Lobban, C. (1991) *Ethics and the Profession of Anthropology: Dialogue for a New Era*, Philadelphia: University of Pennsylvania Press.

Foucault, M. (1972) *The Order of Things*, New York: Vintage.

Geertz, C. (1973) 'Thick description', in *The Interpretation of Culture*, New York: Basic Books: 1–23.

Geertz, C. (1983) *Local Knowledge*, New York: Basic Books.

Geertz, C. (1988) *Works and Lives: The Anthropologist as Author*, Stanford, CA: Stanford University Press.

Grimshaw, A. (2001) *The Ethnographer's Eye*, Cambridge: Cambridge University Press.

Latour, B. (1999) *Pandora's Hope: Essays on the Reality of Science Studies.* Cambridge, MA: Harvard University Press.

Marcus, G. and J. Clifford (1986) *Writing Culture*, Berkeley: University of California Press.

Marcus, G. and D. Cushman (1981) 'Ethnographies as texts', *Annual Review of Anthropology* 11: 25–69.

Marcus, G. and M. Fischer (1986) *Anthropology as Cultural Critique*, Chicago: University of Chicago Press.

Moore, R. (1994) 'Marketing alterity', in Lucien Taylor (ed.) *Visualizing Theory*, New York and London: Routledge: 126–39.

Pels, P. (1999) 'Professions of duplexity: a prehistory of ethical codes in anthropology', *Current Anthropology* 40 (2): 101–36.

Pels, P. (2000) 'The trickster's dilemma: ethics and the technologies of the anthropological self', in M. Strathern (ed.) *Audit Culture: Anthropological Studies in Accountability, Ethics and the Academy*, London: Routledge: 135–72.

Rabinow, P. (1996) *Essays in the Anthropology of Reason*, Princeton, NJ: Princeton University Press.

Ruby, J. (1995) 'Out of sync: the cinema of Tim Asch', *Visual Anthropology Review* 11 (1): 19–36.

Scheper-Hughes, N. (1995) 'The primacy of the ethical: propositions for a militant anthropology', *Current Anthropology* 36 (3): 409–39.

Scholte, B. (1974) 'Towards a critical and reflexive anthropology', in Dell Hymes (ed.) *Reinventing Anthropology*, New York: Vintage: 430–57.

Strathern, M. (2000) *Audit Cultures: Anthropological Studies in Accountability, Ethics and the Academy*, London: Routledge.

Tierney, P. (2000) *Darkness in Eldorado: How Scientists and Journalists Devastated the Amazon*, New York: Norton.

Trouillot, M.-R. (1992) 'Anthropology and the savage slot: the poetics and politics of otherness', in Richard Fox (ed.) *Recapturing Anthropology: Working in the Present*, Santa Fe, NM: School of American Research: 17–44.

Wagner, R. (1975) *The Invention of Culture*, Chicago: University of Chicago Press.

Wagner, R. (1986) *Symbols that Stand for Themselves*, Chicago: University of Chicago Press.

Wagner, R. (2001) *The Anthropology of the Subject*, Berkeley: University of California Press.

White, H. (1981) *Tropics of Discourse*, Baltimore, MD: Johns Hopkins University Press.

Winston, B. (1995) *Reclaiming the Real*, London: British Film Institute.

INDEX

(AAA) American Anthropological Association 207, 208
Aboriginal Australians 81, 141
abstraction 145, 219
aesthetics 3, 14, 101, 151, 164, 167, 179, 180, 185, 216; of representation 142–7, 149, 181
Africa 30, 36, 77; *see also* North Africa
after-image 148
agency 113, 127, 128
Algeria 115–19
Algonquin 99, 103
alienation 98, 100, 101, 106, 108, 111, 133, 137, 138, 140, 147, 173, 174, 184, 203
alliance theory 87, 119, 120
Amazon 32–4, 37, 82, 87, 208–11
America 7, 93, 176; *see also* North America; South America
American Indians 7, 40–1, 99–103, 111, 155–62
L'Année Sociologique 9, 60, 61
anthropology: and technocracy 181–6; assumptions of 8; biological 28; British social 25; economic 67; feminist 53–5, 92; historical 37; holographic 178, 220; interpretive 52, 57, 217; linguistic 78; 'literary turn' in 216; modernist 12, 94, 133, 134; of the present 15; postcolonial 97, 101, 106, 111; postmodernist 12, 176; psychoanalytic 154, 178; reflexive 11; Victorian 25; visual 15, 33, 148
Appadurai, A. 192, 194, 195, 203
archaeology 107, 155
Aristotle 206
Asad, T. 27
Asch, Tim 33, 209–10; *The Ax Fight* 33, 209–10; *The Feast* 33
Association for Social Anthropology 207
audit culture 184, 206
Augé, M. 77
Australia 7, 8, 141, 179
autobiography 118
Aztecs 163

Banks, Mrs Linnaeus 136
barter 42, 43
Bastar 199
Bataille, Georges 14, 151, 155, 161, 162, 163, 167, 168
Bateson, Gregory 177, 178
Battaglia, D. 175
Baudelaire, Charles 135–6
beauty 152–3, 174, 179, 216
'begging' *see* Kerekere Vakavidi
Benedict, Ruth 7–8, 72, 160, 162, 217
Berbers 115–19, 122, 123, 124–6
Best, Elsdon 67
biodiversity 189
Blake, J. 189
Boas, Franz 1, 13, 27, 38, 40–1, 57, 63, 72, 156–7, 160, 162
body, the 49, 101, 113, 129, 133, 150, 172, 175, 178, 211, 219, 220
Bolshevism 60, 61
Bourdieu, Pierre 14, 113, 115–19, 122–3, 125, 127, 128, 129, 194
Bourgeois, Léon 60
bourgeois subject 14, 133–50, 151, 173; critique of 138–42, 147, 148, 150; *see also* subjectivity
Brown, M. 196–7, 203
Buddhism 155
Burma 121
Byzantine power 31

Calcutta 98, 104, 106
Cambridge expedition 25–7, 39
camera obscura 138–9, 142
Canada 7–8, 40, 72–3, 155–61, 197, 198
capitalism 2, 4, 5, 14, 31, 62, 63, 100, 109, 115, 137, 142, 147, 148, 150, 156, 159, 160, 161, 168, 198
Cartesian: philosophy 5, 133, 134, 172, 176–8, 185, 218, 219; subject 172, 173, 176, 219, 220
caste system 104, 105, 109, 111, 191, 199
Chagnon, N. 33, 34, 208–11
challenge 118, 119
chaos theory 178
China 6
Clifford, J. 38, 51, 77, 216
Codere, H. 157
codes of practice 108, 205–8, 211, 221
cold societies 86
Cold War 76
collective 194–5, 203; memory 126–7
colonial relations 6, 13, 20, 28–32, 34, 35, 37, 39, 46, 55–6, 58, 72, 97–111, 124–6, 137, 158, 161, 167; *see also* postcolonial society
commodity exchange 5, 14, 62, 91, 110, 135, 161, 182, 183
common wealth 23, 24–5, 188–90, 192, 194, 198, 203; *see also* culture
commons *see* common wealth; culture
communication 77, 78, 81, 82, 84–5, 87–9, 125, 178, 179, 180, 185, 216, 217, 218, 221; technologies of 172, 173, 174–5
communism 61
comparative approach 11, 13, 60, 61, 64–8, 71, 72, 74, 129
competition 68, 69, 71–2, 75, 118–19, 123, 156–61, 192; *see also* tournaments of value
complexity 181
Comte, Auguste 9
consumption 142
context 14, 111; *see also* historical context
Cook, Captain James 21
Coombe, R. 197, 203–4
Coronation Street 140
Counterfeit Coin 135–6
creativity 200
Cree 92
cultural diversity 189, 203
cultural property 15, 187–204
culture 1, 15, 40, 58, 100, 108, 109, 113, 163, 197, 217; as the new commons 189–90, 203–4; popular 171–2, 173, 174, 179, 184
Cushman, D. 216
custom 6–7, 64, 68, 106, 108, 164, 193
customary belief *see* custom
cyberspace 171, 172

D'Andrade, R. 31
Daribi 78, 215
Darwin, Charles 27
dead: spirits of the 159, 166, 168
death 163, 164–8
debt 97, 99, 103, 104, 111, 126
deconstruction 139, 148
Demian, M. 200
democracy 9, 24, 62, 102, 103, 107, 180, 189
Derrida, Jacques 14, 135–6, 138, 146, 147, 167
description 20, 28, 40–1, 46, 57, 157, 173, 176, 181, 184, 217, 218–19; technologies of 173, 174–9, 184–5, 218; thick 218, 219
Diamond, S. 30–1
difference 100, 110, 148, 167, 182, 182–3, 219, 220; cultural 188; social 76–9, 91, 93, 121, 127, 199
disappearing communities 41, 102
discovery: age of 6
displacement 175
Diwali 109
Dobu 7–8, 42
double consciousness 128
Dumont, L. 134, 149
Durkheim, Émile 1, 4, 9, 60, 61, 79, 81, 123; *The Elementary Forms of the Religious Life* 8, 10
Dutfield, M. 197

economic man 62, 73, 98, 110, 111, 149, 187
economics 2–3, 5, 12, 13, 53, 60, 62–4, 67, 73, 75, 159, 187; *see also* natural economy; political economy
education 9, 24, 35
elitism 34
empathy 177, 178, 179, 184, 185
Engels, Friedrich 141, 150
England 136–8, 139, 143–6
Enlightenment, the 3, 5, 6, 21, 30, 133, 134, 188–9; legacy 8, 10, 19–37, 218
epistemology 6; *see also* knowledge

equality 9, 21, 28, 31, 61, 86, 111, 116, 121, 151
essay form 6–8, 23
ethics 12, 15, 25, 69, 74, 136, 138, 151, 159, 167, 184, 185, 187, 192–4, 197, 200; anthropological 205–21; of representation 15, 209
ethnicity 20
Europe 7–8, 30, 31, 32, 43, 50, 61, 93, 102, 105, 129, 139, 162, 176, 182, 184, 202
Evans-Pritchard, Edward 36
evidence 11, 38, 57, 70
evolutionary theories 25–8, 33–5, 37, 38, 39, 49, 50, 57, 76, 79; criticisms of 40–1, 43–6, 86, 128, 129, 209, 210, 211, 217
excess 14, 151, 154, 155–61, 162, 163, 166, 167; of affection 153–5
exchange: of people 77, 79, 82–5, 94; of women 79, 81, 82–94, 119–21, 198; *see also* commodity exchange; gift; matrimonial exchange
exogamy: rule of 83–4, 122
experience-distant knowledge 52, 219
experience-near knowledge 52, 219
exploration 20, 21, 97

Fabian, Johannes 217, 218
Fair Trade movement 187
fantasy 128; bourgeois 150; English 21, kinship theory as 36; Noble Savage as 21–2, 25, 36, 47; of power 160
fascism 161–2; *see also* National Socialism
feasting 153, 159–64, 177, 181, 211–12; marriage 115–19
feminist: analyses 13, 53, 58, 81, 85, 87–9, 90–4; ideology 79
feudal systems 105
Fiji 14, 98, 105–9, 111, 179–81, 185; trade in 105–7
First World War 9, 10, 39, 56, 60, 61, 76, 104
Firth, Raymond 50
Fischer, M. 216
Flaherty, D. 210
forgiving 2
Fortes, Meyer 36
Fortune, Reo 42, 192–3
Foucault, Michel 176, 217, 218
fractals 178, 184–5
France 118; revolutionary 22–4, 35
free gifts 64, 69, 75, 135, 146, 147, 195–6
freedom 20
friendship 136, 172, 177
functionalism 49–50, 57, 90, 128; structural- 50

gambling 165–6
gatekeepers 57
Geertz, Clifford 52, 55, 115, 124–6, 129, 166, 173, 206, 217, 218, 219
Geertz, H. 117
Gell, A. 48, 86, 129, 192, 193, 199
Gellner, Ernest 49, 50, 115
gender relations 79, 85–94, 182–3
genealogy 9–10
Germany 155
Ghassyia caste 199
gift: as communication 77, 81, 82, 84–5, 94; how of the 113; spirit of the 65, 67, 68, 69, 71, 74, 75, 81, 185, 191; timing of the 114, 118, 119–23; as a total social fact 3–5, 12, 63–4, 70, 75, 123, 185, 187, 196, 198; virtually real 172, 175; *see also* exchange
giving voice 88
giving while keeping 68–9, 70, 73
Gledhill, J. 31, 32
globalization 12, 15, 187, 192, 194
Goddard, Jean-Luc 174
Godelier, Maurice 13, 60, 63, 68, 71–5, 81, 87, 121, 159; thesis 13, 60, 64–8
gods 159, 163; gifts to 74–5
Gofman, A. 3–4
Graeber, D. 99, 101, 102, 103
Gregory, C. 5, 161, 198, 199
Grimshaw, A. 33, 209
guidelines 205–7, 209–11

habit 112, 113, 123, 124, 126, 138, 146, 166, 175, 220; *see also* habitus
habitus 113, 129
Haddon, A.C. 1, 9, 25–7, 39
hau 13, 65–8, 71, 73, 114, 158, 166, 167, 185, 191
Hawaiians 7, 21, 196
Hertz, R. 73
Hill, Christopher 189
Hinduism 109
Hirst, Damien 203
historical consciousness 12, 13, 14, 87, 129
historical context 97, 100, 110–11
historical experience 113

historical particularism 13, 40–1
history 34, 35, 37, 49, 57, 85–6, 90, 94, 97, 103, 106, 110, 112, 157, 195, 196, 216, 217; collective 127; *see also* historical consciousness; historical particularism
Hobbes, Thomas 25, 190, 194, 195
Holi 109
holistic approaches 47, 57, 73, 128, 184
holographic reality 176, 184
Homo economicus *see* economic man
hot societies 86
household work 113, 117; *see also* women
human: nature 23, 32–4, 38, 45, 47, 50, 73, 110, 146, 195, 196, 209; what it means to be 3–6, 12, 20, 50, 185–6, 217
Hume, David 8
Hunt, George 72, 156, 157
Huron 100, 101, 103
Hutnyk, J. 161, 162

ideology 28, 34, 35, 50, 53–5, 61, 88, 90, 92, 94, 106, 117, 119, 121, 122, 159, 160, 217; of anthropologists 110; feminist 79; gender 128; of modernity 41
imaginary 142
imperialism 105
incest: prohibition of 83
indebtedness *see* debt
indenture 103–5, 111
independence 20
India 199
Indian votive sacrifice 109
individuals 59, 73, 74, 138, 149, 194, 203; possessive 134; *see also* bourgeois subject
Indo-Fijians 109, 179–80
inductive reasoning 45, 46, 47, 48
inequality 21, 22–5, 28, 30–2, 36, 67, 79, 85, 87, 111, 116, 121, 126; gender 91–3
integrated holistic description 13
interest 190–2
internet 172
interpretation 52, 57, 108, 125, 174, 206, 218, 219; rational 153
irony 7–8
Iroquois 13, 98, 99, 100, 101–3, 107; confederacy 102–3
irrationality 15, 151, 155, 156, 161–4, 166–8, 174
Islam 115
isolates 74, 183; *see also* individuals

Jajmani system 104
James, William 48–9
Jati 13, 191
Jenkins, R. 118
Jews 124–7

Kant, Immanuel 8
Kaplan, M. 106
Kawelka Big Man 121
Kelly, J. 105, 106, 109
Kerekere Vakavidi 98, 107–8
kinship 1, 9–10, 36, 79, 81, 87, 90, 102, 152, 154, 157, 158, 177–8; as communication 81, 82; diagrams 122, 129, 141, 209
Kiriwinians 59, 64
Kisian 193–4
Klima, A. 165, 167
knowledge 8–10, 52–3, 56, 62, 79, 81, 113, 121, 128, 138, 182, 183, 215, 218, 220; anthropological 206, 207, 211; cultural 163, 187, 203; habits of organising 6; indigenous 187–8, 189, 197–8; practice 113, 125, 180, 186; secret 214; as social 10, 11; unconscious 115; visual 146
Kohut, H. 52
Kuklick, H. 25, 27
kula trade 13, 41–3, 46, 48, 53–4, 59, 64, 65, 68, 69, 71, 72, 73, 129, 153, 180, 190, 192–4, 200, 214
Kuper, Adam 27, 36
Kwakiutl 7–8, 65, 72–3, 155–62, 198

Ladaven 211–14
Latour, Bruno 175, 176, 178, 181–2, 185, 218, 219, 220
law 64, 67–8, 73, 177, 187–8, 190–1, 192, 195–7, 199, 200, 209; customary 124–6, 129; international 187, 188
Leach, Edmund 48, 121, 200
Leacock, E. 92
Leahy brothers 78
Lévi-Strauss, Claude 13, 14, 30, 32–4, 65, 78, 90, 91, 94, 119–21, 129, 157, 183, 209; *Elementary Structures of Kinship* 81, 82, 86, 85; *The Savage Mind* 86; *Tristes Tropiques* 32;
linguistics 107–8
London 62
long-cycle of exchange 119–20, 121
loss: experience of 98, 99

love 171, 172, 173–4, 177–8, 183, 184, 185, 196, 220; parental 151–2, 153–5
Lowry, L.S. 142, 144–7, 150

Mabo decision 141
Macaulay, Thomas B. 103
Mach, E. 49
McLuhan, Marshall 171
Macpherson, C. B. 134, 149
magic 42, 43, 48, 63, 70, 121, 153, 154, 162
malanggan 162–3, 164, 177, 200–3, 215
Malinowski, Bronislaw 13, 15, 38–58, 59, 63, 64, 68, 69, 73, 75, 89, 90, 152, 154, 156, 190–4, 195–6, 200, 203, 206; *Argonauts of the Western Pacific* 41, 44, 48, 50, 53, 64; *Crime and Custom in Savage Society* 50, 64, 190; diaries 51, 55–6; functionalism 49–50, 57; pragmatism 48–9; *The Sexual Life of Savages* 50; subjective bias of 50–3, 58
Manchester 2, 14, 140, 141, 148, 150; School of Political Economy 36, 137
Manchester Man 136–8, 146
Mandeville, Bernard 190
Manhattan: Indians 99, 111; transfer of 99–103
Maori 65–8, 71, 73, 74, 81, 191
mapula 63–4, 68–71, 74, 75, 153–5, 167, 196
Marcus, G. 216, 217, 218
Marx, Karl 23, 91, 138
matrimonial: exchange 13, 14, 32, 34, 85, 91, 94, 121, 182; transactions 112 *see also* women: exchange of
mats: ceremonial 180–1
Mauss, Marcel 1–4, 10, 12, 15, 60–75, 79, 81, 98, 110, 113, 123, 129, 134, 149, 158, 160, 167, 190, 191–2, 198, 199, 203; comparative approach 13, 60, 61, 64–8; *The Gift* 4, 33, 61–3, 73
Maybury-Lewis, D. 34
Mead, Margaret 112
megalomania 160, 162
Melanesia 28, 35, 53, 128, 155, 176, 184, 198
Melpa people 78, 79, 183
memory 183–4, 193; *see also* collective memory
merographic 183
metalogue 178
metaphor 173
Métraux, Rhoda 112
mind 133, 172, 178, 219; unconscious 91, 115, 154
misconnaissance see misrecognition
misrecognition 115, 122, 126, 128, 129, 194
misunderstanding 114, 119, 125, 127–8
models 178, 179; network 179–81
modernism 12, 94, 113, 135, 182; nostalgia in 12
modernity 22, 41, 76–7, 93, 135, 175, 177, 182, 218–20; failure of 114
Montaigne, Michel de 6–7, 23
Morgan, L.H. 91, 100, 102
Morocco 115, 126, 127
motive 68, 69, 73, 75, 151, 155
Munn, N. 179
Muria castes 199
mystification 138

National Socialism 155, 162; *see also* fascism
natural economy 13
nature: state of 20–1, 23–5, 28, 31, 35
Needham, Rodney 79
networks 179–81, 182, 218, 219
New Guinea 77–8, 79, 82, 93, 121, 155, 161, 166, 176, 182–3, 184, 197, 198, 200–3
New Ireland 155, 162–3, 164, 166, 176, 177, 200–3
New Zealand 65–8
NGOs (non-governmental organizations) 179–81, 185–6
nihilism 135
Noble Savage 5, 12, 13, 103, 188, 209, 211; as fantasy 21–2, 25, 36, 47; legacy of 19–37, 91, 93, 133; *see also* 'savage slot'
non-conscious beliefs 113, 114, 117, 129
normative theories 20
North Africa 115–19, 123, 127, 129
North America 6, 7, 14, 32, 72, 76, 98, 99–103, 111, 177, 182
numayn 157–8

Obeyesekere, G. 21
obligations 4, 10, 25, 59–75, 106, 114, 133, 147, 153–4, 167, 168, 191, 198, 203; of anthropologists 11, 206, 207; regulation of 2; to reciprocate 59, 63–8, 74, 75, 86
Onga's Big Moka 79–80, 82
ontology 12, 15, 146, 182, 188–92, 195, 196, 197, 203, 217

oppositions 78, 91
Ortner, S. 92–3, 113
Orwell, George 62, 142–4, 146, 147, 150
others 30, 173, 191, 217
ownership *see* property

Papua New Guinea *see* New Guinea
Pardee, L. 148
Paris 62, 142
Parry, J. 190–2, 195, 196
Parsons, A. 154
participant observation 13, 38–9, 41, 46–8, 56–7, 220; as subjective 39, 50–3
Pels, P. 206, 207
phenomenology 40, 48, 49
Plato 174
political economy 5, 13, 59, 67, 146, 198
politics 12, 22, 28, 34, 37, 64, 67, 135, 137, 187, 189, 194–5, 197, 209; Algerian 117; American Indian 102; Fijian 106; postcolonial 109; South Asian 104; *see also* political economy
Polyani, Karl 115
Polynesia 28, 35
popular culture 171–2, 173, 174, 179, 184
Posey, D. 197
postcolonial society 13, 30, 31, 94, 97–111
postmodernism 12, 13, 176, 185, 218, 220; critique of subjectivity 134
postmodernity 15
poststructuralism 176, 178, 218; critique of subjectivity 136, 138, 146, 147, 149
potlatch 7, 13, 14, 65, 71–3, 75, 155–62, 167, 198
Pottage, A. 182
poverty 20, 36, 111, 136–7, 146, 151, 221
Powdermaker, H. 200
power 30, 31, 71–3, 91–4, 114, 115–19, 123, 126, 127, 129, 153–6, 160, 162, 194; of women 117, 214
practice theory 14, 113, 114, 119, 123, 126, 128, 129, 194
pragmatism 48–9, 58
Prakash, G. 103, 105
prestige 68, 69, 71, 75, 86, 87, 118, 121, 128, 129, 156, 157, 159, 192, 194
primitive 44, 63, 175
principle of reciprocity 82, 84, 85, 86, 90, 119
Principles of Professional Responsibility 207, 208
property 24, 190; communal 62, 67; cultural 15, 187–204; debates 188–90, 199, 203; intellectual 197, 203; private 62, 67, 184, 188, 189, 195
psychoanalysis 154
public persona 134

racism 28, 31, 34, 50, 76, 129
Radcliffe-Brown, Alfred R. 50
rationality *see* reason
realism 142, 144, 146, 185, 216, 219
reality 138–9, 142, 173–4, 175, 178, 185, 218, 219; *see also* holographic reality; virtual reality
reason 8, 14, 20, 22–8, 37, 48, 77, 79–81, 91, 115, 133–5, 155, 159, 160, 166, 168, 194; critical 8–9; economic 2, 11, 36, 98, 110, 115, 134, 136, 148, 160, 166; native 7, 27; natural 6, 7, 13, 23, 35, 134; scientific 136, 216, 219; social construction of 134; unconscious 154; *see also* inductive reasoning; irrationality; scepticism
recording experience 211–15
Reed-Danahay, D. 118
reflexive sociology 113
relationships 59–75, 88, 191, 203; ideal 59; managing 65; sentimental 70
religion 9, 10, 48, 74, 109
repayment equivalent 64
representation 138–47, 150, 173, 176, 178, 180, 218; aesthetics of 142–7, 149, 181
responsibilities of anthropologists 206–7, 208, 218, 220
rice gifts 98, 104
rights: natural 23–4, 103
Riles, A. 179–81
riposte 118
ritual 8, 9, 33, 46, 70, 71–2, 77, 102, 106, 109, 121, 156–62, 164–6, 168, 178, 197, 202, 214
Rivers, W.H.R. 1, 9, 11, 25, 141
Rosen, L. 115, 127
Rouche, Jean 33
Rousseau, Jean-Jacques 12, 19–25, 30, 35, 37, 91, 93, 188, 195; *A Discourse on Inequality* 22–5; *Émile* 22, 24; *On Aesthetics* 22, 23; *The Social Contract* 20, 24
Royle Family 140
Rubin, G. 91
Ruby, J. 33
Russell, Bertrand 178
Russian Revolution 61, 76

sacred 13; object 69, 72–3, 74, 159
sacrifice 109, 163, 168
Sahlins, M. 21, 27, 28, 67, 68, 71, 74, 106, 107, 108, 109, 113, 191, 195, 196
Saussure, Ferdinand de 79
'savage slot' 35, 36, 37, 210–11, 221
scepticism 4–12, 21, 133, 172, 177, 217–8, 219, 220, 221
Scheper-Hughes, N. 31
Schneider, David 81, 154, 177–8
Scott, D.C. 72
Second World War 27, 56, 76, 77
secular humanism 74
self 50, 134, 173, 174, 185, 191; private 134; technologies of 172
self-interest 2, 69, 151, 153, 190, 192–5
self-scaling 178
Seligman, Charles G. 25, 39, 40
Service, E. 27
short-cycle of exchange 119, 121
small societies 12, 13; integrated 12
Smith, Adam 134, 137, 150
social construction 134, 149
social contract 103, 111, 190, 191, 195
social interconnectedness 10
social reproduction 85–7, 90, 116
social theory 10, 65, 184
socialism 60, 61
solo research 39, 40
South America 32, 76
South Asia 98, 103–5, 111, 190, 191, 199
spiritual 12, 63, 64, 66, 71, 75, 81, 101, 102, 114, 159, 174, 187, 198
state 20, 28, 30, 31, 35, 66, 93; power 13, 37, 91, 92
stereotypes 14, 124, 125
Stocking, G. 25, 27, 49
Strathern, A. 121
Strathern, Marilyn 10, 12, 13, 53, 55, 74, 81, 93, 113, 121, 128, 129, 147, 175–8, 181–5, 206, 218, 219–20
structuralism 13, 30, 32, 34, 35, 76–94, 108, 119, 129, 183, 209; as theory of difference 76–9, 119, 129
subjectivity 12, 13, 81, 94, 129, 134, 151, 177; critiques of 136, 141; visualization of 133; women's 81, 85, 87–9, 90, 94; *see also* bourgeois subject; self
superstition 7
symbolic: exchange 152–3; representation 218; thought 77, 78, 176
synchronic approaches 50

taxation 104–5
technocracy 181–6; of virtually real exchange 179
technology 171, 176, 184–6; descriptive 173, 174–9, 184–5, 218; as virtually real exchange 172–4
television 140, 171: reality 90
Thailand 165–6
theft 124–6, 129
Thomas, N. 28, 97, 106, 108
time 86, 114, 118, 119–23, 127, 129, 216–17
tobacco use 135
Torres Straits 25–7, 39, 141, 146
total approach 1, 12, 13, 129
total social fact 3–5, 12, 63–4, 70, 74, 75, 111, 123, 185, 187, 196, 198
totems 8, 71, 157, 158
tournaments of value 192–6, 197, 203
trade 66, 68, 100, 102, 110; age of 5–6; Berber 116, 124–6; Fijian 105–7; free 134, 137, 148, 149–50; fur 99; international 2; law 124–6; *see also* kula trade
traditional lifestyles 76, 114
translation 67, 124–6, 174; ethics of 218–20; politics of 215
treaties 103
Trobriand islanders 39, 41–56, 65, 68, 69, 72, 90, 152–3, 166, 167, 187, 192, 196, 200
Trouillot, M.-R. 35, 36, 210, 221

unconscious mind 91, 115, 154
United Nations 187; Convention on Biodiversity 189; Declaration on cultural diversity 189, 203
United States of America 102, 105, 184; *see also* North America
utilitarianism 2, 3, 12, 59, 60, 75, 198

value 100; aesthetic 101; ontological 199; symbolic 199; *see also* tournaments of value
Vico, Giambattista 216
Vietnam War 56
violence 20, 31, 33–4, 101–3, 105, 106, 151, 209, 210, 221; *see also* warfare
virtual reality 171–81, 184–6
virtual society 12, 15, 46, 150, 171–86, 187, 218
virtue 179, 185, 196
vision 138–41, 144, 147, 149, 150, 184–5, 186, 200, 203, 204, 221; *see also* after-image

visualization *see* vision
vulnerability 15, 205–8, 211, 221; exchanging 220–1

Wagner, Roy 78, 173, 174, 176, 178, 181, 184, 185, 215, 218–19, 220
Walbiri 179
Wallace, A. 102
wampum 98, 99, 101, 103, 111
warfare 32–4, 56, 66, 101, 102, 121, 150, 209, 210; *see also* violence
wealth 59, 62, 69, 73, 75, 87, 110, 153, 155, 158, 159, 161, 162, 164–5, 166, 184, 198, 200; bride 82, 84, 88, 91, 97, 121, 168, 182–3, 195, 198; cultural 197; excessive 155–6; private 189; *see also* common wealth
Weiner, Annette 53–5, 63–4, 68, 69–70, 73, 74, 159; *Inalienable Possessions* 63–4; *Women of Value, Men of Renown* 53
White, Hayden 216
Whitehead, Alfred North 178
Wolf, Eric 28, 72, 157, 160, 161, 163, 167, 198; *Europe and the People without History* 30
women 93, 117, 179, 180–1, 185, 211–15; as object 87–9, 94; as subject 81, 85, 87–9, 90, 94, 182; as supreme gift 85–7, 90–1, 94; exchange of 79, 81, 82–94, 119–21, 198; work of 85, 94, 112, 117; *see also* household work; matrimonial exchange
World Trade Center 148
World Trade Organization 2
Wyandot *see* Huron

Yanomami people 33, 208–11
Young, M. 152

Zeno 49
Zuni 7–8

Related titles from Routledge

The Reinvention of Primitive Society: Transformations of a Myth

Adam Kuper

The Invention of Primitive Society, Adam Kuper's decisive critique of ideas about the origins of society and religion that have been debated since Darwin, has been hugely influential in anthropology and post-colonial studies. This iconoclastic intellectual history showed that 'primitive society' was the imagined opposite to Western civilisation. By way of fascinating accounts of classic texts in anthropology, classical studies and law, the book revealed how wholly mistaken theories can become the basis for academic research and political programmes.

The publication of this expanded and radically revised new edition, now entitled *The Reinvention of Primitive Society*, coincides with a revival of the myth of primitive society by the 'indigenous peoples movement', which taps into a widespread popular belief about the noble savage, and reflects a romantic reaction against 'civilization' and 'science'. In a new final chapter, Kuper challenges this most recent version of the myth of primitive society. Another new chapter traces conceptions of the barbarian, savage and primitive back through the centuries to ancient Greece. The remaining chapters have all been recast and updated to take new research into account.

The Reinvention of Primitive Society: Transformations of a Myth is essential reading for readers interested in anthropological theory and current post-colonial debates, and indeed for anyone who is curious about the ways in which we systematically misunderstand other peoples.

Related titles from Routledge

Anthropology:
The Basics

Peter Metcalf

The ultimate guide for the student encountering anthropology for the first time, *Anthropology: The Basics* explains and explores anthropological concepts and themes in a highly readable and easy to follow manner.

Making large, complex topics both accessible and enjoyable, Peter Metcalf argues that the issues anthropology deals with are all around us – in magazines, newspapers and on television. Engaging and immensely interesting, he tackles questions such as:

- What is anthropology?
- How can we distinguish cultural differences from physical ones?
- What is culture, anyway?
- How do anthropologists study culture?
- What are the key theories and approaches used today?
- How has the discipline changed over time?

A strong addition to this established and successful series, this exciting text presents students with an overview of the fundamental principles of anthropology, and also provides a useful guide for anyone wanting to learn more about a fascinating subject.

Hb: 0–415–33119–6
Pb: 0–415–33120–X
Available at all good bookshops
For ordering and further information please visit:
www.routledge.com